Women's Science

Women's Science

Learning and Succeeding from the Margins

Margaret A. Eisenhart and Elizabeth Finkel

with Linda Behm, Nancy Lawrence, and Karen Tonso

THE UNIVERSITY OF CHICAGO PRESS / CHICAGO AND LONDON

Margaret A. Eisenhart is professor of education and anthropology at the University of Colorado, Boulder. She is coauthor of *Educated in Romance: Women, Achievement, and Campus Culture*, also published by the University of Chicago Press. Elizabeth Finkel, formerly assistant professor of science education at the University of Michigan, Ann Arbor, now teaches Science at Noble High School, an innovative public school in Maine.

The University of Chicago Press, Chicago 60637
The University of Chicago Press, Ltd., London
© 1998 by The University of Chicago
All rights reserved. Published 1998
Printed in the United States of America
08 07 06 05 04 03 02 01 00 98   5 4 3 2 1

ISBN (cloth): 0-226-19544-9
ISBN (paper): 0-226-19545-7

Library of Congress Cataloging-in-Publication Data

Eisenhart, Margaret A.
    Women's science : learning and succeeding from the margins /
Margaret A. Eisenhart and Elizabeth Finkel ; with Linda Behm, Nancy
Lawrence, and Karen Tonso.
        p.   cm.
    Includes bibliographical references and index.
    ISBN 0-226-19544-9 (alk. paper). — ISBN 0-226-19545-7 (pbk.: alk.
paper)
    1. Women in science—United States.   2. Women in engineering—
United States.   3. Women science students—United States.   4. Women
engineering students—United States.   5. Marginality, Social—United
States.   I. Finkel, Elizabeth.   II. Title.
Q130.E38   1998
305.43′5′0973—dc21   98-16867
                                                                                CIP

This book is dedicated to my husband, Joe Harding, whose love and care, during the years of this project and before, have meant more than I could ever write about, no matter how many drafts.

— Margaret Eisenhart

This book is dedicated to my mother, Constance Urdang, whose clear vision, stubborn strength, and loving words will always be with me.

— Elizabeth Finkel

 Contents

Illustrations

 Preface

[T]here are kinds of [ethnographic] texts imagined that are not yet fully achieved. . . . What we have in mind is a text that takes as its subject not a concentrated group of people in a community . . . but the system itself—the political and economic processes . . . [that] are registered in the activities of dispersed groups or individuals whose actions have mutual, often unintended, consequences for each other. . . . [This] may entail a novel kind of fieldwork. Rather than being situated in one, or perhaps two communities for the entire period of research, the field-worker[s] must be mobile, covering a network of sites that encompasses a process, which is in fact the object of the study. (Marcus and Fischer 1986, 90, 91, 94)

This book was initially conceived as a result of Margaret Eisenhart's interest in opportunities for women (and men) to pursue academic knowledge outside the school setting. Throughout her career as an anthropologist of education, Eisenhart has been interested in what people learn in and around schools about the nature and value of academic knowledge in relation to gender. In her long-term study of women's career-related experiences in and after college (with Dorothy Holland; see Holland and Eisenhart 1990), she found that for many college women academic knowledge is relatively unimportant compared to social activities, especially romantic relationships with men. Approximately three-quarters of the bright young women she studied, who came to college expressing serious commitments to careers (including careers in mathematics or science), graduated with diminished interest in academic work, reduced career commitments, and increased investment in romantic relationships; shortly after graduation, these women were married and working in part-time or non-career-track jobs.

Some women, however, stood out as different. Roughly 22 percent of the women maintained a commitment to academic work throughout college and seemed able to balance their academic and career-related interests with their social and romantic interests. When these women graduated from college, they went on to graduate school or into careers (see Eisenhart and Holland 1992, for a discussion of these patterns). In a very few cases, the researchers noticed that these "nontraditional" women were also involved in extracurricular groups or activities in which academic knowledge was valued and used for some environmental, political, or other practical purpose. These groups included women and men who worked together to accomplish the organization's tasks and agenda.

Eisenhart speculated that such groups might provide contexts in which women and men learn to interact closely in nonromantic relationships and in which they might develop a commitment to academic knowledge because it was being used for worthwhile purposes, rather than simply in exchange for a grade in a course. This speculation led her to wonder about how groups outside of school use academic knowledge, how women and men interact in nonschool groups that use academic knowledge in some way, how such groups nurture and extend academic interests and learning in ways that coursework does not, and how information from such groups could help educators think about educational alternatives. These questions were the impetus for Eisenhart's study of the conservation corporation—the "CC site" of chapter 6—and for her interest in and encouragement of the other studies presented in this book. In 1992, she received grants from the Women's College Coalition and the Spencer Foundation to support a comparative study of women's scientific learning outside of school.

In 1992, Karen Tonso began work on a doctorate with Eisenhart at the University of Colorado at Boulder. Tonso had come to the study of education looking for a new career, having left engineering in 1987. After fifteen years as an engineer, she had proved that she could do engineering on a daily basis and found that she could no longer work "in the trenches." Simultaneously, Tonso became annoyed that the classrooms of her three daughters, who were in upper elementary and middle school at the time, perpetuated rigid gender-role expectations. Though her daughters were far more successful in mathematics and science than she had been at comparable ages, all three decided against continuing these studies by the time they entered ninth grade. Tonso was disappointed that there had been so little progress in the twenty or more years since she had passed through elementary school. She decided to study gender issues in mathematics and science education, because she did not understand how schools could be so static for so long. In 1990 she earned a Master of Arts in Content and Instruction (Secondary Mathematics) from the University of Colorado at Denver. She studied there with Lyn Taylor, pursuing gender issues in mathematics education, particularly the so-called "gender-difference" literature.

Eisenhart suggested that Tonso study engineering students, because she knew that Tonso had personal insights into the obstacles to becoming an engineer. Tonso's experiences in engineering—during both her education and her career—had made her better prepared than other researchers for such a study. In addition, her status as a former engineer allowed her access to engineering sites that was not likely to be available to other researchers.

Nancy Lawrence became interested in politics at the age of eight, while living in Arizona, when she asked her parents why "Goldwater" was spray-painted on so many stop signs in and around Tucson (to form the phrase "STOP Goldwater"). Later, in junior high, she got valuable grassroots experience while working on her first U.S. Senate campaign—stuffing envelopes and delivering campaign literature door-to-door for a "Watergate baby" candidate in 1974.

Lawrence remained politically active in high school and college—serving as a precinct caucus chair, spending a couple of years on electoral campaigns, and volunteering for different issues campaigns. She spent the 1992 election year examining the construction and negotiation of the word *choice* in the context of political debates: the debates surrounding public schools of choice; public/private schools of choice, and abortion rights. One chapter of Lawrence's study, "The Language of Science and the Meaning of Abortion," examined how science was used by opposing sides of the abortion debate to persuade, motivate, challenge, and defend respective positions. Although Lawrence's chapter is not included in this book (see Lawrence 1993, 1994), her work on the meaning of *science* in the abortion debate influenced the development of our argument.

Linda Behm's interest in informal science education prompted her initial participation in the project. A middle-school science teacher for many years, Behm believed that many groups provide contexts for informal science learning: museums, support groups for health concerns, science clubs, nature centers, mentoring programs, and similar settings.

Since informal education can enhance one's level of scientific knowledge, especially for nontraditional students, Behm wanted to investigate a group of people in an informal context where science learning was likely to take place. Like many of us, Behm had the experience of a canvasser (typically a young adult) coming to knock on her door and request funds for environmental protection. Behm became interested in understanding how the members of such an environmental group learn about and use science.

Behm searched for and found an environmental group (the Environmental Legislation Action Coalition; see chapter 5) in which there were approximately equal numbers of young adult men and women with a variety of college majors. She was interested in determining how they went about their work and how they thought about science and about the need to learn and use science to be successful in campaigning for the environment. She also wondered if gender differences existed in the method or extent of canvassers' learning about environmental and science-related issues. She felt that studying those who are under-represented in science (including women) in situations in which they use science, might suggest more effective methods for getting them in-volved in school science.

Elizabeth Finkel was a graduate student in science education at the University of Wisconsin–Madison and lived in Boulder on a fellowship during the 1992–93 academic year. Prior to returning to school for her Ph.D. in science education, Finkel had pursued a career in geology, completing B.S. and M.S. degrees in geological sciences. After completing those degrees, Finkel spent four years teaching earth science, chemistry, physical science, and environmental science to middle-school and high school students. It was during that time that she decided to return to school to earn a Ph.D. in education.

At the University of Wisconsin, Finkel began work with Jim Stewart, a professor of science education who had an interest in applications of the history and philosophy of science to understanding the teaching and learning of science at the secondary level. Through her work with Stewart, Finkel began a study of a high school genetics classroom that would become her dissertation. As part of her work in science teaching and learning, and as a result of her own experiences (not all positive) as a woman in science, Finkel was also very interested in the role of context and gender in explaining the experiences of girls and women in work and learning settings that involve science, although this was not the focus of her dissertation.

Finkel arrived in Boulder in the summer of 1992 planning to spend the year writing her dissertation. She and Eisenhart met early in her stay and began to talk about their common interests. After several conversations, Eisenhart asked Finkel to join her, Lawrence, Behm, and Tonso for a series of informal discussions about the work they were all pursuing. For more than a year the five women met regularly to share findings from the individual case studies they were conducting, and to read and comment on each others' case study drafts. All five were preparing papers for a national conference, and used the group as an opportunity to develop and refine presentations and final drafts.

Conversations, while not always focused on finding similarities in their work, did turn up a number of similar patterns among the cases, and it was this ongoing conversation that eventually culminated in the ideas in this book. Once these meetings ended, Eisenhart proposed developing a book based on the work of the group. As Finkel prepared to leave Boulder for a job in science education at the University of Michigan, Eisenhart asked her if she would be interested in becoming coauthor, and the two agreed to pursue the project.

Thus, over a two-year period (1992–94), the five of us collected data, discussed our preliminary findings, and challenged each other with competing theories of "what was going on" regarding science, women, and learning in the different sites. Each researcher produced a case study, which was then reviewed and critiqued by the others. The complete case studies are available from each author (Behm 1994; Eisenhart 1993; Finkel 1993; Lawrence 1994; Tonso 1993). Behm, Finkel, and Lawrence completed their dissertations on the same groups they studied for this project. Tonso used the research included here as a pilot study for her dissertation.

Eisenhart became especially interested in knowing what cross-site comparisons would show. Although she had been initially inspired by Lave and Wenger's (1991) theory of situated learning, she found herself increasingly drawn to numerous other perspectives in order to understand different facets of the data from the various sites. This motivated her to develop a more comprehensive argument to explain findings from all the sites. At this point, however, Behm, Lawrence, and Tonso needed to pursue their professional careers in some different directions.

The present authors began to work with the case studies to identify themes across sites and to develop an argument that would integrate the cases. As the argument emerged, we used excerpts from the cases to illustrate various points of the emerging argument, and consulted relevant literature for additional ideas and support. The argument that we finally developed uses the case material more selectively and in some ways differently than did the original case studies. Although we are responsible for the argument put forth here, this book could not have been developed without the hard work and insights of all five women who participated. Finally, we must add that our reading and interpretation of the literature and data we present in this book are necessarily partial; that is, they depend in large measure on who we are and what our experiences and interests have been. We are certain that others, including the women of the sites we studied, will beg to differ with us on certain points. We invite their comments and critiques, as well as those of our readers, and hope that all will consider our account a plausible one that opens up previously unexplored avenues of thought about science and gender. In studying these sites, we have been outsiders looking in. Yet as women, researchers, and teachers in areas also marginal to the centers of elite science and power, we know that the processes we are trying to understand in this book are also our own.

Acknowledgments

Numerous people have contributed to the development of the ideas that appear in this book. Special thanks go to the girls and women who participated in our study and to the schools and organizations where they studied and worked. They are the people and places that brought our sites alive. We appreciate their willingness to be questioned, observed, and recorded, and we are grateful for the many insights they shared with us.

Many of our colleagues contributed intellectual and emotional support. We are especially indebted to Hilda Borko, Ardra Cole, Kathy Davis, Dorothy Holland, Kathy Greene, Maurene Flory, Jenifer Helms, Willett Kempton, Scott Marion, and Jean MacPhail for comments on the manuscript in its various incarnations and for their continuing interest in our work. Abraham and Roberta Flexer provided invaluable editorial assistance; Abe deserves special mention for the gentle way in which he raised questions about our ideas from "a male view" and urged us to write in ways that would broaden our audience.

Support for portions of this project was provided by The Spencer Foundation and The Women's College Coalition. The University of Colorado–Boulder, provided additional support for Eisenhart, and the The University of Michigan did so for Finkel.

Finally, and most important, we want to thank Joe Harding and Scott Fletcher. They have supported, encouraged, cajoled, and endured us in every stage of this work.

Introduction

Learning and Succeeding from the Margins

> The point of this book is to develop a different set of conceptual tools for thinking about out-of-the-way places. . . . I use the concept of *marginality* to begin discussion of such distinctive and unequal positions within common fields of knowledge and power. (Tsing 1993, x–xi)

Tsing wrote about a marginalized group who live deep in the rainforest of Indonesia. Our book is about a less exotic but similarly positioned group—American women in science and engineering. Tsing's analysis of the Meratus Dayaks set the stage for a reexamination of anthropologists' familiar notions of culture, power, and gender. Our aspirations are similar: We hope to provoke a reconsideration of conventional ideas about where science is practiced, what it looks like, and how it is learned by taking the perspective of women and applying concepts such as power relations and culture.

In the United States today, there are places where women learn about science and technology and learn to become scientists or engineers. The women know and can use technical facts, academic theories, and scientific ways of viewing the world. They enjoy their work and their colleagues, and they are recognized and promoted for their proficiency in fields historically associated with men. Some of these places and women constitute the subject of this book.

The places we examine are not the ones most readers will expect. Our sites are not conventional classrooms or laboratories, although they depend in part on what goes on there. Nor do our sites enjoy spectacular discoveries, large federal grants, or media fanfare. In many respects, our sites are on the margins of established communities of scientific or technical practice. They are usually not counted when demographic trends for women (or anyone) in science are studied. They are not mentioned in discussions of opportunities available for learning about and practicing science or engineering. Many such places are eschewed by the scientific establishment, which believes that little or no "real" or "serious" science is practiced there.

At the same time, our sites are thriving places where unsung women work hard, do well, and feel rewarded for their efforts. Almost unanimously the women in these places express interest in science and a desire to know more about it. To varying degrees, they also feel accepted and accomplished in the science practiced at their sites.

What should we make of this situation? Why have places where women practice and succeed at science been ignored in the national conversation about participation in science, mathematics, and engineering? What is happening in these sites to attract, motivate, and support women? What kind of scientific or technical knowledge is being used and learned in these sites? How do these places differ from conventional sites at which science is learned and practiced? What is the social and cultural significance of these unusual sites? Are the women who practice science in such sites merely learning to fit themselves into old, subordinate roles in new communities, or are they actively participating in reconstructing the social relations of scientific practice? These general questions frame this book.

Although our questions can be stated simply, they are not quickly answered. Also, as might be expected, the situation is more complex than we have depicted. Not all the places we studied were good places for learning science. Not all the women we studied challenged traditional expectations. They did not all act alike, and they were not equally successful or equally satisfied. All of our sites were marked by patriarchy—traditional male-dominated power structures and assumptions—despite women's presence and success. Yet, as a whole, our examples will challenge some popular assumptions about women's participation in science and engineering and about the obstacles to learning and using more science in contemporary United States society.

The Popular View

In recent reports about science, mathematics, or engineering in the United States, the numbers of men and women who are proficient or actively involved are discouragingly low. In a study for the National Science Foundation, Jon Miller (1991) found that only 7 percent of

American adults qualify as "scientifically literate"—that is, possessing a basic understanding of the terms, processes, and impacts of science and technology.[1] In addition, women's level of literacy is lower than men's. Miller reported that while 9 percent of adult men are scientifically literate, only 6 percent of adult women are. Controlling for level of education, the overall numbers improve somewhat with increased schooling, but the gap between men and women widens. Among college-educated men and women, 23.6 percent of men qualify as scientifically literate, while only 17.1 percent of women do (Miller 1991, 19–21).

Others have reported that the gender gap in scores on standardized tests of science achievement (e.g., the National Assessment of Educational Progress [NAEP] test) is small or nonexistent in early grades. But it grows larger and in favor of boys as age and grade level increase (Jones et al. 1992; National Science Foundation 1996). The NAEP 1996 science assessment found that male and female students had similar scores in grades four and eight; however, in grade twelve, male students scored higher than females (O'Sullivan, Reese, and Mazzeo 1997, 28–29).

Blame for the low levels of literacy and the gender gap in science achievement usually goes to schools. The Educational Testing Service, developer and administrator of national standardized tests such as the Scholastic Aptitude Test, tells us that

> [f]ar too many [young Americans] emerge from the nation's elementary and secondary schools with an inadequate grounding in mathematics, science and technology. As a result, they lack sufficient knowledge to acquire the training, skills, and understanding that are needed today and will be even more critical in the twenty-first century. (Educational Testing Service 1988, 4)

Two leading science educators point out that

> [m]ost Americans are not scientifically literate. One only has to look at the international studies of educational performance to see that U.S. students rank near the bottom in science and mathematics—hardly what one would expect if the schools were doing their job well. (Rutherford and Ahlgren 1990, vii)[2]

Articles in both the popular media and academic journals emphasize that many elementary and secondary teachers are not qualified to teach science or mathematics:

> Few elementary teachers have even a rudimentary education in science and mathematics, and many junior and senior high school teachers of science and mathematics do not meet reasonable standards of preparation in those fields. (Rutherford and Ahlgren 1990, viii)

In addition, school science curricula and activities (as taught) are said to be poorly designed. "[T]raditional lesson plans are overstuffed with detail, alienate students, and often create confusion about the nature of science" (Culotta 1993, 498).

Studies of elementary-, middle-, and high-school science reveal a persistent pattern in which teachers give more attention to boys' scientific interests and provide them with more science experiences. Girls develop more negative attitudes toward science, and by the end of high school, they take fewer mathematics and science courses, and score lower on most achievement measures (Oakes 1990; Sadker and Sadker 1994). Citing a number of recent studies, Baker and Leary report as follows:

> Teacher-student interactions are biased in favor of boys. . . . In the face of failure boys are encouraged to try again, and girls are allowed to give up . . . [moreover] girls have less access to science equipment, hands-on activities, and computers. (1995, 5)

Numerous examples of classroom treatment biased against girls are described in Sadker and Sadker's comprehensive review (1994) of the research on gender in schools. They report on girls who were told that they "had no need for physics" (120); girls who enrolled in a high school chemistry class, only to be seated on the far side of the room from the teacher, and then told "to be quiet and not cause trouble [so] they would not fail the class"; girls who encountered male mathematics teachers "who felt girls didn't need math, [and so there was no need to] . . . work very hard at teaching [them]" (121). In one particularly blatant example, a girl who repeated a question in a science class had water thrown on her by the teacher, who commented after class that "girls weren't suited to 'do' science" (124). By the time they leave middle school, most girls and boys agree "that science has moved out of the neutral zone" and belongs to boys (123).

Recently, the increasing use of new technologies in educational settings has widened the gap between boys and girls. Sadker and Sadker found that "more than 60 percent of boys but only 18 percent of girls had a computer at home" (1994, 122). And in a study of an innovative, technology-rich, science classroom, Yates and Finkel (1996) found that while girls were skilled at and interested in using computers, they could not be persuaded to bring those skills into the classroom; as a result, girls used computers far less frequently than their male peers in their science class and learned less about the new technology.

For women who persevere through high school with an interest in science or mathematics, higher education seems to present additional obstacles. In large-scale surveys of national trends in college science, several writers (Green 1989a, 1989b; Astin 1985; Astin and Astin 1993) have documented a sharp overall decline in science-oriented enroll-ments since 1983, consistently smaller percentages of female science majors compared to men, and a disproportionate loss during college of women from majors in science, mathematics, and engineering. Jacobs (1995) demonstrates that the rate of improvement in gender balance in scientific fields slowed substantially in the late 1980s after increasing markedly during the late 1960s, 1970s, and early 1980s. He concludes that "women remain segregated from men" in all science fields of study at the college level (81).

Ethnographic studies of college science and engineering suggest that gender imbalance is attributable to stereotyped expectations about who should participate in science and engineering. Gary Downey and his colleagues (Downey, Hegg, and Lucena 1993) and Jan Nespor (1994) have demonstrated that women who enter engineering or physics with academic backgrounds that are as strong or stronger than those of men may, nonetheless, be described by male professors and students as "aca-demically weak" or "not the real engineering type." Eventually, the women come to view themselves that way and leave engineering.

If women somehow persist in science or engineering despite these school-based obstacles, they encounter further difficulties in the work-place. Research on employed women indicates that they are far less likely to have careers in the "hard" sciences (e.g., in physical science, where 9 percent are women; environmental science, 9.7 percent women; or engineering, 3.4 percent women) than in psychological science, where 38 percent are women (National Science Foundation 1994). For the most part, women's salaries start and remain below men's. They suffer various forms of sexual harassment at work, and few women ad-vance to the high, prestigious ranks of their professions:

> Relative to men with similar credentials and experience levels, women in all of the sciences earn lower salaries, experience higher unemployment rates, are more likely to be employed in temporary

positions, and find fewer and slower opportunities to advance, either
in rank or toward management, or to obtain security in the form of
tenure. (Vetter 1992, 18)

The women we discuss in this book challenge this popular view (and
the general trends on which it is based) in several ways. Among our sites,
we found one where the women were considerably more "scientifically
literate" than in Miller's study. In another, 50 percent of high-status
positions and 46 percent of environmental scientist positions were held
by women. In another, women and men made equal performance gains
in engineering, and women's enthusiasm for engineering work exceeded
men's. The sites where we found these successes are a political action
group, an environmental protection group, and a school-to-work engineering internship. Against the backdrop of the widely documented,
dismal statistics on women's participation in the conventional sites of
science, mathematics, and engineering practice, our findings are remarkable, indeed. They illustrate that whereas women's achievements
in science are discouragingly low in general, they are not everywhere
so low, nor everywhere below those of men.

Exceptions to the Rule

As a group, the women we studied are exceptional. Although some described negative experiences in school science, schools had not perma-
nently distanced these women from science or its promise, and the
women entered our sites excited about science and the possibility of
learning more of it.

Nor were the women we studied alienated from wanting to put scientific information to worthwhile, publicly responsible use. This, too, is
in contrast to a large body of literature. In a recent book, Philip Wexler
(1992) compared students in three high schools: one working-class, one
middle-class, and one underclass. He argues that U.S. schools are currently functioning (inadvertently and regardless of class standing) to reduce students' interest in academics and their commitment to social
or political issues. He finds that high school students are subjected to
repetitive and boring classes, disparaging labeling and tracking procedures, and cold, "professional" teachers, to which they respond with
virulent defensive strategies. These defensive strategies focus on
avoiding academic work and pursuing individual success in the eyes of
their friends and peers, among whom success is calculated in terms of

mass media fads, physical attractiveness, and individual exploits (see Eckert 1989; Foley 1990; and Willis 1977 for similar findings among diverse student populations). The responses Wexler observed differed somewhat depending upon the social class of the students, but the students in all three schools achieved "being somebody" in roughly the same way: in response to cold, depersonalizing treatment at school, students found it more rewarding and satisfying to pursue individualistic identities and personal pleasure with the resources favored by peers.

Dorothy Holland and Margaret Eisenhart, in their study of black and white college women on two university campuses (1990), found similar patterns among college students. Most of the young women in their study did not find their college coursework worthwhile or interesting and turned instead to peer groups for identity, status, and personal enjoyment. As a result, they finished their school careers poorly prepared for work, with only vague career aspirations. Most of them did not organize or join collective groups. They did not engage in social activism on campus, and they did not leave college with articulated social or political commitments.

Again, many of the women in our study proved to be exceptions to these patterns. As they entered and remained in the sites where we found them, most saw themselves developing careers, extending their academic learning, and pursuing strategies for responsible and public uses of science and technology. They had somehow developed an interest and commitment to exactly those things and identities that Wexler, Holland and Eisenhart, and many others would not expect of them.

Another area in which the women at our sites surprised us concerns their learning. Recently, some prominent theorists have argued that learning is not best thought of as a cognitive phenomenon that occurs in individual minds. Instead, they view learning as "situated," that is, dependent on the *social practices* in which knowledge is made available to participants in those practices and on the ways participants actually engage (or do not engage) in social practices. In this view, to understand learning, researchers must understand the knowledge made available and actually used in "social practices," defined as the concrete activities (tasks and relationships) of everyday life (Lave 1988a, 1993; Lave and Wenger 1991; Nespor 1994). One of the major contributions of this body of work is the idea that to learn means to change one's "identity" (i.e., to develop a new or different sense of self) as a consequence of active participation in a social practice. The measures of learning become new ways of being—new ways of talking, acting, describing oneself, or relating to others. These new ways of being develop when, for example, one changes from novice to expert, newcomer to old-timer, or naive to mature practitioner in a social practice such as the activities of a science curriculum or an engineering workplace.

From this perspective, the most important condition for learning to be a scientist (or any expert) is participating in the relevant social practices: taking part in coursework, degree requirements, homework study groups, lab groups, apprenticeships, internships, work tasks, professional meetings, and career associations. These activities involve individuals in specific tasks, social relationships, and networks *through which* a body of knowledge is presented, used, and interpreted. Only when individuals are allowed or encouraged to participate in the tasks, relationships, and networks relevant to mature practice can they be exposed to the full meaning of being an expert, and have the knowledge and connections to act (and be recognized) as experts.

We were persuaded that learning is first and foremost a social phenomenon, and believed that the body of scholarship on "situated learning" made clearer why so many women have been unsuccessful in science and engineering. If women's participation in constructive tasks, social relationships, and networks in science and engineering is blocked, which many have suggested it is, then women will not gain access to the forms of social involvement that increase their expertise (see also Atkinson and Delamont 1990; Bourdieu 1977). But what of women who do succeed? Are some women simply smart enough or do they persevere long enough that these necessary forms of social involvement are opened to them? Or are the places where we found successful women somehow more receptive to their participation, and if so, how and why? Or does something else account for their learning and success?

The theoretical perspective that guided our resolution of these questions and our analysis of the findings we present in this book is described in chapter 2; we were forced to reconsider existing theories about the social reproduction of scientific power, the theory of situated learning, and the formation of women's identities. Our findings contain implications for thinking about the place of scientific knowledge in society, about women's participation in science and technology, and about how science is taught and learned in the United States. In developing an argument to explain our results, we draw on literature from several areas normally considered separately: the history of Western women's participation in science and technology; the status hierarchies among and within science and engineering disciplines; current theories of learning from anthropology, psychology, and cognitive science; and studies of gender identity and women's responses to the opportunities they have and the situations they face. Each of these topics is taken up in some detail in at least one chapter of the book and referred to in others.

In order to explore various opportunities and experiences of science and technology, we considered a range of sites within the broad arena of contemporary scientific or technical practice: from school-based programs (most conventional) to political action groups (most unconventional). Further, we decided to focus in all cases on sites where women were present in greater-than-usual percentages. Thus, our sites came to include an elective, senior-level high school genetics class; an engineering design internship for prospective engineers at a selective engineering college; an environmental legislation action group; and a nonprofit conservation corporation. The general characteristics of each site are listed below.

1. Innovative Genetics Course (IGC) is an elective, senior-level, high school science course. It was designed as a constructivist-oriented science curriculum that would engage a wide range of students, including those previously unsuccessful in science. Fieldwork in IGC was conducted by Elizabeth (Liza) Finkel in 1992. During her study, 40 percent of the students enrolled in the class were girls.

2. Engineering Design Internship (EDI) is a required, sophomore-level, college engineering course. EDI was introduced over ten years ago as a course requirement in the otherwise traditional academic degree programs of a selective engineering college. EDI is designed to ease the transition from school to work by requiring students to solve "real-world" engineering problems contracted to them by industry or the public sector. Fieldwork in EDI was conducted by Karen Tonso in 1993, when 26 percent of the class were women, compared to 15 percent in engineering colleges nationally.

3. Environmental Legislation Action Coalition (ELAC) is a nonprofit, environmental action organization providing mostly summer employment for college-aged students. As employees of ELAC, young people canvass residences to solicit financial and political support for

legislative actions that protect the environment. Fieldwork in ELAC was conducted by Linda Behm in 1992; during the study, 50 percent of ELAC employees were women.

4. Conservation Corporation (CC) is a nonprofit enterprise that provides permanent employment to biologists, botanists, ecologists, lawyers, and fund-raisers who work to protect threatened species and habitats. Fieldwork in CC was conducted by Margaret Eisenhart in 1992–94, when 46 percent of the environmental scientists at CC were women. Thus our sites included two school-based programs (IGC and EDI) and two workplaces (CC and ELAC).

Organization of This Book

Chapter 1, "Women (Still) Need Not Apply," begins with an investigation of the distribution of opportunities and places for learning and doing science or technology in contemporary U.S. society. We examine the trends in women's and men's participation and success. In general, we find that despite indicators of academic preparation and interest that place women and men at equal levels, and despite some narrowing of the gender gap during the 1970s and early 1980s, women have been and continue to be underrepresented in science or engineering workplaces, and they remain concentrated in places and work practices of lower prestige.

In chapter 2, "In the 'Heretical' Sectors: Where the Women Are," we look more closely at the places where women have been well represented over time and across disciplines, and we consider how well previous theories of women's participation in science can explain their persistent underrepresentation in elite practices and overrepresentation in lower-status ones. Finding limitations (as well as strengths) in these theories, we propose an alternative that we refer to as a "historical-relational perspective," based in the tradition of practice theories.[3] This perspective led us to focus on two things not usually taken up in accounts of women in science: (1) how everyday practices in high- and low-status sites relate to each other and (2) how women come to be constrained agents in the world of scientific action as well as coproducers of that world. Put in less formal terms, we came to be interested in how and why bright, young women, interested and prepared to work in science or engineering, could not only end up in lower-status work, but actively seem to choose that work and status for themselves.

With chapter 3, we launch our in-depth examination of the four sites and the women in them. Chapters 3 through 6 provide careful looks inside our four sites; we first explore and then compare the "science practices" in each site. By "science practices," we mean the concrete, everyday tasks and social relationships in which scientific information of some kind is used. We include for each site the various representations of expertise and identity that give value and direction to the group's practices and individuals' contributions to them. These "representational devices" (after Nespor 1994) define what it means to be a "scientist," an "engineer," a "good worker," a "woman," a "man," and so forth in each site. Next, we consider how the representational devices connect participants to wider networks of power in science, engineering, or political action.

We found that scientific or technical information fit differently into practice at each site, and each place organized tasks, relationships, and individuals' contributions in distinctive ways. We also found that *science* meant something quite different in each site. Yet, despite the differences, all of the women were involved in worthwhile activities, and most were successful at using and learning the knowledge available to them. They actively participated in activities that included scientific or technical information; they were rewarded and advanced about as often as men; and for the most part, they enjoyed what they were doing, felt empowered by virtue of developing competence in an area they associated with men, and believed they were making an important contribution, both scientifically and politically.

In three of the four sites, however, (all except the genetics classroom), the practices, meanings, and networks of "science" that women developed were distinctly different from those characteristic of elite science sites. In some cases, the women became "experts" in work disdained as "not real science"; in other cases, women became "experts" in activities dismissed as unimportant by the men who worked with them; and in still others, women became "experts" in activities supported only precariously by the public. Thus, as women came to participate in, enjoy, and get better at "science" in the ways they did, they also came to occupy particular status positions—mostly lower-status positions—in the hierarchy of science, occupations, or both. We take a hard look at this situation, asking why it is that the science women do is so consistently thought of as low-status.

In chapter 7, "Women's Status and the Discourse of Gender Neutrality at Work," a closer look at three of the sites—the engineering internship (EDI), the environmental action group (ELAC), and the conservation corporation (CC)—reveals an even more complicated picture. The women and men in these three sites relied on what we call a "discourse of (alleged) gender neutrality."[4] This discourse both attracted women to the site and hid some of its features that disadvantaged women more than men. Women were attracted by the discourse because it suggested that everyone was treated equally at work. But they were disadvantaged to the extent that "good work" was talked about and acted upon *as if* it were genderless or gender-neutral, when in fact it incorporated features that were prototypical of white males. For the most part, the women actually found easy access and success only insofar as they worked as if they were prototypical white males. That is, successful women (as well as men) had to conform to work practices culturally and historically associated with male professionals who have wives at home and who enjoy the prerogatives of adults who feel safe in public spaces.[5] The discourse of gender neutrality made it possible for workplaces to encourage and support women's participation while simultaneously denying the existence of features that disadvantaged women.

Chapter 8, "In the Presence of Women's Power," asks whether women at the three sites (EDI, ELAC, and CC) attempted to resist or change the conditions of their work. Although the women's challenges were few, some disrupted both the science and the work-practice status quo, often in small and unacknowledged, but potentially consequential, ways. These challenges were generally not viewed by the women themselves as political efforts. The women believed they simply acted in response to their individual needs. Yet, the ways of talking and acting that sprang from these actions carried the potential for progressive institutional change—potential that probably would not have arisen if women had not been present in significant numbers and willing to take some risks with their prestige.

In chapter 9, "Situated Science, the Presence of Women, and the Practices of Work and School," we try to make sense of the patterns in women's successes and difficulties in science, social life, and politics across the four sites, and to draw out the implications of these patterns for theories of the social reproduction of (scientific) power, situated learning, and women's participation in science and engineering. We argue that our "lower-status" or "marginal" sites are not simply receptacles for people who "can't make it" or are excluded from higher-status sites, although this is part of the situation. In addition, the sites are attractive alternatives to sites of privileged science, and women view them as places to pursue their scientific or technical interests in more satisfying ways. At the same time, however, women (and men) use ideas about gender neutrality (e.g., equal opportunity, gender equality, "everyone's treated the same here") to celebrate and legitimize lower-status sites for something they are not. These women may be conceived to be "in struggle" (Holland and Lave, forthcoming) to define themselves and their work as important, legitimate, and rewarding amidst many possible competing definitions. In the sites we studied, in this particular historical moment and for these women who were in various stages of making the transition from school to professional work, women's work-related struggles were not primarily over access, opportunity, or promotion in male-dominated places. Rather, their struggles concerned how to be successful, satisfied, gendered, *and* "safe" in work worlds that are normatively defined as gender-neutral or genderless but are not.

In chapter 9 we also discuss the implications of our findings for schools and school science. We believe that the findings from our sites contain important insights for school and community science. For example, our findings suggest that many people, including women, want to learn more about science and technology and try to do so, though not in school. Unlike so many young people today, the women in our sites found legitimate public spaces in which to learn and use science and to act on at least some of their critiques of the establishment. In so doing, they appropriated science and developed it in a context with public and personal relevance. Although their efforts were constrained by existing power relations, they nonetheless pointed out the value of looking at science—the sites of its use and learning—more broadly than is normally done in discussions of school science or scientific literacy. On the other hand, our findings suggest that for girls and women to overcome current barriers to meaningful involvement in science or engineering, they must also participate in activities which offer them experiences and a critical language by which to assess their practices in gendered terms. In the sites of our study, women may gain entry and do well in science, but the discourse of gender neutrality by which they make sense of their experiences hides many prototypically male characteristics of workplaces that jeopardize the promise of women's presence.

 Part One

The Gendered Landscape
of Science and Engineering

Science and knowledge will always be deeply permeated by the social relations through which they come into existence, but it is contemporary social relations that create and recreate science and knowledge today. (Harding 1991, ix)

Before turning to the sites themselves, we must take up the large-scale patterns in women's representation in science and engineering, both historically and presently. These patterns alert us to the fact that while our sites are not comparable in the strict sense, they are, together with the more familiar sites of schools and laboratories, part of the system that comprises science and technology in contemporary American society and beyond. They comprise what Marcus and Fischer (1986, in the opening quotation for the preface) refer to as part of a network of dispersed groups with mutual, often unintended, consequences for each other.

 Chapter One

Women (Still) Need Not Apply

[S]tarting in 1968 and essentially complete by 1972, there was a legal revolution in women's education and employment rights. It promised, even seemed to guarantee, broad ramifications for women's careers in science and engineering, but its full implementation would require many battles in the years ahead. One era had ended and a new, more equitable one was beginning. (Rossiter 1995, 382)

[Women's] career attainments continue, on average [as of 1991], to be more modest than those of men in all sectors—in academia, industry, and government—and the gap in attainments grows as men and women age. Moreover, while some distinguished women scientists and engineers have become insiders and members of the scientific establishment, those who have often feel themselves to be outsiders and on the margin. It is not clear at this juncture whether parity will be achieved in the careers of men and women scientists and engineers and, if so, when. (Zuckerman 1991, 56)

Patterns in the Participation of Women in Science and Engineering

Despite the hope for the equal participation of women in science and engineering noted by Margaret Rossiter above, women have been and continue to be found in the lower-status activities and workplaces of science and engineering practice. Although many believe that women in the 1990s are well on their way to achieving parity with men in science and engineering, there is evidence to the contrary. The gap between men's and women's success, especially in elite science and engineering, remains significant.

This chapter begins with an examination of women's involvement in science or engineering in the United States today. We investigate the distribution of women in science and engineering degree programs and workplaces and summarize changes in their participation over the past four decades. We then examine and critique current proposals for educational reform developed with the goal of addressing the absence of women and their inequitable treatment in science and engineering activities in school and at work.

Before proceeding, we want to note that our search for information about where the women are in science and engineering was not easy. Although considerable data are available on the numbers and types of degrees earned by female and male scientists and engineers, there are many fewer sources of information on the employment of men and women in science and engineering. We found, as did Rossiter (1995), that "the statistical picture is badly incomplete, . . . [has] many gaps, and fail[s] to probe very deeply or meaningfully into . . . aspects of the women's situation" (95).

Particularly significant in our opinion were the limited trend data on the employment of scientists who do not have doctoral degrees (not available during the period 1970–1995) and the lack of information on employment of scientists in nonprofit organizations (with the exception of government). Given Rossiter's finding that (as of 1966), of people employed as scientists, 38.1 percent of the women (26.5 percent of the men) held master's degrees (1995, 105), and our own finding of large proportions of female scientists in environmental and other nonprofit organizations, the absence of detailed information in these two areas was especially notable.

A Brief History of Women in Science and Engineering

Rossiter's description, quoted above, of the optimism about women's increased opportunities in science and engineering produced by the passage of equal rights legislation in the late 1960s and early 1970s initially appeared to be well founded. The number of science and engineering doctorates awarded to women rose from a mere 7 percent in 1970 to 24 percent in 1985 (Zuckerman 1991, 29), and in engineering alone the number of bachelor's degrees awarded to women rose from only 385 in 1975 (less than 1 percent of all undergraduate degrees awarded in engineering) to more than 11,000 in 1985 (approximately 16 percent of the total) (National Science Board [NSB] 1993, 79). Similarly, the percentages of white females with doctoral degrees in science or engineering employed as academic faculty increased from 12.1 percent in

1979 to 18.1 percent in 1989 (NSB 1993, 409–11). At the same time, the numbers of men in these fields also increased, thus making women's achievements all the more impressive (NSB 409–10).

Unfortunately, by the mid-1980s the picture seemed to be changing, and the late 1980s brought sobering news. Analyzing the enrollment of men and women in college-degree programs, Jerry Jacobs (1995) found that the rate of improvement in what he refers to as the "integration," or balance, of women and men in twenty-four degree programs slowed substantially in the late 1980s after increasing markedly from the late 1960s through the early 1980s. Among those receiving bachelor's degrees in computer science, life sciences, mathematics, and engineering, increases in the proportion of women during the period of 1980–85 slowed during the period 1985–90, and except in the life sciences, women's percentages remained considerably below men's (Jacobs 1995, 88). In the physical sciences, small increases occurred over the entire period 1980–90, but women's enrollment had reached only about 30 percent in 1990. Jacobs concludes his report with this ominous note:

> The results discussed here present some reason for concern among those who are interested in women's economic prospects. The data indicate that the 20-year trend toward greater integration among college majors that began in the early 1960s slowed markedly during the late 1980s and, in some contexts, came to a complete stop. (96)

Thus the picture of women's opportunities in science and engineering is not currently as rosy as that predicted in the 1960s, nor even as rosy as that described by people examining trends in enrollment, hiring, and employment between the late 1960s and the mid-1980s. In fact, current figures on women's participation in science and engineering, as well as the details of women's increased participation in scientific and engineering fields between 1960 and 1985, reveal that although there are currently more opportunities for women to become scientists and engineers than in the past, the opportunities are still limited.

Figures on the percentages of women receiving master's and doctoral degrees in natural science or engineering show a pattern similar to that reported by Jacobs (National Science Foundation [NSF] 1996). Although the percentages of women in these fields have increased dramatically since 1971, their percentages continue to be considerably lower than those of men, as tables 1.1 and 1.2 reveal. Thus, despite substantial

Table 1.1   **Percentages of women receiving master's degrees, 1971 and 1991**

Field	1971	1991
Engineering	1.1%	14.0%
Natural sciences	22.2%	35.6%

Source: National Science Foundation, Division of Research, Evaluation, and Communication, Directorate for Education and Human Resources, *Indicators of Science and Mathematics Education, 1995*, ed. Larry E. Suter (Arlington, VA: National Science Foundation [NSF 96-52], 1996), 186.

gains, women continue to be underrepresented in science and engineering degree programs.

Even women who do succeed in academic science or engineering have more trouble than men do in finding satisfying and rewarding employment. Rates of unemployment and underemployment among scientists and engineers (those looking for work) are consistently higher for women than men (Vetter 1992; Zuckerman 1991, 32). Harriet Zuckerman's (1991) study of the careers of male and female scientists and engineers reveals that even when men and women are similarly qualified and get jobs, their career trajectories tend to be different, to women's disadvantage.

Beginning with their initial qualifications, Zuckerman traces scientists' careers between 1970 and 1980. She includes indicators such as the timing of tenure and promotion; salary; research impact; honors; and reputation. She reports that the intellectual caliber of men and women entering science or engineering with doctoral degrees is the same (as measured by either standardized test scores or by prior academic performance) and that men and women now earn their doctoral degrees at much the same age (34). These similarities, as well as the fact that approximately equal numbers of women and men are awarded and accept postdoctoral positions (an expected step in the trajectory toward high-status academic positions in most science fields), suggest

Table 1.2   **Percentages of women receiving doctoral degrees, 1971 and 1991**

Field	1971	1991
Engineering	0.5%	8.7%
Natural sciences	9.7%	26.0%

Source: National Science Foundation, Division of Research, Evaluation, and Communication, Directorate for Education and Human Resources, *Indicators of Science and Mathematics Education, 1995*, ed. Larry E. Suter (Arlington, VA: National Science Foundation [NSF 96-52], 1996), 187.

that men and women begin their careers as scientists equally well prepared for success (34–35). However, female scientists in academe are
considerably more likely to hold their first professional position as instructors, lecturers, and other "off-ladder" academic positions, whereas
men are more likely to work first in tenure-track positions (36).

The initial tendency for female scientists to fill lower-status positions
continues into the later stages of their careers. While data on women's
positions in educational institutions, industry, and government are less
than thorough,

> they are relentlessly consistent; . . . women, on average, started out
> in lower ranks than men, and the disparity in their ranks continues.
> . . . [For] example, Ashern and Scott . . . report that among matched
> men and women who received Ph.D.'s in the 1940s and 1950s, 86
> percent of men had become full professors by 1979 as against 64
> percent of women (a ratio of 1.3:1). In the cohort that got Ph.D.'s
> in the 1960s, a smaller proportion of both men (52 percent) and
> women (30 percent) had become full professors by 1979, but men
> proportionately outnumbered women by a ratio of 1.7:1. . . . And
> finally, among those who had gotten Ph.D.'s between 1970 and 1974,
> just 6 percent of men and 3 percent of women had become full pro-
> fessors [by 1979]. (Zuckerman 1991, 37)

Salary figures for male and female scientists and engineers reported
in 1991 reveal another disparity between men and women. Despite the
calls for more women to be employed in science or engineering, median
annual salaries for full-time employed civilian scientists and engineers
are less for women at every level of experience, beginning with scientists
and engineers employed less than five years. For people employed less
than five years, the median salary for men is $48,000, and that for
women is $42,000 (NSF 1994, 374). The disparity remains even after
more experience, with women consistently earning between 87.5 percent and 83.6 percent of men's salaries.

The statistics cited above from Zuckerman's review reflect a picture
of women in science that is particularly grim: in general, while women
and men seem to be completing doctorates with similar credentials and
experience, the positions and rewards they find are not comparable.
While many of the reports Zuckerman summarizes were produced in
the late 1980s and based upon studies conducted between 1970 and
1980, her conclusions are not out of date.

In a recent review of trends in the production of doctorates in science and engineering, Smith and Tang (1994) report findings similar to those of Zuckerman. While the majority of all academic scientists and engineers are tenured, men are more likely than women to hold tenured positions as scientists in universities. As of 1989, 65 percent of men and only 40 percent of women held tenured positions (115). At the same time, more women than men (37 percent vs. 21 percent) were in non-tenure-track jobs (115). In addition, only 29 percent of all scientists and engineers employed as assistant professors in four-year colleges and universities were women (NSF 1994, 376–77). As Smith and Tang comment,

> Surprisingly, this pattern remains the same even in fields where women have relatively high representation in doctoral training. In 1989, less than half of all female doctoral scientists and engineers held full professorships in psychology or the social sciences, compared to two-thirds among males. Experience apparently only explains a portion of the gender disparity in academic rank. (117)

According to the National Science Board (NSB 1993), "no profession exhibits a greater disparity in the employment of men and women than engineering" (79). As of 1991, women made up 3.4 percent of the U.S. engineering workforce. Due in large part to the scarcity of qualified female engineers, starting salaries for women in engineering are higher than those for men and higher than those offered to women in any other field (Vandervoort 1985, 140). However, a salary gap begins to appear after several years. According to Vandervoort, "women engineers who have worked fifteen years have salaries only 84.9 percent of men" (140). And we find that "men's salaries continue to increase with years of experience, but women's reach a plateau. The chief explanation for this widening gap is that significantly more men are promoted to managerial positions than women" (NSB 1993, 79).

According to a study by Judith McIlwee and Gregg Robinson (1992), many female engineers graduate from college and find well-paid jobs, receiving starting salaries at or above those of their male counterparts. However, within ten years, women occupy lower-status positions than men. According to the authors, "men who had been out of school longest and with their current employer longest held the highest ranked jobs. In contrast, there was no similar association for women" (84). Furthermore, "a significant number of women who started their careers in high-status design jobs actually experienced downward mobility over time" (84).

Thus, despite increases in women's involvement in science and engineering degree programs after the passage of equal rights legislation in the late 1960s and early 1970s, women's participation in the work of science and engineering remains unequal to that of men, and is less well rewarded. Women tend to be concentrated in fields of low prestige and in jobs and positions with less status and less salary, than those enjoyed by men. This distribution of people in the disciplines and places of scientific and engineering practice suggests why, when we went looking for women practicing science, we found them where we did: in lower-status workplaces, and in lower-status activities of science and engineering.[1]

This continued disparity has not escaped the notice of educators and policymakers, who have proposed a series of educational reforms designed to rectify some of the inequities that still exist for women interested in pursuing careers in science and engineering. Although these reforms do not directly address women's concentration in lower-status and lower-paying science positions, they seek improvements in science education that will raise the number of well-trained women prepared to enter science or engineering fields.[2]

The Effort to Improve Opportunities for Female Scientists and Engineers through Education[3]

For many people, the key to solving the problem of women's underrepresentation in science and engineering lies in increasing the numbers and improving the academic preparation of girls and young women in science and mathematics. If schools did a better job of teaching science and mathematics, more people, especially women, might pursue degrees and jobs in science or engineering and be more successful in them. Concerns such as these have led to the recent development of three national-level proposals for science education reform, including the American Association for the Advancement of Science's [AAAS] Project 2061 (AAAS 1989, 1993; Rutherford and Ahlgren 1990); the National Science Teachers Association's [NSTA] project, *Scope, Sequence, and Coordination of Secondary School Science* (Aldridge 1992; NSTA 1992, 1995); and the National Research Council's [NRC] *National Science Education Standards* (1994, 1996). In one way or another, all three reform proposals aim to improve science education for the benefit of girls (among other goals). For example, the NRC makes equity for all students the first principle of its reform agenda. Its first principle reads as follows:

> Science is for all students. This principle is one of equity and excel-
> lence. Science in our schools must be for all students: All students,
> regardless of age, sex, cultural or ethnic background, disabilities, as-
> pirations, or interest and motivation in science, should have the op-
> portunity to attain high levels of scientific literacy. The standards
> . . . emphatically reject any situation in science education where some
> people—for example, members of certain populations—are discour-
> aged from pursuing science and excluded from opportunities to learn
> science. (NRC 1996, 20)

This goal is also addressed in both the NSTA and AAAS proposals,
although to different degrees. NSTA's scope, sequence and coordination proposal (1992) includes a more general statement about equity,
focusing on the need to develop "instructional strategies [that are] . . .
appropriate for heterogeneous groups, with no tracking" (15), and aim-
ing at what they describe as "an ambitious, but not unrealistic" final
goal: "Science learning for all students that is interesting, relevant, challenging, and personally rewarding" (16). The authors of AAAS's *Science
for All Americans* (1990) are more explicit:

> The recommendations in this report apply to all students. The set
> of recommendations constitutes a common core of learning . . . for
> all young people, regardless of their social circumstances and career
> aspirations. In particular, the recommendations pertain to those who
> in the past have largely been bypassed in science and mathematics
> education: ethnic and language minorities and girls. (Rutherford and
> Ahlgren 1990, x)

Despite these goals, we are not optimistic that current plans to imple-
ment these reforms will produce the desired results. Our pessimism is
fueled by the failure of reform proponents to take seriously the many
ways women (and minorities) are discouraged, barred, or chased from
science.

The processes thought to contribute to the underrepresentation of
girls and women in science are many and varied. They include the mass
media's stereotyped portrayals of scientists as nerdy and male (e.g., Nelkin 1987); the "chilly climate" of science classrooms and degree programs (e.g., Hall and Sandler 1982; Sadker and Sadker 1994; Seymour
and Hewitt 1997; Tobias 1990); the ways women and minorities are
culturally defined as the type of "people who leave" science and engineering programs (Downey, Hegg, and Lucena 1993); the known ma-
nipulation of some scientific findings for corporate or political gain

(e.g., Greider 1992; Nelkin 1987); and the systematic exclusion of non-Western, nonmale interests and perspectives from science (e.g., Harding 1991; Keller 1985).

Yet the current reform proposals suggest that relatively minor changes in science content and classroom instruction can overcome these barriers. The following excerpt from *Science for All Americans* is illustrative:

> We are convinced that—given clear goals, the right resources, and good teaching throughout 13 years of school—essentially all students . . . will be able to reach all of the recommended learning goals by the time they graduate from high school. (Rutherford and Ahlgren 1990, x–xi)

In essence, the reform proposals suggest that better teaching, higher standards, and sensitivity to differences among students can overcome long-standing obstacles to participation. The proposals do not address feminist or minority critiques of science.

Over a decade ago, Evelyn Fox Keller (1982) argued that feminist and minority critiques of science could be arranged on a four-point continuum from liberal to radical. The liberal critique suggests that women and minorities are underrepresented in science because they have not been treated in the same encouraging way as have men. The liberal solution is to find ways for girls, women, and minorities to gain equal access to the range and depth of positive science experiences already available to boys and men.

This is the approach taken by AAAS, NSTA, and NRC. An excerpt from NRC's national standards provides an example. The second underlying principle of the national standards (after the principle of equity) states that "[a]ll students will learn all science in the content standards" (I-7). Later in the document, NRC explains what teachers should do to meet this principle:

> Teachers of science orchestrate their classes so that all have equal opportunities to participate in learning activities. Students with physical disabilities might require modified equipment; students with limited English ability might need to be encouraged to use their own language as well as English. . . ; students with learning disabilities might need more time to complete science activities. (1996, II-13)

Yet in Keller's scheme, the liberal approach is the most conservative one.

A second, more radical, critique by Keller suggests that the predominance of men in the sciences has led to a bias in the choice and definition of the problems scientists have addressed. For example, in the health sciences, problems associated with conceiving a child have, until very recently, received little attention. The focus of work (generally by male researchers) has been on contraceptive techniques and devices to be used by women to prevent conception. From this perspective, science is likely to discourage women and minorities because it does not address many of the topics that concern them.

Other, more radical critiques advanced by Keller question the fundamental processes and foundations of science. A third critique suggests the possibility of bias in the design and interpretation of research. The study of primatology provides a good example (e.g., Haraway 1989). When white males were the only primate researchers, they viewed the primate troop, composed of a single adult male with several females and young, as a harem and interpreted their data from the assumption that the male was the troop leader. Years of field observation studies by female researchers (e.g., Jane Goodall and Dian Fossey) have shown that the social organization of some primate troops is better explained by matriarchy: males are used by females as a resource for sperm, protection, and friendship. The possibility of this type of bias suggests that science discourages women and minorities because its theoretical stances tend to privilege white male standpoints.

The most radical critique of science offered by Keller is a challenge to the truth and warrant of the conclusions of natural science on the grounds that they reflect the judgments of only one group of people: men. Keller writes, "It is not true [that] 'the conclusions of natural science are true and necessary, and the judgment of man has nothing to do with them'; it is the judgment of women that they [the conclusions of science] have nothing to do with" (1982, 590).

The means of lowering barriers for women and minorities suggested by AAAS, NSTA, and NRC address only the type of bias identified in Keller's first and most conservative critique. The changes are all "compensatory" strategies (e.g., Howe 1993) to provide access to science for previously underrepresented groups. Compensatory strategies treat disadvantaged persons according to their special needs, but only with the aim of enabling them to measure up to a standard already set by the advantaged group. The content and modes of inquiry in the science activities of the current reform projects in science education are not open to the kind of revisions that Keller's other three critiques suggest. In all three proposals, the nature of the science to be learned is specifically described in the content standards, and they describe, almost exclusively, the content and methods of conventional science.

The same criticisms can be made of college-level reform efforts. Programs such as those for "women in engineering" or those that encourage cooperative work groups and single-sex classes are usually compensatory in that they aim to raise women's performance to the level of men's (see Tonso 1997 for an extended discussion in the case of engineering).

If we are serious about increasing the numbers and kinds of people in science, new curriculum plans and outcome measures that focus on conventional science do not seem to be promising directions to take. Given the apparently low level of student interest in conventional academic work (see, for example, Holland and Eisenhart 1990; Lave 1990) and the findings of feminists and others about the biases inherent in conventional science, efforts to involve more people in science, especially women and minorities, may fail precisely because conventional science and modes of practicing it are stressed in school. Without considering questions about the nature of science itself, such as those raised by Keller, it seems unlikely that improving the content of science education will help to attract or retain more women or minorities.

In the course of this book, we will suggest some broader ways of thinking about scientific practice—activities that include science in some way—by looking at places where women are currently engaged in such practice. In some of these places, contrary to the general trends reported in this chapter but consistent with Keller's ideas, women in about the same proportion as men are engaged in scientific practice that interests and rewards them. Our findings also make evident that such places are not normally counted and evaluated by government agencies and researchers. In other words, they are not locations of elite scientific practice.

 Chapter Two

In the "Heretical Sectors": Where the Women Are

> As *authorities*, whose position in social space depends principally on the possession of cultural capital [wealth derived from prestige], a subordinate form of capital, university professors are situated rather on the side of the subordinate pole of the field of power and are clearly opposed in this respect to the managers of industry and business [who hold economic and social capital, the dominant forms of capital]. But, as holders of an institutionalized form of cultural capital, which guarantees them a bureaucratic career and a regular income, [professors] are [also] opposed to [freelance] writers and artists . . . the occupants of the less institutionalized and more heretical sectors of the field. (Bourdieu 1988, 36)

In Pierre Bourdieu's account of the status hierarchy of university professors in France during the 1960s and 1970s, scientists—among all professors—were the most dependent for their prestige on cultural capital. By this he means that while professors of medicine, law, the arts, and even the social sciences relied at least in part on some social and economic capital (theirs by virtue of their class backgrounds, membership in powerful social networks, and access to money) to establish their prestige, science professors and science researchers did not or could not. Among scientists, whose origins were in the lower and middle classes, prestige was derived almost exclusively from one form of cultural capital—access to, and command of, scientific knowledge. Once having gained a reputation, some scientists extended their prestige through social networks of students, former students, laboratory assistants, research associates, and administrators of funding programs; yet as a group, scientists remained socially subordinate, albeit intellectually dominant, in the French university community, at least until the 1970s.

In the United States, studies of scientists' social origins suggest that until World War II, the same profile existed. Before that war, more than two-thirds of people receiving doctorates in science were from middle- or lower-class backgrounds (Zuckerman 1977, 66), and prestige in science in the United States, as in France, depended on contributing to scientific knowledge.

> Prestige in the scientific community is largely graded in terms of the extent to which scientists are held to have contributed to the advancement of knowledge in their fields and is far less influenced by other kinds of role performance, such as teaching, involvement in the politics of science, or in organizing research. Even great influence in national politics and science policy, for example, does not earn a scientist the same kind of esteem as scientific contributions judged to be truly important. (Zuckerman 1977, 9)

On the face of it, this situation should have boded well for women who wanted to pursue a profession. Usually lacking the social and economic capital available to men, women might have found their fair share of places among scientists. Bourdieu suggests why:

> The fact that the social origins of professors . . . tend to become lower as we move from the faculties of medicine and law to the arts and above all to the science faculties . . . can no doubt be explained by the fact that . . . the procedures and processes of production and acquisition of knowledge are objectified in instruments, methods, and techniques—instead of existing only in a personally internalized state. . . . [O]utsiders, and notably those among them who lack inherited capital [surely most women], have more chance and earlier opportunities in competing with the insiders, if the capacities and dispositions required place less emphasis . . . on experience in all its forms and on intuitive knowledge arising from a long process of familiarization. (1988, 59)

As we saw in chapter 1, however, women have not been able to take their fair share of academic or other elite positions in science. Rather than holding high-status and secure university or laboratory positions, they have become (after Bourdieu) "occupants of the less institutionalized and more heretical sectors of the field." In fact, since the emergence of science in the Western world, women have participated in the "heretical sectors," first as active and accepted contributors in science when science itself was heretical, and then as occupants of its heretical sectors when it became prestigious. The next section explores these patterns.

Heretics in Science[1]

Patterns in Women's Participation across Time

While science itself was heretical, women played prominent and central roles in it. From the sixteenth century until well into the nineteenth century, the pursuit of expertise in scientific knowledge was considered a heretical alternative to the pursuit of classical knowledge. During this period, proponents of anticlassical education actively encouraged women to pursue science, and many did (Phillips 1990). Popular science books were written by women and specifically for them. Women also wrote science textbooks in which they presented science through female characters. Women wrote for scientific journals and were members of scientific associations. "Certainly by the end of the eighteenth century, ladies seemed to take for granted their appearance at scientific meetings" (Phillips 1990, 79). During this period, women were expected to be interested in science and especially inclined toward it (see Phillips 1990, chap. 6).

Yet by the end of the nineteenth century, as research science began to replace the classics as the preeminent form of intellectual knowledge, women's representation, particularly their involvement in the central activities of science, began to decline. Once scientific knowledge became culturally dominant after the turn of the twentieth century, women came to be concentrated on its margins.

Margaret Rossiter's book, *Women Scientists in America: Struggles and Strategies to 1940* (1982), takes up the history of U.S. women in science at the end of the nineteenth century and follows it to 1940. Rossiter argues that during this period, new roles were being defined both for scientists and for women. In this process, *science* and *womanhood* came to be rhetorically cast as opposites. The scientific ideal became rigorous, rational, impersonal, and competitive behavior, while the ideal woman was supposed to be delicate, emotional, unobtrusive, and noncompetitive. Science was to be "upgraded" to a profession through the application of standards that would exclude "amateurs" (i.e., those who did not meet the new ideal). Women were to become better mothers and household managers (but not "professionals") through increased education. Thus, the prototype of a scientist came to be associated with masculinity, and "female scientist" became an unnatural, unexpected conceptual category. Previewing this outcome in introductory remarks about her book, Rossiter writes,

[T]his conceptual [cultural] element meant that much of the history of women in science would be worked out not simply in the realm of objective reality, of what specific women could or did do, but covertly, in the psychic land of images and sexual stereotypes, which had a logic all its own. (1982, xv)

Thus, while the status of scientists might depend on access to cultural capital, as Bourdieu suggested, and cultural capital might be the easiest form of capital for women to get, the cultural meaning of "being a scientist" did not fit easily or naturally with "being a woman" after the turn of the nineteenth century.

In her subsequent book, *Women Scientists in America: Before Affirmative Action, 1940–1972* (1995), Rossiter continues the historical narrative. During World War II, with so many men away fighting the war, women were needed to take up important jobs in science and related fields. The demand for women with scientific training was high. Women answered the call in record numbers and performed well in these jobs.

In light of this success, the rhetoric about women's suitability for science might have changed; it did, but not in a way that made subsequent access easier. After the war, women's numbers in high-status positions again declined, although the demand for people with scientific training remained high.

Soon after the war ended, official U.S. sources began to emphasize the need for women (as well as men) to prepare to come to the nation's defense during the Cold War. Increasingly, the official view stressed that women would be needed as scientists and engineers. Women were encouraged to enter these fields, and employers were urged to hire and employ them fully (Rossiter 1995, 54). By the mid-to-late 1950s, this rhetoric began to correspond to slight increases in women's representation in science and engineering training programs. Yet, as these women started to look for jobs, the rhetoric began to change again. Rossiter writes, "Starting around 1954–1955 there was a sudden explosion of articles urging women to study science, primarily in order to become laboratory workers or public school teachers" (1995, 56). Rossiter quotes an unnamed author, who explained the situation as follows:

[While] laboratories are interested in training and ability regardless of sex, . . . women are most successful and appear happiest in the position of technical aide to scientists and engineers engaged in research and development programs. They are more willing than men

> to do routine, repetitious work. They are patient, faithful, and dexterous. They are subjective rather than objective in attitude. (Rossiter 1995, 56)

Thus it appears that the U. S. government, the science establishment, and the public as a whole alternately applauded women as a new source of scientific expertise and then restricted or minimized the roles they might play. "Any increased numbers of 'scientific womanpower' could be safely channeled into traditionally feminized roles, where they would reinforce rather than threaten existing sex segregation" (Rossiter 1995, 57).

Another significant cultural theme also emerged in the media of the 1950s and early 1960s: women's preparation in science and engineering should be used only in case of dire national emergency. For example, the high proportion of women scientists in the Soviet Union was often mentioned in the media as evidence of women's potential for success in technical fields (as well as evidence of what the enemy was up to). However, as Rossiter explains,

> [A]fter presenting all the statistics on Soviet women engineers, a journalist would point out (usually emphasizing the point with a photo) how unattractive (plain and stocky) these Soviet women were by Western standards. They were never shown with children, although statistics showed that most were married and mothers. Thus the journalists, female as well as male, usually ended up showing not that a normal American girl should want to become an engineer like Olga but that she should be relieved that her country was not yet so badly off that she had to. (Rossiter 1995, 65)

Rossiter ends her chronicle in 1972, just as new federal legislation was passed to provide "equal employment," "equal pay," and "equal treatment" of women in higher education programs. She expresses optimism that the growing political movement to ensure equality for women and the legislative victories it helped to produce would pave the way for many more women to enter and succeed in science and engineering. As the statistics presented in chapter 1 attest, her hope has not yet been realized.

Patricia Phillips' (1990) account of how science education for girls—a strong feature of British single-sex schools prior to 1868—was transformed by 1918 into "needlework, cookery, laundrywork, housekeeping, and household hygiene" hints at another cultural reason why the hope Rossiter expressed and many shared has not been realized. In 1864, the British government commissioned an assessment of girls' education. The Taunton Commission's final report, coming after four years of study, praised the high level of science education available in girls' schools but expressed shock at the generally inferior level of girls' classical education compared to that of boys. Stating categorically that no evidence existed to suggest that girls could not or should not be educated in the same way as boys, the commission concluded that the only way to improve girls' education, and *thereby to assure girls' equality*, was to give them the same education—an education in the classics—that was provided to boys. As this change was being implemented, hard economic times led some prominent figures to suggest that the economic problems stemmed in part from women who, while engaged in educational and occupational pursuits previously available only to men, were neglecting their traditional family responsibilities. In this political climate—and in the name of equality for girls—the portion of the curriculum which had been devoted to science education in girls' schools was paradoxically replaced. A curriculum that had included in some cases "the property of matter, the laws of motion, mechanical powers, simple chemistry, electricity, geology, botany, natural history and astronomy" (Phillips 1990, 248) was replaced by the classics and a new "science for girls" that was "domestic science" only.

In these ways, women have been moved to the margins of science as it became prestigious. Women's opportunities in elite science have been compromised by expectations, rhetoric, and programs which assume that women will play supportive roles. Further, in the name of "equality" coupled with ideas about traditional female responsibilities, opportunities for women have come to be different and generally of lower status than those for men. Such contradictory cultural impulses—which on the one hand encourage girls and women to pursue mainstream science and on the other hand constrain them in the margins—concern us still. In chapter 7 we will discuss a contemporary American "discourse of gender neutrality"—a way of talking and acting which suggests that things are "neutral" and thus "fair" for both women and men when women are treated "just like men." This discourse, which we found in lower-status sites of scientific practice, appears to be a descendant of the earlier cultural assumption that if girls and women were to have "equal" opportunities, then they should be treated as if they were men. Although ameliorative efforts based on this idea, both in Britain and the United States, have been and continue to be well-intentioned and helpful to women in many instances, we will argue that the contemporary discourse of (alleged) gender neutrality supports women's participation in lower-status science while simultaneously obscuring or contradicting workplace expectations that are especially troublesome for women. Thus, four hundred years after women first began to be involved in science and two decades after a flurry of political and legislative activity to achieve gender equality, women continue to face cultural obstacles to their participation in high-status science. The contemporary obstacles may look somewhat different from those of the past, but we will argue that in many respects they are not.

Patterns in Women's Participation across Disciplines

The same pattern of women's underrepresentation in elite sites and overrepresentation in lower-status sites appears when we make comparisons across scientific and engineering disciplines, *although the indicators of high status differ from discipline to discipline.* Regardless of how high status is constructed (i.e., culturally defined), women (as a group) never seem able to measure up. In the high-energy physics laboratories studied by Sharon Traweek (1988), for example, status is calculated by "intelligence" and "reasoning" capabilities. In the idealized form, laboratory scientists who win awards, receive prestigious appointments, and get published are "rational, open-minded investigators, proceeding methodically, grounded incontrovertibly in the outcome of controlled experiments, and seeking objectively for the truth" (Traweek 1988, 80). Among the physicists, theoretical physicists ranked at the top of the status hierarchy, followed by experimentalists. Similarly, physics as a discipline ranks above all others, followed in order by chemistry, engineering, biology, the social sciences, and finally the humanities (Traweek 1988, 79). By these criteria of intelligence and reasoning, theoretical physics deserves the highest status because it is the most demanding. The humanities, in contrast, deserve to be at the bottom, because they demand the least. Also, in terms of this logic, women are not expected to make good physicists (Traweek 1988, 103–4). In general, as one descends this status hierarchy, the percentages of women (compared to men), which are quite small at the top, become much larger.

In contrast, in engineering, the top of the status hierarchy is management (upper management, followed by mid-management, then senior and project engineers), followed by engineering design, and then research and development (Evetts 1996; McIlwee and Robinson 1992). Lower down the status hierarchy are activities that support design (analysis or test engineering) or production (manufacturing engineering). As in the science hierarchy, as one descends the engineering hierarchy, the small percentages of women at the top grow larger (McIlwee and Robinson 1992, 81–82).

Judith McIlwee and Gregg Robinson (1992) give careful attention to a comparison of women's experiences in the two largest engineering fields, electrical engineering and mechanical engineering. Among engineers, electrical engineering is generally perceived as a good specialty for women because it is "abstract, math-based, and 'clean' work" (106). Note the contrast with physics, where abstract, theoretical work is not expected of women. Mechanical engineering, by contrast, is associated with the image of a "'tinkerer,' building prototypes in a shop" (106) and is thus closely tied to the image of a male. Nationally in the United States, slightly more undergraduate women engineers choose electrical engineering (13 percent) than mechanical engineering (11 percent), but once in a job, women in mechanical engineering are treated better and more equally than they are in electrical engineering. McIlwee and Robinson explain this finding by reference to workplace cultural norms that distinguish the sites where the two specialties are practiced; we will return to this explanation shortly.

Our point here is that despite the fact that status hierarchies in science and engineering are diversely constructed, women are consistently underrepresented in the high-status categories. When high status is defined by abstract, theoretical work (as in physics), women are underrepresented. When high status is defined by management skills and interests (including interpersonal skills, surely an area in which women might be expected to do well), women still are underrepresented. Capabilities identified as high-status in one field (physics) may be associated with women in another (electrical engineering), but women are underrepresented in both fields.

Some have suggested that as women's numbers increase in historically male-dominated fields or sectors, these status differentials will diminish. For example, Rosabeth Kanter, in her influential book *Men and Women of the Corporation* (1977), argued that women's difficulties in high-status jobs arose from being tokens. She found that tokens received heightened scrutiny because they stood out as different, felt isolated from social and professional networks, and were expected to act in gender-stereotyped ways. Kanter posited that as women's numbers increased, the negative consequences of tokenism would be reduced. However, Janice Yoder (1991) has recently discovered that this is not the case. First, she found that when men inhabit a mostly female domain, they avoid the negative consequences that women suffer (181). Second, as women's numbers increase, backlash against their presence also increases. Thus the trend moves in the wrong direction and the effect is the opposite of what Kanter predicted. Yoder's explanation is that women's intrusion into a male-dominated area threatens the area's prestige, while men's infiltration into a female-dominated area increases its stature (184). Thus, quoting Barbara Reskin, Yoder believes that "[m]en resist allowing women and men to work together *as equals* because doing so undermines differentiation and hence male dominance" (Yoder 1991, 181; Reskin's emphasis).

As a group, the studies cited above make clear that women's difficulties in moving into high-status positions in science and engineering are endemic. Yet the persistent fact of women's underrepresentation in the high-status areas of science and engineering, over time and across disciplines, is a challenge to most popular explanations of women's representation in science and engineering.

Popular Explanations for Women's Participation in Science

The pattern of women's underrepresentation in elite science or engineering cannot be adequately explained by theories that depend on differences in biological characteristics, stubborn gender-role stereotypes, or recurring socialization patterns. In this section, we begin with a brief review of these popular theories. We will show why they lack explanatory power for the processes and outcomes we wish to address. In fact, we believe that the virtually exclusive focus on these theories among many academics and the public makes it essentially impossible to gather the kinds of information needed to appreciate the circumstances of women's underrepresentation in high-status science. From this review, we will move on to discuss more adequate explanations from the tradition of social reproduction theory and then to develop our own approach to these issues.

"Gender-difference" theories focus on biological, social, and cognitive processes that begin as early as the moment of birth and function to differentiate the inclinations, skills, and attitudes of girls and boys as they grow up. Although various theories of gender difference emphasize different processes and outcomes (see Eisenhart and Holland 1992 for an extended review), in general they posit that socialization pressures, alone or in combination with biological factors, lead American girls to develop strengths in nurturing, building relationships, and caring for others. In turn, girls become interested in, better at, and committed to play, tasks, cognitive abilities, jobs, and moral perspectives that draw on their strengths (see, for example, Belenky et al. 1986; Chodorow 1978; Eccles 1987; Eccles and Jacobs 1986; Gilligan 1982; Maccoby and Jacklin 1974). In consequence, girls and women are likely to choose activities, coursework, and jobs or careers that coincide with their socialized strengths and interests.

These gender-difference theories can explain why relatively few girls or young women *ever* enter science, mathematics, or engineering, but they cannot adequately account for the patterns of underrepresentation among those who do enter. They cannot explain why women, over time and across disciplines, are not better represented and more successful in high-status science or engineering. If childhood socialization and relatively enduring abilities and skills were the cause of women's career patterns in science, then we would expect to find women choosing, working, and doing well in elite science or engineering positions that call for the skills women have developed through socialization. As we have demonstrated in the previous section, this does not often happen.

Some gender-difference theorists posit that career choice is better explained by the way childhood socialization pressures encourage girls and boys to develop different priorities for adulthood (Astin 1985; Goffredson 1981; J. Holland 1985; Tittle and Weinberg 1984). In the United States, girls and boys are socialized to different views on educational and occupational achievement and the importance of work versus family. Girls learn that the family is primary; boys, that work comes first. Girls learn to view work as something that must fit around family responsibilities, whereas boys learn to view family as something that must fit around work. If men but not women are found in science or science-related careers, the reason is that these pursuits are perceived as too demanding for people who want to put family first. If this were the cause of women's underrepresentation in science, we would not expect to find many women pursuing advanced coursework or degrees in fields known to lead to demanding careers. Yet many women now do so, both in and outside of science. Gender-socialization theories are unable to explain why relatively large numbers of women would pursue advanced degrees in science only to devote themselves instead to having families when they finally finish their preparation for careers.

In light of the shortcomings of gender-difference theories, others have suggested structural explanations, the simplest being that women have been barred by men, either officially or behind the scenes, from access to elite positions in science and engineering because of their gender. Considerable evidence exists of structural discrimination in the past (e.g., Rossiter 1982, 1995), but this explanation is less persuasive now that more than two decades have passed since formal gender barriers were removed—after years of affirmative action in education and employment, job growth in science and related fields, funding initiatives reserved for women interested in elite science or mathematics, support programs designed specifically to encourage girls and women to pursue these fields, and employers' increased acceptance of women's need and desire to work (see, for example, Dinnerstein 1992). Although many observers have noted the limitations of formal remedies (e.g., Howe 1993; Stromquist 1993), we find it curious that these remedies have produced so little change for women employed in science or engineering. Certainly formal barriers had to be removed, but once they were, and once incentives were offered to overcome the legacy of discrimination, one would expect more positive results if these barriers had been major impediments to women's participation.

Others have focused on the "culture," or "hidden curriculum," of some elite workplaces. McIlwee and Robinson (1992), in their comparison of electrical and mechanical engineering, discovered that electrical engineering workplaces were organized so as to celebrate and reward a "culture of engineering," while in mechanical engineering, a "bureaucratic culture" was more evident. Engineering culture stresses the centrality of technology via "tinkering" and the acquisition of administrative power as the marker of engineering success. Bureaucratic culture, in contrast, relies on governmental rules and regulations (e.g., seniority, academic credentials, affirmative action) for measuring and attaining success. McIlwee and Robinson found that in workplaces dominated by bureaucratic culture, women's chances for success are protected from some of the male-oriented engineering customs that disadvantage them. In workplaces dominated by engineering culture, women are not similarly protected, and they do less well there.

Still others have noticed the numerous, small, interactional routines by which women are treated poorly in elite workplaces. Ample evidence shows that women are treated rudely, excluded from important decision making, overlooked for promotion, and made the brunt of jokes (Evetts 1996; McIlwee and Robinson 1992; Traweek 1988). However, these difficulties hardly seem sufficient to deter strong-minded women who have no doubt endured years of such treatment as they pursued science and mathematics in schools. Further, these interactional difficulties, as well as the organizational and cultural ones referred to above, appear to be as likely to occur in lower-status occupational sites and traditionally female-dominated workplaces as they are in high-status ones. Studies of high- and low-status workplaces in science, medicine, engineering, politics, universities, and public schools all suggest that women face cultural and interactional disadvantages in both kinds of workplaces (see, for example, Aisenberg and Harrington 1988; Kleinman 1996; McIlwee and Robinson 1992; McNeil 1986; Seager 1993).

More to the point are explanations of the reproduction of subordinate status. These explanations seem highly relevant to women's experience in science and engineering, yet they have not consistently been part of the conversation about it. Instead, such conversation tends to focus on childhood socialization or the structural, cultural, and interactional pressures outlined above, and the ways these pressures result in women's being unprepared, uninclined, or excluded. This is where most accounts of women in science or engineering end. In one way or another, previous accounts reveal subtle and not-so-subtle pressures and barriers that are said to exclude women; they deplore the apparent permanence of these forces and call for their change or removal. Discussion of the reproduction of subordinate status would give equal attention to how women face and respond to these forces.

The Reproduction of Subordinate Status

In now-old accounts of social reproduction, theorists assumed that social institutions, especially schools, were responsible for transmitting (reproducing) society's differential status expectations to the next generation. Samuel Bowles and Herbert Gintis (1976) and Jean Anyon (1981), for example, argued that schools teach students that they are suited to perform certain tasks, make certain choices, and fill certain jobs by the ways schools divide children for instruction, present different curricula to different groups, and evaluate individual and group successes and failures. Working-class children learn, for example, that they are expected to perform menial tasks under the close supervision of others, "choose" coursework to better develop these skills, and make educational and occupational plans accordingly. Upper-class students, of course, learn to perform quite different tasks, select different coursework, and make different plans. Both groups also learn that the work performed by the working class is culturally valued less than the work performed by the upper class. Similarly, girls and women learn from the organization of schools that they are expected to perform certain tasks and that these tasks are less valuable than those men perform.

More recent accounts have demonstrated that children do not simply agree to the school's sorting of them; they may end up in lower-status positions with fewer opportunities, but for reasons of their own as much as those given by others (see, for example, Connell et al. 1982; Gaskell 1985; Valli 1986; and Willis 1977). In Paul Willis's study of working-class boys (the "lads") in a British secondary school (1977), the lads actively produced social practices and a meaning system (cultural forms) that opposed school practices and culture. Willis argues that these young men, and by implication other subordinate groups in a society, come to realize that school culture offers people like them (members of the working class) false hopes for opportunity and advancement. Their collective response is to produce a counterculture, that is, a set of practices and meanings that deny the value of the school culture that lies to them. The lads came to value such things as manual (rather than mental or academic) labor and behaviors such as drinking, smoking, and sleeping around that were discouraged by the school. This counterculture was organized around working-class models of adult masculine identity, which the lads appropriated to challenge the school's ideology and to construct a more satisfying alternative by which they could interpret and act in the school. Later, Willis defined such alternative behaviors as "cultural productions": the emergent outcomes of societal subgroups using "discourses, meanings, materials, practices, and group processes to explore, understand, and creatively occupy particular positions in sets of general material possibilities" (Willis 1981, 59).

In the case of the lads, their cultural productions that opposed the school cut off their chances to benefit from school and eventually led them to be prepared only for working-class jobs. The more the lads acted in school in accord with their counterculture, the less access they had to the benefits that schools offer (good grades, help from teachers, a degree) and, consequently, the less prepared they were to do anything other than work in factories. Thus their cultural productions led them, through their own actions, to reproduce their subordinate class position in society. Their cultural productions also led them to a virulent form of male privilege, thus reproducing the male position of dominance over working-class women. The important point, however, is that neither the school nor the family alone socialized or forced the lads to their position in society; the lads themselves, through the social practices in which they participated and the cultural productions they themselves constructed, were very much a part of the process (Levinson and Holland 1996, 9).

Jennifer Pierce, in her book, *Gender Trials: Emotional Lives in Contemporary Law Firms* (1995), provides a more recent example. In a study of two large law firms, Pierce found that female lawyers were routinely criticized, often harshly, if they did not play both aggressive litigator roles and friendly, nurturing roles at work. This situation created special problems for them: to be considered good litigators, they had to act aggressively, and to be considered women, they had to act nice. If the women were nice, they weren't good litigators; if they were ruthless, they weren't women. For women alone, the meanings inescapably attached to them because of their gender were opposed and subordinated to those attached to the professional role (litigator) they were trying to fill.

One might think that female litigators, facing such a double bind, would simply quit. However, many in Pierce's study chose to stay, and they responded to the tension at work in several ways: "Some practiced an ethic of care in the resolution of legal disputes, others adopted the adversarial model for the courtroom and a more care-oriented approach in the office, and a small minority conformed to the male model" (104). Like Willis's lads, most of the female attorneys developed their own cultural productions; that is, their own ways of solving the dilemma of being both litigators and women.

Regardless of their strategy, however, female attorneys could never measure up to the male-oriented standard for both "good litigator" and "woman." Continuing to work as litigators and developing their identities within the limits set by the firm's culture, these women contributed to the double bind that trapped them.

Further, male attorneys used sexual harassment and traditionally male activities (e.g., drinking competitions, golf weekends) to keep female attorneys on the margins and to "underscore the differences between women and men, thereby constantly reminding the women that they [were] different and [did] not fit in" (107). For the most part, female attorneys did not or could not mount serious challenges to these attacks.

In these law firms then, the meaning of being a woman was used repeatedly to encourage women to engage in traditionally female behaviors *and* simultaneously to reduce their professional prestige and status relative to men's. Both male and female attorneys relied on the cultural categories of "litigator" and "woman" to make sense of their own and others' behaviors at the firms, and in so doing, they regularly reproduced a cultural system that subordinates women relative to men.

From this perspective, subordinate status is reproduced as individuals "choose" and then respond to activities which often appear as appealing alternatives to hegemony but which actually organize power relations in the same old way. By this logic, if women consistently end up in lower-status positions in science or engineering, they must do so in part by virtue of their own social practices and cultural productions, by which they learn to accept an enduring relation of subordination to a dominant group as "just the way things are." This brings an explanation for the pattern of women's participation in science into sharper focus: as the meaning of being a scientist changes from one historical period to another, one discipline to another, or one site to another, the "material possibilities" for women's social participation and cultural productions may vary, but the power relation apparently remains the same. In other words, while the content of what it means to be a woman in science has changed rather dramatically across time and space, the power relation between women and a dominant group in science has somehow been maintained.

Thus the possibility that a "historical-relational" perspective could provide an explanation for the pattern of women's representation in science became one of the central themes of our work. We began to wonder how the women in our four sites might be contributing to this historical-relational pattern: What social practices were the women and men in our sites participating in? What cultural productions emerged there? How were women and men learning to relate to each other, and how did their practices and productions in these local sites link participants to wider relations of power? Would it turn out that the practices in places where women "do" science were leading them to reproduce their subordinate status?

One other insight from Willis's work and the studies it inspired (e.g., Apple and Weis 1983; Foley 1990; Holland and Eisenhart 1990; Weis 1990; and Wexler 1992) led us to another, more appealing, question. These studies have demonstrated how students' identities in schools develop in the context of social practices (ways of acting) and cultural productions (collective means of understanding or interpreting actions) that both respond and contribute to larger social structures, movements, and discourses beyond the school. In most cases, these processes were the mechanism of both individual learning and social reproduction. In a few cases, however, notably Lois Weis's (1990) example of young women from working-class families whose future in manufacturing jobs had virtually disappeared, social reproduction was not inevitable. In the face of job opportunities drastically different from those of their parents' generation, these young women moved toward feminist views of their futures, rather than toward the traditional models of womanhood offered by their community (unlike the young men in their community, who moved toward especially virulent forms of working-class masculinity). In Weis's study, some young women found ways to critique their circumstances as women and hoped to live out their critiques in ways that could lead to change or transformation. Thus we wondered if something like this was happening among the women in our sites. Would any of the social practices and cultural productions of the women in our sites turn out to be harbingers of social change or transformation in women's status in science?

Literature in the area of practice theory guided the approach we took to investigating these questions.

Practice Theory

The theoretical perspective that focuses on social practices and cultural productions has been termed *practice theory* (Bourdieu 1977; Connell 1987; Holland and Eisenhart 1990; Ortner 1984). Practice theorists focus on the generation of meaning systems by people as they participate in everyday, local activities (or "social practices") and on the way these meaning systems connect people to broader patterns of social reproduction or change. Practice theorists have been especially interested in three conceptual issues: (1) what meanings are produced within and about everyday activities; (2) how knowledge, identities (e.g., the meaning of being a scientist, a woman, an expert, etc.), and learning are made socially available (or "situated in practice") in the activities in which people actually participate; and (3) how everyday activities and meanings organize participants in wider relations of power. These are the three issues we addressed in our study; we did so with reference to three corresponding conceptual categories: "cultural productions," "situated learning," and "networks of power." We hoped that by investigating women's involvement in science through the lenses of these categories and in a variety of different sites, we could better understand the pattern and implications of women's contemporary participation in science and engineering.

Cultural Productions

Work on cultural productions, defined as meanings developed by groups in their everyday activities and based largely on Willis's insights, is one version of practice theory. *The Cultural Production of the Educated Person* (1996), edited by Bradley Levinson, Douglas Foley, and Dorothy Holland, is a collection of articles illustrating various aspects of this approach: it deals with schools as sites of cultural production, and the cultural production of the "educated person" in various places and discourses. Margaret Eisenhart's article in this book, "The Production of Biologists at School and Work," focuses on the cultural productions of the meaning of the term *scientist* in three sites. It illustrates how the meaning of being a scientist is constructed differently depending upon the organization of activity in the sites. Yet the different meanings and activities are related: the activities and the meaning produced in one site figure into the organization and meaning of the others, which are sometimes consistent with the those of the first, sometimes opposed to them, and sometimes modifications of them. These relational features are especially important because they reveal the workings of power, that is, how some "scientist identities" and the activities associated with them are made the prototype, norm, or "center," while others become unusual, "marginal," or "heretical." Although Eisenhart's article does not address gender, it begins to suggest the approach we will take in the next several chapters to understanding how the meanings of *science* and of *being a scientist* were produced in the sites of our study.

The Cultural Production of Scientists

Eisenhart's article compares the meaning of being a scientist suggested by Jan Nespor's study of a physics degree program (1990) first with the meaning of being a scientist in an environmental biology degree program, and then with its meaning in the conservation corporation, CC, where she conducted the study reported in this book. In Nespor's account, the curricular structure of physics activities encouraged students to develop identities as scientists who solve abstract, theoretical problems and are headed for success in laboratory and university research settings. Environmental biology, in contrast, prepared students to become scientists who apply scientific principles to real-world issues and are headed for success outside the university as conservationists, ecologists, wildlife managers, and forest rangers.

As in Nespor's physics program, coursework in environmental biology encourages students to work in groups to solve problems. However, unlike the physics program, where the problems are theoretical and abstract, environmental biology's problems involve applying scientific principles to conservation policy, forest management, and other current environmental issues.[2] Problem solving in environmental biology requires more broadly focused and more contingent approaches than does the abstract problem solving of physics. Excerpts from two upper-division environmental biology course announcements reveal this focus:

> Microbial approaches and solutions to environmental problem areas in which microorganisms play favorable or unfavorable roles: in . . . soil, water and waste management, current pollution problems, resource recovery, energy production, ecological control of pests, and biotechnology.

> Demanding, problems-oriented methods course . . . emphasizing techniques appropriate to realistic biological problems.

Unlike the physics program studied by Nespor, the environmental biology program encouraged students to make extra-academic social contacts with practicing conservation scientists and their constituents. Class assignments included internships and field placements with local environmental agencies and demanded that students work out solutions to realistic environmental problems by taking into account the views and needs of different groups. Thus environmental biology required out-of-school contacts that aligned students' academic and social relationships in specific ways that served its academic purposes. The environmental biology program encouraged students to develop identities as scientists who would spend their time working with others on contemporary environmental problems. Heavy course demands in environmental biology's curriculum, coupled with the additional demands of internships and field placements, suggest that the program exerted powerful pressures on students to develop strong commitments to applied biology and environmental activism.

The meaning of *scientist* produced within environmental biology was, in some ways, pointedly in opposition to (or "against") the one produced in programs like physics. In environmental biology, the view of a scientist was a kind of challenge to the hegemony of the theoretical, laboratory, or research scientist who is widely celebrated in the physical sciences (see, for example, Traweek 1988) and touted as the best model for elementary and secondary school science (American Association for the Advancement of Science 1989). The hegemonic model of science that appears, for example, in undergraduate physics textbooks and courses suggests that "science is . . . independent of all social or political contexts; [and] that all knowledge is dependent on or derivative from physics" (Traweek 1988, 78). In the textbook materials Traweek studied, she found a public image of scientists as rational, dispassionate, and open-minded investigators that was used explicitly to inspire students to pursue a career in physics.

Environmental biology's insistence that biological science be applied to real-world environmental problems makes this degree program an institutional dare to the hegemony of laboratory science. Whereas the hard sciences, such as physics, define controlled, cumulative, abstract problem solving and knowledge production as the *sine qua non* of "real scientists," environmental biology defines a good scientist as someone who contributes to species and habitat protection. Where the hard sciences portray science as separate from political or social issues, environmental biology places itself in the midst of such issues. Thus the curriculum structure of environmental biology produces an identity for the scientist that is at least in some ways counterhegemonic to the one produced in physics.

In one sense, environmental biology's challenge to the hegemony of the laboratory scientist is minor. It does not oppose laboratory science *per se*, but only how and where its principles are used. The power, politics, and privileges of laboratory science and university hard science are not directly confronted in the program.

On the other hand, many of the students majoring in environmental biology were dropouts from physics, chemistry, engineering, and medicine. They chose environmental biology as a major after leaving the so-called harder sciences. Thus the environmental biology program seemed to offer a "space" in which some students could articulate and further develop a critique of the hard sciences.

Eisenhart's investigation of environmental biology did not include observations or interviews with students. However, a comparative study conducted by Elaine Seymour and Nancy Hewitt (1997) of college students who did and did not switch out of science, mathematics, or engineering programs provides some clues to student perceptions of degree programs in science. Seymour and Hewitt interviewed 335 students (54.6 percent switchers; 45.4 percent nonswitchers) on seven college campuses, including the one where Eisenhart studied environmental biology, about the factors that influenced their decisions to stay in or switch out of science, mathematics, or engineering. A major finding was that switchers and nonswitchers differed very little in their statements about science, mathematics, and engineering degree programs. Both groups had various similar and sometimes radical complaints about the programs. Some illustrative comments follow; page references are to Seymour and Hewitt (1997).

Many of the students viewed science, mathematics, and engineering coursework as too demanding of their time and attention:

> There was no possibility of taking the time to do some of the classes I enjoyed. Like, I couldn't find time for a foreign language. There just wasn't any opportunity for it. You start to realize that you really don't want to go on doing this, because it's not exciting enough to allow you to put on blinkers as far as the rest of the world is concerned. (White male mathematics switcher; 60)

> You can never sit down and read a book that's not related to school—that's a luxury. (Male white engineering nonswitcher; 103)

> It's a hard field. It's risky to study it, I think for your ego, and friendships suffer. (Female white engineering switcher; 103)

> It takes everything from you. It takes all the time you've got. I think I had one Saturday off the whole semester. (Female white engineering nonswitcher; 103) . . .

> I have a friend who managed to complete a civil engineering degree in four years—one of the few who could pull that off. But it cost him his girlfriend—quite literally. 'Cause I've seen him look at his watch, and say, "I haven't talked to her in a month." He'd wake up

and realize it had been that long. Eventually, she said, "Sorry, I don't remember what you look like anymore." (Male white science non-switcher; 104)

You think, "Well, all I have to do is make it through the weed-out courses and then it'll start getting interesting," but you're completely wrong. There's no room in the sequence for humanities, and you find out you'll be taking six aerospace courses a semester. And that's just inconceivable. You'd have to be a some kind of drug addict. (Male Asian-American engineering switcher; 180)

Others complained that coursework was made harder than it needed to be:

This ridiculous computer programming and graphics stuff needn't have been so heavily emphasized in the first semester. A lot of it was really bogus. (Female white engineering nonswitcher; 105)

I don't think the fundamentals of chemistry are that difficult to grasp. It's very logical. But I think they do *make* it harder than it needs to be. (Female Asian-American science switcher; 105)

It's ridiculous that they make you learn that much in so much detail—because you never, ever need it all. You can just look it up in a book if you need it. (Male white engineering nonswitcher; 124)

For many, the work was simply too boring:

I had enough of the sciences, largely because the classes were so boring. I found there was a lot more to learn, to expand your mind within the social sciences. With strict science, it's just textbook, textbook, textbook. (Male white engineering switcher; 178)

I've found that there's very little tolerance for anything that has any kind of subjective quality. It got to the point where it was very boring. (Male Hispanic science switcher; 180)

Finally, many complained about the lack of relevance:

To me, it's sanity to take other courses because if I had only engineering courses, I would feel like my mind was in a box and that I couldn't relate to the real world. (Female black engineering nonswitcher; 180)

I was trying to double major in personal relations. I couldn't find any professor that was even thinking that had anything to do with engineering. There's a certain way the two intertwine, and they just can't see it. (Male white engineering nonswitcher; 181)

Given these students' concerns for increased breadth, greater interest, and more relevance, it seems reasonable to assume that degree programs like environmental biology offer some students a context where they can express their discontent with the hard sciences. Like Willis's lads when frustrated by their school, students disillusioned with the hard sciences probably look elsewhere for activities in which they can more fully participate and excel. Although the environmental biology program does not completely address the students' concerns and contains its own set of limitations (as did the working-class culture appropriated by the lads), it seems to provide an alternative for students who object to the practices and identities of the hard sciences produced in the university.

Environmental biology's applied-science identity is produced *in relation to*, that is, *within and against* (not separate from) the image of the laboratory scientist that is hegemonic in the university and in American society. The identity produced in environmental biology is consistent with hegemonic science in the sense that "serious science" is expected but it differs from hegemonic science in that real-world applications, rather than controlled and abstract problem solving, are considered the context for scientific work. Again, this institutional challenge to the hegemony of laboratory science is minor: the power, politics, and privileges of laboratory science are not directly confronted by or in the program. Nonetheless, environmental biology offers an alternative set of activities and meanings of *science* and *scientists* for students who have experienced "minor liberations" (Willis 1981) from hegemonic science in the university.

In our view, it seemed too simple to assert that students who choose environmental biology as an alternative to the hard sciences are participating in unwitting social reproduction, that is, scaling down their activities to fit some social stereotype of the kind of person they are or the job they are suited for. At least some of the students who oppose the hard sciences appear to do so with a clear sense of what they are rejecting and what the alternatives and their advantages are. To the extent that alternative social practices and cultural productions gain a following and social salience, they could undermine the prevailing hegemony. We hoped to explore this possibility further in the case of women who participate in alternative sites of science.

Situated Learning

Jean Lave and Etienne Wenger's theory of situated learning (1991) is another version of practice theory. Whereas studies of cultural productions focused our attention on meanings produced in activity, Lave and Wenger's work alerted us to the importance of carefully examining the content and organization of the activities in which people actually participate over time.

As described in our introduction, Lave and Wenger argue that human knowing and self-identification develop in social situations: that is, learning is "situated" in social phenomena. Thus, in order to understand what individuals come to know, how they come to view themselves, and how these things change and develop over time, we must first understand their social practice: how group activities are organized; how knowledge and identity are represented in activity; and how individuals can change their participation over time. This became the first priority of our analysis and we present it first in our discussion of the sites in chapters 3–6.

But Lave and Wenger's approach does not end with an analysis of local practice. They make clear that local practices are local realizations of broader sociohistorical structures: as individuals participate in local practice, they simultaneously take up features of broader structures which are manifested in that practice. Any analysis of practice, and thus of knowing, identifying, and learning, must include an analysis of how structure is realized in local practice.

In a more recent article, Lave suggests that situated learning be viewed as the exploration of "how it is that people live in *history*, and how it is that people *live* in history" (1993, 21). By this brief phrase, she means to indicate the importance of understanding how the legacies of history are reproduced and how they provide resources that help individuals to act purposively and to value and enjoy their everyday lives. About this, Levinson and Holland say,

> Reshaped by the more recent focus on practice and production, the larger question is now one of how historical persons are formed in practice, within and against larger societal forces and structures which instantiate themselves in schools and other institutions. (1996, 14)

In this book we will try to develop a clearer understanding of how history—operationalized as struggles over status in science and engineering—becomes part of people's lives and identities via the organizational activities through which they come to participate in institutions and sometimes try to affect them.

Relations of Power

The approach of one other practice theorist, Jan Nespor, has been particularly helpful to our analysis because of its explicit focus on how power, not simply history, is reproduced by individuals as they participate in specific activities. In his recent book, *Knowledge in Motion* (1994), Nespor outlines an approach to learning conceived as a process of moving individuals into and through specific organizations of time and space: for example, a university degree program or a workplace. These organizations of time and space also connect individuals to each other in relations of power. Different sites—in Nespor's case, the degree programs of physics and management—organize time and space differently, thereby connecting individuals in power networks of distinctly different kinds. Nespor writes,

> I've written about those programs [physics and management] because they're areas where education and power come together in crucial ways. Physics and management are disciplines deeply implicated in the domination of the physical and social worlds. The fact that both regulate membership and participation in their realms through educational requirements makes them prime areas for exploring how students get connected to core disciplines of modern society, and how they become parts of durable networks of power. (1994, 1)

Following Nespor,[3] we see that each degree program has a distinctive spatial-temporal arrangement. This arrangement represents, physically and symbolically, what individuals are supposed to do in a "space" and how they should use "their time"; it includes notions about the kinds of persons who are (and are not) supposed to be in a "space" and take up "time"; and it creates the opportunities for certain kinds of social and power relationships, while making others unlikely or impossible. Newcomers gain proficiency ("learn") as they participate in specific spatial-temporal representations that are increasingly inaccessible to outsiders or the less proficient.

Nespor's theoretical formulation is illuminated in his discussion of the undergraduate physics and management programs he investigated. The two degree programs organized space and time in substantially different ways, and the kind of power relationship each program fostered was different.

Nespor finds physics to be an especially "greedy" degree program (or "major"). It requires a precise sequence of increasingly advanced coursework, concentrates that coursework (and thus the students) in one building, demands significant academic work outside of class, permits only a narrow range of "good-student" identities, and focuses the course content on abstract, "mathematized," and invariant models that separate it from everyday referents. Thus the program channeled students into a tight spatial-temporal regime that demanded virtually all their time, separated them from other students and activities, reconstructed their social activity and talk, and headed them toward a single endpoint (identity): graduate work and a career in physics. As students were moved through and came to use space and time in the "way" of the program, their connection to other physicists was strengthened, while their ties to nonphysicists were weakened. As their involvement in the network of physicists increased, so did their proficiency with increasingly abstract, mathematical, and invariant models of physics knowledge. According to Nespor, proficiency with abstract, invariant knowledge entails a special kind of power: Abstract, mathematical knowledge allows people in widely dispersed situations and with very different backgrounds (e.g., workers in a laboratory in Berkeley, California, and others in another lab in Geneva) to use the knowledge consistently and in coordination with each other. Despite background differences, situational differences, or language barriers, physicists in Berkeley and Geneva can communicate effectively and build on each other's work, thanks to the abstract, mathematical models they share. Invariant models, such as the laws of physics and other principles modeled on them, also facilitate social control: they can become the principles that guide national policies (e.g., in energy or the military) in ways that are virtually impervious to local needs or objections.

The management program organized students' time and space in looser but nonetheless consequential ways. Management created a form of the corporate world at school. In this world, official hierarchy was spatially and temporally marked (e.g., professors had plush spaces that students could not enter without permission), and students were encouraged to spend time developing social ties outside of class, for example, in fraternities, sororities, or business associations. In consequence, management students learned to integrate schoolwork into the spatial and temporal course of social activities and to develop a demeanor that linked them to networks in the corporate world beyond the school. Thus the program established its own dominant regime, and students who moved into its time and space configurations became more firmly attached to business networks, while their connections to other networks were weakened. But the power gained by these business students was considerably different from that of physicists. In business, power derives not from invariant intellectual models, but from connections to wealth and consumers. In the management program, students learned how to build and exercise power through social contacts and connections, not through rational intellectual prowess.

New Questions about Women's Participation in Science and Engineering

We relied on Nespor's ideas to help us identify how time, space, and other representational tools were organized for individuals in our sites. We also examined the kinds of power relations to which individuals were being connected in each site. These ideas, together with those about cultural productions and situated learning, led us, finally, to approach the studies of our four sites by addressing the following four questions.

1. What forms of science (or engineering) practice occur in each site, and how do these practices compare to each other and to the sites of elite science?

2. What meanings of *science* and *scientist* are produced in each site, and how do these cultural productions compare to each other and to those produced in elite science?

3. What relations of power are organized and represented in these sites, and how do these relations compare to each other and to those in elite science sites?

4. How do women participate and fare in these sites?

Our answers to these questions define some of the central features of the dynamic of opportunity and privilege in contemporary American society. We reveal how science privilege is developed, sustained, made "natural," and brought home in the social practices of smart, active, and well-intentioned women and men.

To begin to answer these questions, we now move inside our four sites for a closer look at the heretics. When Bourdieu named writers and authors "heretics," he implied that they held unorthodox views and behaved in unorthodox ways. In consequence, they were likely to deviate from "normal trajectories" within the field and not to experience the psychological and social security associated with "normal" practice (Bourdieu 1988, 105–8). For these reasons, we expected that innovations and demands for change were also considerably more likely to arise in such places.

Apparently heretical places have played an important role for female scientists in the not-so-distant past. Rossiter, for example, has this to say about women employed by nonprofit organizations:

> In contrast to the reluctant recruitment, systematic ghettoization, and minimal advancement facing women scientists in other sectors in the 1950s and 1960s, their participation was relatively welcome, and their achievements were substantial at many nonprofit institutions. Although only a tiny proportion (about 1 percent) of the nation's scientists and engineers worked at such institutions, several of the more talented and dedicated women researchers of the time, unwelcome or not advancing in academia [notably Barbara McClintock, winner of the Nobel Prize], capitalized on the opportunities there to do good science. Many service-oriented women scientists, [who worked] as librarians, editors, abstractors, educators, and association staff members, upon whom so much of the scientific community relied but preferred to keep invisible, also worked [in nonprofit organizations], as did those "institution builders" who, finding existing job opportunities closed to them, . . . created alternative organizations to fit their own as well as some larger scientific needs. [And] certainly a large proportion of the top honors going to any women in science went to those, especially biologists, from the nonprofit sector. (1995, 235, 255)

What would we find in such heretical places in the early 1990s?

Part Two

Practice on the Margins: Getting in, Doing Well, and Gaining Power

The dry sciences of academic abstraction involve a particular institutionalization of masculinity. . . . The view of the natural world that mainstream science embodies, the language and metaphors of scientific analysis—a discourse of uncovering, penetrating, controlling—have some of their deepest roots in the social relations between men and women. A different kind of knowledge could have been produced, and to some extent is produced, by people whose thinking is shaped by experience of a different location in gender relations. For instance, a science constructed by women might be more likely to use metaphors of wholeness than metaphors of analysis, seek cooperations with nature rather than dominion over it. . . . [The dry] sciences are connected to power . . . the organized, collective power embodied in large institutions like companies, the state, and property markets. This is power that delivers economic and cultural advantage to the relatively small number of people who can operate this machinery. A man who can command this power has no need for riding leathers and engine noise to assert masculinity. His masculinity is asserted and amplified on an immensely greater scale by the society itself. (Connell 1993, 200–201)

Historically, women have had very limited access to the kind of power described above by Connell. Although a few biographies and autobiographies of notable exceptions exist, women as a group have been and continue to be poorly represented among the scientific elite. This demographic finding is surprisingly robust, holding true through history and across scientific fields, although the definition of "elite" has changed over time and varies by field. On the other hand, women are relatively well represented in lower-status science.

As we began our study, we were astonished to realize that no one had closely examined the sites of science where women are well represented.

Apparently almost everyone has assumed that such sites are irrelevant to "real" science and to women's opportunities in science. But if some women actively choose unconventional or marginal sites, are treated well there, and find the work satisfying, might these assumptions be misleading? We wanted to examine the similarities and differences of local practices in elite and marginal sites of science, and to ask about the ways in which marginal sites might be good, as well as not so good, places for women.

In the next four chapters, we move inside our four sites—two school-based programs (the genetics classroom, IGC, and the engineering school-to-work internship, EDI) and two workplaces (the environmental action coalition, ELAC, and the conservation corporation, CC)—to examine and compare their characteristics. The sites represent four points along a continuum of site types for "unconventional" science practice: from the least unconventional (the IGC classroom, an innovative practice but at a place most people associate with opportunities to learn elite science or engineering), to the slightly more unconventional (the EDI school-to-work internship), and to the even more unconventional (the CC workplace and especially ELAC), where most people would not expect to find opportunities to learn "serious science."

As indicated in the introduction, the four sites that are the focus of our study are unusual in several ways. First, they are not sites like laboratories or conventional classrooms that most people think of as places for learning science. Two of the four are outside of school, a third is a program designed to ease the transition from school to work, and the fourth is an innovative high school genetics classroom. In selecting these sites, we took seriously the work of researchers who have suggested that "authentic learning" (learning that is uncoerced) is more likely when situated in so-called real-world activities, such as apprenticeships, that embed goals, relationships, skills, and identities that have meaning for participants beyond the immediate context of learning (Lave and Wenger, 1991). Lave and Wenger make the provocative suggestion that, in contrast to contexts like apprenticeships, most in-school learning is coerced by the teacher's authority and not really valued by students. Students do the work and perform on the tests because teachers (and other authority figures) force them to, not because the students believe the work or skills have real value for them. For this reason, real-world activities are expected to motivate learning more successfully than conventional school activities. Ideas such as Lave and Wenger's have influenced the designers of some school programs, such as the genetics and engineering programs we studied, to make them more similar to real-world activities and thus to inspire better learning. Working with these ideas, we planned to investigate and compare activities and learning in sites where knowledge of science or engineering was embedded in real-world activities.

All four of our sites met this criterion, although in varying degrees. The environmental action coalition (ELAC) and the conservation corporation (CC) relied on conservation science to justify the environmental actions they promoted. ELAC, for example, is one branch of a nationwide organization that aims to convince the public to support its legislative positions on environmental issues. Branches are visible to the general population as the result of fund-raising activities mainly in the form of door-to-door canvassing done by hired college students. A canvasser must convince the person at the door of the importance of the group's environmental positions in order to solicit funds both for legislative action and for the group's continued existence. Within the organization, knowledge of science related to the environment is said to be a desirable and even necessary part of convincing the public to support ELAC.

CC is in the land-protection business. Its activities include identifying land parcels where species, habitats, or ecological processes are threatened; developing protection plans for these parcels; raising money to buy or manage such parcels; and convincing landowners to accept CC's decisions about how to "take care of the land." CC's success, like ELAC's, is said to depend on using conservation science to convince the public of the credibility and importance of CC's work and positions.

The two environmental workplaces were, however, perceived quite differently by the scientific establishment. Because environmental action groups such as ELAC do not engage in laboratory research and do engage in political activity, they are not generally regarded by the scientific community as good or legitimate sites for learning and doing science. In fact, most of the scientists and science educators, including two dissertation-committee members with whom Behm consulted as she searched for nonschool sites that used science, disparaged ELAC's work as "unscientific." In contrast, CC has a reputation for doing serious and respectable scientific work, albeit outside of the laboratory. Unlike ELAC, CC explicitly refuses to engage in organized political activity, to take public stands on environmental legislation, and to support political candidates. Instead, CC presents itself as an environmental business dedicated to both conservation science and sound business practices. When Eisenhart was searching for potential research sites, she asked a number of university scientists and environmental agency employees to suggest groups outside of formal schools with reputations for "serious science." CC was consistently mentioned as a good choice.

The genetics class, IGC, and the engineering school-to-work internship, EDI, represent the category of innovative school activities in which students' work is modeled on the so-called real world of professional scientists or engineers. In IGC, the teacher explicitly organized the course around a computer program designed to simulate the outcome of breeding populations of fruit flies. Students were presented with problems that professional geneticists might face: the problem of dealing with data that existing models cannot explain and the problem of developing new models to accommodate new or anomalous data. In EDI, all of the coursework was devoted to investigating and determining solutions for actual engineering problems faced by industry or the public sector. An industry or government client formally contracted with student teams in the class to solve each problem. Both IGC and EDI offer the kind of school experiences that many in the educational and scientific establishments consider authentic—that is, both academically and professionally credible—and for which they are currently recruiting more and more schools and classrooms.

The prominence of women in our sites is their other unusual feature. In the elective genetics class, 40 percent of the students were girls.[1] In the engineering internship, 26 percent of the students were women (compared to 15 percent in engineering classes nationally). In the political action group and the conservation corporation, approximately 50 percent of employees were women, and 50 percent of high-status positions were held by women. In the conservation corporation, 46 percent of the environmental biologists (with master's or doctoral degrees) were women.[2]

Most people concerned about the representation of women in science and engineering have investigated sites where there were few women and asked, "Why so few?" We decided to ask instead, "Why so many?" We wondered, Where are women already engaged in science (or engineering), and what does their practice there look like? We hoped that our inquiry would reveal information that could lead to a better understanding of the differences between contexts that encourage or discourage women's participation in science or engineering.

Our decision to select sites where newcomers were engaged in real-world activities and where the proportion of women was unusually high resulted in a sample composed of nonprofit organizations, which differ in numerous ways from the public or commercial laboratories that have been the focus of most discussions and studies of science or technology. We simply could not find conventional sites that met our selection criteria. We also found that the population of our sample of sites was primarily white.

Our sites were not randomly selected; they served different purposes than science laboratories or research universities, and women may have chosen them in lieu of more conventional science sites. Therefore our findings about science practices and women's experiences may not be generalizable beyond other settings with similar characteristics. Nevertheless, we believe our findings have important implications—both positive and negative—for those who are trying to design more authentic contexts for learning science and for those who are searching for new ways to involve more women in science. Each of the four sites offers a different picture of the ways women found to become involved in science or engineering, as well as a different set of possibilities and constraints for women. To the extent that our theoretical concepts allow us to make sense of findings about science practices and women's experiences *across* the different sites, we think that our conclusions may be generalizable to other professional fields in which women have historically been relegated to the margins.

In chapters 3–6 we focus specifically on the science related practices engaged in at each site, the meanings of *science* and *scientists* that were produced and learned in these practices, and the relations of power that were organized and represented there. Working with these features, we discuss similarities and differences across the sites and make comparisons to others' accounts of elite sites.

At the end of each of these chapters, we discuss the differences we found in the way men and women participated at each site. With reference to other literature on science and women, we attempt to make sense of the patterns in their participation.

From the outset we anticipated that social practice in each site would call for a specific kind of relevant knowledge and skill, privilege different identities, and enable newcomers' movement into forms of contemporary science practice in distinctly different ways. To the extent that women were numerous in our sites and that the sites were marginal places of science practice, we also expected that women would find at least some opportunities not widely available in elite sites. What we did not know was how diverse the sites would turn out to be.

Chapter Three

Learning Science in an
Innovative Genetics Course

[T]he goal here is not to come up with a model. It would be great, but I mean that's not the goal. The goal here is to actually go through the process of trying to develop a model, OK? So it's not that the people who get a model are going to [get] A's, everybody will get an A if they are model developing and model revising, OK? Have fun, get frustrated, [or] a combination of the above. (Teacher, Innovative Genetics Class, on the first day of model revising)

The Innovative Genetics Course (IGC) is a nine-week, elective course for high school seniors. The course was developed and taught by an experienced biology teacher at a public high school of approximately five hundred students. The student population of the high school and the class is largely white, middle-class and working-class. By state law, all students are required to complete two years of high school science in order to graduate.

The science program in this high school is organized around the concept of Unified Science. When they enter the high school, teachers place students according to previous academic success in science classes in an advanced track (Science A) or a remedial track (Science B). During the first three years of high school, students do not enroll in biology, physics, or chemistry classes; instead they study all three disciplines concurrently in a sequence of classes designated Science I, II, and III, each with A- and B-tracks. Once they have completed the two required years of science (I and II), students have the choice of taking an additional year of Unified Science (III) and then, in their senior year, of electing one of several discipline-specific science courses. These elective courses are each nine weeks long (one academic quarter) and cover a variety of

Primary data about IGC were collected and analyzed by Elizabeth (Liza) Finkel.

topics, including comparative anatomy, organic chemistry, the physics of electricity and magnetism, and genetics.

At the time of our study in the winter of 1992, the elective genetics course had been previously taught five times. Students who had elected the course ranged from those with a preexisting interest in genetics to those who had very little knowledge of genetics but had heard that the class was "fun." Some students had excellent academic records in science (i.e., they had come up through the A-track) and expressed a desire to study science after high school; others had done less well in science classes (they came up through the B-track) and did not intend to study science beyond high school. During our study, approximately half of the students enrolled in IGC were either from the B-track or had low grades (2.0, or Cs) in the A-track.

Elizabeth Finkel, the researcher, was present in all class sessions during the winter of 1992 and interacted with students as a second teacher, working individually with student research groups by responding to questions and leading some class discussions. Twenty-five students were enrolled in the class; fifteen were boys and ten (40 percent) were girls; all but one were white. Class activity was conducted in self-selected "research" groups of three or four students each. Four of eight research groups working in the class were the focus of the study described here. These four groups were chosen because they were homogeneous with regard to gender (two groups consisted of three boys, two of three girls), and they were homogeneous with regard to previous success in school and in science classes: two groups consisted of students who were all previously successful in science, and two consisted of students who were not. Their performance in this class ranged from unquestioned success (one group of girls and one of boys), through moderate success (a second group of boys), to unquestioned lack of success (a second group of girls). Each of the research groups was referred to in the class by the surname of a famous geneticist. The group of successful girls was called Franklin (after Rosalind Franklin); the unsuccessful girls' group was called Watson (after James Watson); the clearly successful boys' group was called Sutton (after Walter Sutton), and the moderately successful boys' group was called Crick (after James Crick).

The data for this study were gathered as students worked with populations of organisms similar to fruit flies that were simulated by an educational software program called *Genetics Construction Kit* (Jungck and

Calley 1993). As student research groups revised models to account for anomalous (previously inexplicable) data, their conversations were recorded using unidirectional microphones attached to portable cassette recorders. These audio recordings were later transcribed and comprise most of the data used in this study. All teacher and researcher interactions with students were also transcribed from these audio tapes. All written materials produced by students during model revision were also collected.

IGC is a typical high school science course in the sense that it takes place in a classroom setting and focuses on academic knowledge. However, unlike many conventional courses, IGC is consistent with new approaches to science curricula which rely on constructivist learning theory for their ideas about teaching and collaborative learning of science.[1] Key principles of this constructivist approach are (1) that students need opportunities to develop their own understandings of science; (2) that students learn best when the teacher is involved as a facilitator, rather than a disseminator; and (3) that students should be engaged in doing science for its process (e.g., discovering scientific principles while collaborating with peers) rather than its products (e.g., finding the right answer to a problem). In particular, IGC was carefully designed to give students the opportunity to construct an understanding of genetics by participating in activities similar to those of actual geneticists, that is, in "the 'three P's of science' (Peterson and Jungck 1988): problem posing, problem solving, and persuasion of peers" (Johnson and Stewart 1990, 297).

The teacher who developed IGC anticipated that it would significantly raise the interest level of all students in genetics. Although there was no explicit attempt to increase girls' participation, IGC was known as a popular program to most students, including girls. Thus, although IGC took place at a school site, the most conventional site of science practice in our study, it is unconventional compared to many science courses in the sense that it represents an innovative approach to science education. IGC also reflects the spirit of many science-education reforms that aim to increase the participation of girls and minorities by making science curricula more like real science (see chapter 1). Given these unconventional characteristics and the fact that numerous similar science-education reforms are currently being encouraged and implemented throughout the United States (Eisenhart, Finkel, and Marion

1996), we wondered, What are the science-related activities, outcomes, and experiences of young women in such a site, and are such sites actually better places for women than conventional sites of school science?

Our answers are complex. We found that most students, including most girls, were enthusiastic about and successful in IGC. However, a few students, notably girls who were not previously successful in science, did not do well in IGC either.

Genetics in Practice

In IGC, science was practiced as a set of inquiry procedures and commitments for answering the kinds of questions that geneticists ask. The first five days of IGC were spent on a series of whole-class tasks designed to introduce students to the concepts of model-based problem solving, inheritance, and variability in organisms. Tasks in which the teacher and all the students engaged in this part of the course included developing, presenting, and revising models. The first problem was to develop a model to explain the behavior of a detergent box, shaped like a milk carton, that poured a fixed amount of liquid detergent each time it was tipped. The second problem was to compare the characteristics of cookies baked according to five different recipes and develop a model to predict the outcomes from each recipe. In the detergent box problem, the students worked on translating their observations about the box into models for testing. In the cookie problem, students compared the appearances (phenotypes) of cookies with similar recipes (genotypes) in order to develop an understanding of the influence of heredity (recipe) and environment (baking temperature, duration of baking, etc.) on the cookies. The third and final introductory task—a "human variation lab"—required students to compare aspects of their own phenotypes, such as tongue rolling or mid-digital hair, of which some are thought to be inherited and some are not.

Following this introduction, which included definitions of genetic terms and concepts, students read an annotated version of Gregor Mendel's 1865 paper in which he describes the work with pea plants that led him to develop his model of simple dominance. Then a graduate student dressed as Mendel visited the class and, with the help of the students, constructed a model of simple dominance based on Mendel's work. During his one-day visit, Mendel took students through some of his early experiments with peas and pea flowers. For example, after showing pea flowers and the first generation of peas produced from those flowers, Mendel gave out handfuls of second-generation peas (some green and smooth, some green and wrinkled, some yellow and smooth, some yellow and wrinkled) and asked students to count the different kinds. He tallied their results on the board, and together he and the students calculated the ratios of green-to-yellow and smooth-to-wrinkled peas. In this way he helped them to develop the concept of "simple dominance," the idea that one variation of a trait is dominant over another (e.g., green seed color is dominant over yellow; smooth surface is dominant over wrinkled) and that as a result, the proportions of individuals bearing those traits change from generation to generation. A pen-and-paper representation of the simple dominance model was distributed to help students develop a structured way of thinking about the model of simple dominance and about genetic models in general. Hereafter, the students and teacher referred to this model as "Mendel's bible." (Figure 3.1 is Mendel's bible, the pen-and-paper representation given to the students.)

Once they had developed the simple dominance model, students in small groups of three or four used it to explain populations of insectlike organisms generated by a computer simulation. The students were presented with a computer screen depicting a vial of organisms similar to fruit flies. Figure 3.2 illustrates one of the screen displays, which includes the names of the two phenotypes of a trait (eye shape). The students were asked to determine what controls the variation in offsprings' eye shape. Students had previously been told that "genes" (genotypes) are responsible for traits (phenotypes), and that "alleles" are alternative forms of a gene that are responsible for variations in the trait. Simple dominance involves two alleles of a gene; one allele is dominant (i.e., expressed), and the other is recessive (i.e., may be "masked" by its dominant allele). The computer generates a variety of simulated outcomes, of which some can be explained by the model of simple dominance, and others cannot. The latter require students to construct new models: for example, models of codominance, which involves two alleles of every gene, neither of which is dominant; multiple alleles, where there are three or more alleles of every gene, and they can be dominant or not; or linkage, where the inheritance of a particular trait is linked to the inheritance of some other trait.

After the research groups practiced with the first set of simulated crosses (those explained by simple dominance), the teacher asked one group of students to present their model to the rest of the class. Other

OBJECTS in the simple dominance model

Number of traits	1
Number of variations	2
Number of genes	1
Number of alleles/gene in the population	2
Number of alleles/gene in an individual	2
Number of possible allele combinations	3

STATES in the simple dominance model

Type of allele combinations:

(1,1) and (2,2)	Homozygous
(1,2)	Heterozygous

Allele combinations can map to variations in the following ways:

(1,1)	Variation A
(1,2)	Variation A
(2,2)	Variation B

Variation A
(1,2)
(1,1)●——————————●(2,2)
Variation A   Variation B

Tall
(1,2)
(1,1)●——————————●(2,2)
Tall   Short

Cross possibilities:[a]

	Phenotype	Genotype	Possible results
1.	Variation A × Variation A	1,1 × 1,1	All variation A
2.	Variation A × Variation A	1,1 × 1,2	All Variation A
3.	Variation A × Variation A	1,2 × 1,2	Variations A & B (3:1)
4.	Variation A × Variation B	1,1 × 2,2	All Variation A
5.	Variation A × Variation B	1,2 × 2,2	Variations A & B (1:1)
6.	Variation B × Variation B	2,2 × 2,2	All Variation B

[a]If reciprocal crosses were done for cross possibilities 2, 4, and 5, the general ratios would remain the same.

PROCESSES in the simple dominance model
    Segregation:
    Separates one member of a pair of alleles of a parent during gamete production.
    Changes the state of an object (an allele pair) from double to single.
    Independent assortment:
    Assorts allele pairs so that members of the pair for one trait are distributed to
    gametes independently of the members of pairs for other traits.
    Fertilization:
    Joins gametes that have a single member of each allele pair so that a zygote
    has two members of a pair.

Figure 3.1 A model of simple dominance (modified from Hafner 1991)

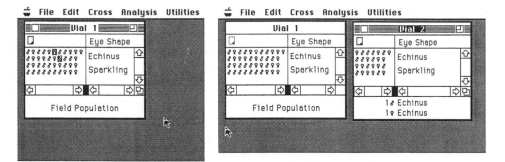

Figure 3.2 Examples of screens from the computer simulation, Genetics Construction Kit. (Left) The field population. The box represents a vial of organisms with distinct phenotypic characteristics. In this case the individuals vary with regard to eye shape, and there are two variations: Echinus and Sparkling. Each organism in the population is represented by a male or female symptom, and possesses a distinct genotype. The field population vial is the first screen encountered by a user of the Genetics Construction Kit. (Right) The offspring of a cross between the two individuals highlighted in the field population; the software calculates the sex ratio among the Echinus offspring.

class members then asked them to predict the results of additional crosses, as a test of the generalizability of the model. Then the teacher changed the underlying genetic principle behind the computer simulation so that when students made crosses, the results were not explained by their previous model: for example, crossing two individuals might produce three phenotypic variations rather than the two observed under simple dominance. Students were then asked to revise the model of simple dominance to account for these anomalies. Cycles of presentation and public tests of a model were repeated for progressively more challenging genetic problems (e.g., sex-linked inheritance).

In the design of IGC, such model revision was the central and ongoing task. Ideally, students' understandings of the process of model revision improved as they developed proficiency with the tools of the preliminary tasks and with the software in the context of small-group work.

During each class period, the teacher moved from group to group modeling the process of model revision. She focused students' attention on aspects of new populations that appeared similar to or different from previous populations. She encouraged students to refer to the previously developed model of simple dominance and suggested that they use the representation of that model as a template for developing new models. She emphasized that she would grade them on model revision rather than on final models.

In addition, she commented frequently on the ways in which classroom events were like those encountered by actual real scientists. Such events included building models to explain and predict data, revising models in light of anomalous data, attempting to deal with competing models which appeared equally "predictive," being frustrated at not being able to explain anomalous data, and even spying on the work of others. The computer simulations, together with the teacher's behaviors, created a classroom environment in which students were encouraged to develop an image of themselves as practicing scientists.

The following sections illustrate in detail the kinds of activities students participated in as part of the small groups in which they regularly worked and how they were encouraged to "act like scientists." After describing each group, we will contrast the experiences of boys and girls in these groups.

Activity in the Franklin Group

From the beginning, the three girls in the Franklin group (whom we call Sandra, Cathy, and Joan, all typically good students and previously successful in science) plunged into the process of model revision and never looked back. On the first day of model revising, they encountered a problem (involving codominance) that two of them (Cathy and Joan) had never seen before. Sandra had transferred from another school and had more previous instruction in genetics than the other two. She had seen such problems before and she identified the problem as one of codominance after less than five minutes of work.

Using genetics terminology, Sandra called the teacher over and tried to find out if what she suspected was true:

Sandra: Yeah, I have a question; . . . you [she says to the teacher] can just kinda say yes or no. OK. Let's say like these [here she points to the computer monitor and indicates two variations, here referred to as "echinus" and "bar"] are codominant, it [one variation] would be [like] a red flower . . . this [another variation] is a white flower, this [their offspring] is a pink flower.

Teacher: If that's your hypothesis, then what would you have to do to test it?

Sandra: We did an echinus and a bar cross and came up with all roughs, and so that would lead me to believe that the red and the white . . . [are codominant].

Teacher: What would you have to do to be sure?

Sandra:	I would want to know why . . . they came up all rough, not some white and some pink. [Teacher leaves.]
Cathy:	That could be it.
Sandra:	Definitely. . . . I know because I took genetics before, and I know about the red and the white makes pink.
Sandra:	[Calls the teacher back] Ms. Roberts, we figured it out.
Cathy:	No, we don't have a model yet, we just . . . have a theory.
Sandra:	[To the teacher] We have a model using codominance.

This excerpt illustrates some of the central features of the group work that IGC was designed to elicit from the students. First, Sandra drew attention to the model she was working on. She was eager to ask questions of the teacher and draw attention to her work. Second, she demonstrated her understanding that in this class, the teacher was unwilling to give away the answer: She told the teacher that she could just "say yes or no" and then went on to give her own explanation of the phenomena she had observed. Finally, she explained her idea in terms of a concrete example, in this case, one that is commonly (in traditional genetics classes) used to teach students about codominance: According to the model of codominance, crossing a plant with red flowers with a plant with white flowers produces offspring with pink flowers.

When Sandra's idea was shown to work, the other two girls in the group were dismayed. Instead of being pleased that they had a solution for the first problem, they were upset because they did not fully understand Sandra's explanation. They described her to the teacher as someone who "knows too much" and commented that they didn't "know how they would have figured this out if [Sandra] didn't know it already." When they began work on the next problem, Cathy suggested that Sandra be quiet "so Joan and I can get a chance to do it by ourselves." In the next excerpt, we see that Sandra contributed very little, while Joan and Cathy talked about the data, another expectation of IGC.

Joan:	Listen, can you guys explain what's the difference between a variation and a trait again?
Cathy:	A trait is something like blue eyes, brown eyes.
Sandra:	Eye c- [stops]
Cathy:	It's . . . a description of an actual thing, and then a variation is the differences within it.
Sandra:	Are you sure?
Cathy:	Yeah
Sandra:	I thought a trait was like eye color.
Joan:	So then these are traits?

Cathy: No that's variation.

Joan: Wait, oh no, now I thought that you just said the other way
              around, so that I thought you just contradicted yourself, re-
              peat what it is.

Cathy: A trait would be like the fact that it's there like you have a
              eye.

Sandra: Eye color.

Cathy: And eye color is the variation

Joan: OK, so then these are variations.

Cathy: Right.

Joan: OK.

Cathy: Wing shape is the trait.

Sandra: Trait

Cathy: Variation is . . .

Joan: Oh! Thank you, OK gotya [What Joan "got" is an understand-
              ing of the difference between a trait (particular feature, e.g.,
              wing shape) and variations of that trait (e.g., the shapes wings
              can be).]

Cathy: Good, OK, now . . .

Activity in the Sutton Group

The three boys in the Sutton group (whom we call John, Andy, and
Kevin) appeared at first to be quite unlike the Franklin girls. The three
boys were not good students and had not previously been successful in
science.

Despite their previous lack of success, however, the boys in Sutton
seemed anxious to succeed in this class. Although they had no difficulty
working on their own, they frequently called out to the teacher or researcher with questions and announcements of success. For example,
before beginning to work on the first day of model revision, they engaged the researcher in the following exchange:

John: We have to figure out what's dominant [and] recessive
              out of these three [variations]?

Researcher: You gotta make a model that explains how there can be
              three [variations], you gotta figure out what to do.

John: We have to figure [which variations are] dominant and
              [which are] recessive, just like before. OK. That can't be
              that hard.

Researcher: You gotta figure how can there be three variations. Get
              out your—do you have Mendel's bible [the representation
              of the model of simple dominance, figure 3.1]?

John: Yeah but . . .

Researcher: You should have a copy of that, and you should [use] your [lab] notebook.

John: Do mutations, do mutations count?

This exchange illustrates the boys' interest in and willingness to use scientific terms to describe their understanding of what they are supposed to be doing. In addition, it illustrates the genetics vocabulary they have been able to develop over two weeks of introductory work in IGC. Like the conversations of the girls in the Franklin group, the Sutton group's conversations with the teacher and among themselves frequently contained references to genetics concepts, both concepts developed earlier in the class (such as "dominant" and "recessive") and concepts which had not previously been addressed in class discussion (such as "mutation").

The following excerpt illustrates the ways in which tools introduced by the teacher (including the computer simulation and Mendel's bible) came to structure the boys' work in a manner congruent with the practice of science as modeled in IGC. Prior to the excerpt below, the students had been working independently for about fifteen minutes. Their problem involved one trait (eye color) with three variations (vermilion, rosy, and white eosin). They hit a snag and called the teacher over to ask her advice. At the end of their conversation, she gave the following advice: "Try and think about [model revision] in terms of the way you did last time and rewriting the [model of simple dominance]. . . . That might help. Remember last time when you were sort of at this stage it [looking at Mendel's bible] kind of helped you to figure out what [to do next]."

After the teacher left, the students turned to look at a copy of "Mendel's bible." Beginning at the top of the page, they replaced the variables in that model with numbers derived from the population they were currently studying. In the process of replacing variables, the students realized that they needed to clarify some genetics concepts before they proceeded.

Kevin: OK. Now how many traits do we have?
John: OK. Number of traits, one.
Kevin: What are traits?
John: This [pointing to "eye color" on the computer screen] is the trait.
Kevin: OK.
John: Eye color's the trait.
Kevin: Number of traits, one.

In a second discussion, the boys focused on the first aspect of their model, which they recognized as anomalous (i.e., different from what they would expect from problems involving simple dominance). They commented that since there were three variations in this problem, they must need three alleles in their model.

John: Number of alleles per gene in the population [reading from the sheet in front of him] . . . for our [model] we have to change it [because there are three variations in this problem]. . . . Number of alleles per gene in the population . . . in the population it's three.
Andy: What?
John: Hey, put three for that.
Andy: Oh. [Andy writes "three" in the team's laboratory notebook.]
John: Put three, three for that.
Andy: I was just . . .
John: 'Cuz we added a third one [allele, in order to explain three variations].

As they continued, the boys discussed and developed a new method for determining the number of possible allele combinations for the model they were describing. In the new model, they suggested that there were three alleles in the population and two alleles in each individual:

John: Number of possible . . . allele combinations, nine? [John is multiplying three alleles by three, the number of variations, in an attempt to determine how many combinations of the three alleles are possible.]
Kevin: What?
John: How many are there? Six? [multiplying three alleles by two, the number of alleles in a pair of alleles, to determine the number of possible combinations]
Kevin: What's that?
John: There's six.
Kevin: For what?
John: Number of possible allele combinations.
Andy: It's more than six, how do you figure six?
Kevin: 'Cuz two times three is six.
John: Here I'll show you, I'll show you the different ones. We can have a one-one, a two-two, a three-three, a one-two . . . [John lists the possible allele combinations to illustrate his hypothesis that there are six different combinations of two each that the three alleles can form.]
Andy: That's how you figure that out!

John: Yeah, 'cuz that's the number of possible allele combinations with this theory [their new model] . . . OK. Do you see how I came up with all these numbers?

Kevin: Yeah.

After establishing that everyone understood how to calculate the number of allele combinations in the new model, or were at least willing to agree that there were six possible allele combinations, the students moved on. As they considered how to represent the possible allele combinations, they discovered that this new model included an allele combination and a relationship they had not previously considered; in this problem, organisms exhibited four variations, and their model postulated six possible allele combinations. The boys now had to struggle with explaining how there could be more allele combinations than variations:

John: OK. Type of allele combinations. Put one, one-two, no, put one-one, two-two, three-three, colon homozygous. [Here the boys are listing homozygous allele combinations, in which both alleles are the same.]

Kevin: Just wait . . . a minute. Hold it . . . I don't think there's a three-three [a homozygous allele pair with two number three alleles in it.]

John: There has to be when you cross 'em. . . . Say you cross a one-three with a one-three?

Kevin: Yeah but we're . . . not getting a fifth thing [variation], and that's what we'd have to get. [Kevin suggests that if there were a three-three allele combination, there would have to be a fifth variation.]

John: Well maybe . . . three-three and two-three are the same variation.

Kevin: Oh, oh maybe three's dominant over two, ah . . . that's what it is. [Kevin suggests that the two-three allele pair and the three-three allele pair result in the same variation because the number three allele is dominant over the number two allele.]

John: Just put three-three down . . . homozygous, and then there's one-two, one-three, and two-three [that are] heterozygous. [Here John goes back to his original intent, writing a list of the homozygous allele combinations, a list that appears on the original representation of the model of simple dominance on which they are basing their new model.]

Finally, as they neared the end of their work, the students realized that they did not know enough to proceed. At this point, they were able to recognize what they needed to do to finish the model they had been building and to decide how to structure the remainder of their work on this problem. John saw that until this point, they had been able to work on their model by "filling in the blanks": looking at the computer screen and copying down numbers (e.g., the number of traits or variations) or using a formula to determine the number of possible allele combinations. Now, as he put it, came the "hardest part," determining how to associate allele combinations with variations in a pattern that was consistent with the offspring of the crosses they made:

> John: OK, so then . . . allele combinations can map to variations in the following ways. This [mapping the six possible allele combinations to the variations they represent] is where . . . we don't know what [to do].

The boys could no longer get their information from looking at the computer screen or listing allele combinations. Now they had to associate the six allele combinations with the four variations in the population they were studying.

> John: Allele combinations can map to variations in the following ways [reading from the model of simple dominance]. . . . This is gonna be the hardest part. If we can figure this out we'd have the rest of it.

The Sutton boys did produce a model, which is shown in figure 3.3. This model is especially impressive because on the one hand, it conforms to the framework provided by Mendel's bible (following its form and including changes to account for the anomalous cross results the Sutton boys observed), and on the other hand, it accounts for the anomalous cross results in a way that explains the outcome of any similar crosses they might make.

The Crick research group included boys who had previously been successful in science, and their group work looked much like that exhibited by the Franklin and Sutton groups. Like those in other groups, the members of Crick worked very hard to develop and revise models that could predict as well as explain, and thereby conformed to the teacher's desire to have them "act like scientists."

The following excerpt from the Crick group illustrates another way in which the teacher characterized their work as scientific, and the boys, having some fun, adopted her characterization. They were struggling

SUTTON BIBLE FOR FOUR VARIATIONS

Number of traits	1
Number of variations	4
Number of genes	1
Number of alleles/gene in the population	3
Number of alleles/gene in an individual	2
Number of possible allele combinations	6

Types of allele combinations:

(1,1), (2,2), and (3,3)	Homozygous
(1,2), (1,3), and (2,3)	Heterozygous

Allele combinations can map to variations in the following ways·

(2,2)	Variation A
(1,2) and (1,1)	Variation B
(1,3)	Variation C
(3,3) and (2,3)	Variation D

Phenotype	Genotype	Possible results
A × A	(2,2) × (2,2)	All A
A × B	(2,2) × (1,2)	A and B (1:1)
	(2,2) × (1,1)	All A
A × C	(2,2) × (1,3)	B and D (1:1)
A × D	(2,2) × (3,3)	All D
	(2,2) × (2,3)	A and D (1:1)
B × C	(1,2) × (1,3)	B, C, and D (2:1:1)
	(1,1) × (1,3)	B and C (1:1)
B × D	(1,2) × (3,3)	C and D (1:1)
	(1,2) × (2,3)	A, B, C, and D (1:1:1:1)
	(1,1) × (3,3)	All C
	(1,1) × (2,3)	B and C (1:1)
B × B	(1,2) × (1,2)	All B
	(1,1) × (1,1)	All B
	(1,2) × (1,1)	All B
C × C	(1,3) × (1,3)	B, C, and D (1:2:1)
C × D	(1,3) × (3,3)	C and D (1:1)
	(1,3) × (2,3)	B, C, and D (1:2:1)
D × D	(3,3) × (2,3)	All D
	(3,3) × (3,3)	All D
	(2,3) × (2,3)	A and D (3:1)

Figure 3.3 Model developed by the Sutton group for a population with four phenotypic variations

to develop a model and decided that the best way to move forward would be to spy on other groups' work.

> Tim: I think we should do a little espionage.
> Evan: Good plan.
> Tim: [He laughs.]
> Evan: Espionage [is the] only way.
> Tim: [If you] can't beat em, take their answers.
> Evan: Right.
> Tim: Can't beat em . . .
> Evan: I, I'll do a little espionage.
> Tim: All right.
> [Evan leaves to spy on other groups.]
> Evan: [He returns and says to the teacher:] Well, I wanted to make this just like real science, try to steal other people's answers.
> Teacher: [She laughs.]
> Rick: [inaudible] I think we would uh . . .
> Teacher: [to whole class] You know it's really interesting about listening to other people's results because there are cases in biotech especially, which is very competitive right now, where they . . . will actually have some people come to work in a new company, and they actually came from another company, and [try] to get information.
> Tim: We were too obvious.
> Teacher: [She laughs.] You just have to be more subtle. [She laughs again.]

Although the teacher had asked the boys not to spy on other groups, in her remarks to the class she compared their actions to those of actual scientists, thereby validating their approach to getting their work done.

In the environment of this classroom, most students, like those in the Franklin, Sutton, and Crick groups, were successful at the classroom's genetic science. That is, they were engaged in using the procedures of model building, testing, and revising to account, in genetic terms, for the variations in the offspring of breeding organisms simulated by the computer software. The students conducted their inquiries by relying on the insights and reasoning of their fellow group members and, in at least one case (when they spied), of members of another group.

The Meanings of *Science* and *Being a Scientist* in IGC

For the students in Franklin, Sutton, and Crick (and most others in this classroom), IGC appears to have provided an educational context in which fairly sophisticated scientific knowledge was actively pursued by a high percentage of class members. The class activities were organized and directed according to a particular model that implied certain meanings for *science* and *being a scientist*. The design of the computer simulation and the words and actions of the teacher repeatedly stressed the guide offered by this model. In a paper in which she discussed the philosophy and goals that guided the development of the course (Johnson and Stewart 1990), the teacher wrote (p. 297),

> The problems being tackled here are not the predetermined, end-of-chapter type, but rather ones that the students pose in response to their own observations of phenomena. "Solutions" cannot be obtained from the teacher nor found in the back of the book; students' solutions (models) are judged on how well they explain the data or make predictions about new data. Finally, students must persuade their peers as to the validity of their models, as do research scientists.

This theme—that students were being asked to do the kind of science that actual scientists do and were thus assuming a scientist-like identity through their work in the class—was communicated regularly.[2] On the first day of class, the teacher explained that "all the practices in the class [were] modeled after those of professional geneticists" and that by engaging in these practices, students would develop "insight into what it is like to do genetics." On the first day of model revision, the teacher gave the explanation quoted at the beginning of this chapter.

The teacher also used her image of how scientists work—building and revising models to account for new or anomalous observations—to organize class activities around the idea of model building. From the first day of class, when she asked students to develop models explaining the behavior of the unusual detergent carton, to the final days of the unit when she asked them to develop models to explain autosomal and sex linkage, she built upon the idea that what matters is "acting like a scientist" by "going through the process of trying to develop a model."

In addition, she supported the development of this identity in her one-on-one interactions with students. During each class period, she moved from group to group structuring the process of model revision. She focused students' attention on aspects of new populations that appeared similar to or different from those of previous populations. She encouraged them to refer to the previously developed model of simple dominance and suggested that they use the representation of that model

Table 3.1 **Summary of students' success in IGC during the five years the course was offered**

	Girls	Boys	Totals
Success in IGC	41 (77%)	27 (75%)	68 (76%)
Difficulty in IGC	12 (23%)	9 (25%)	21 (24%)
Totals	53 (100%)	36 (100%)	89 (100%)

Note: Success in IGC = grade above C; difficulty in IGC = grade of C or below (including incompletes); lack of previous success (difficulties) in science = science GPA of 2.0 or less, or B track. Percentages are rounded to the nearest whole number.

as a template for developing new models. She emphasized that she did not expect them to develop "final" models, and she informed them repeatedly that they would earn A's on days when they engaged in the process of model revision (but not when particular students presented final models). In addition, she commented frequently on the ways in which incidents and experiences in the class were like those experienced by "real" scientists. Such incidents included students from one group spying on others, their frustration at not being able to explain anomalous data, and their development of competing models for which there was no simple or algorithmic way to decide which model was "right" and which was "wrong."

The successful experiences of the Franklin, Sutton, and Crick groups were mirrored in most of the other groups in the IGC class. A review of past performance in IGC revealed that in the five years since the course began, 76 percent of the students, including most of the girls (77 percent), had been successful (see table 3.1; previous success in science is a positive predictor of success in IGC, $\alpha < .001$; gender is not). When we control for previous success in science classes (see table 3.2), previously successful girls, like the Franklin girls, were especially likely to do well in IGC (87 percent were successful). The corresponding figure for previously successful boys is only slightly lower: 75 percent were also successful in IGC. Even among students who had had previous difficulties in science courses, nearly two-thirds succeeded in IGC: 50 percent of girls and 75 percent of boys. What might account for this striking pattern of success over time, especially among girls, in a science subject area often thought of as dry, esoteric, and tedious?

We have no direct evidence of the reasons for IGC's success, but we want to emphasize that the unconventional organization of the class around the processes of open-ended model building and group problem

Table 3.2 **Students' performance according to their previous performance in science courses (data are for five years)**

	Previous success in science			Previous difficulty in science		
	Success in IGC	Difficulty in IGC	Total	Success in IGC	Difficulty in IGC	Total
Girls	34 (87%)	5 (13%)	39 (100%)	7 (50%)	7 (50%)	14 (100%)
Boys	18 (75%)	6 (25%)	24 (100%)	9 (75%)	3 (25%)	12 (100%)
Total	52 (83%)	11 (17%)	63 (100%)	16 (62%)	10 (38%)	26 (100%)

Note: Success in IGC = grade above C; difficulty in IGC = grade of C or below (including incompletes); lack of previous success (difficulties) in science = science GPA of 2.0 or less, or B track. Percentages are rounded to the nearest whole number.

solving, and the active participation of students in these processes are consistent with constructivist ideas about good teaching and successful learning. Further, our findings are generally consistent with larger-scale studies of high achievement in science. In a recent report based on a nationally representative sample of eighth to tenth graders (approximately twelve thousand students), Burkam, Lee, and Smerdon write,

> [Our] results underline the importance of classroom climate, particularly one that is focused on . . . promotion of interest in science and encouragement of advanced study of it, . . . the content and process of science, and a push toward relating science to real-life questions and problems. Students in science classrooms with such climates learn more. (1997, 320)

Although IGC can be faulted for not doing more to relate science to students' real-life questions (we take up this issue later in the chapter), IGC's climate seemed to contain the other elements of success that these authors found.

Burkam, Lee, and Smerdon go on to report that, in their sample, effects of classroom climate were undifferentiated by gender: "Everyone learns more in such classes" (320). However, they did find substantial improvement in girls' science achievement when girls had opportunities to participate in "hands-on laboratory experiences, where students do experiments themselves" (320). In physical science classes (where the gender gap favoring boys is greater than in life science classes), opportunities for girls to participate in hands-on laboratory experiences were associated with a 20 percent improvement in their achievement compared to that of boys (320). In IGC, girls had similar opportunities to experiment with data provided by the computer simulation and to develop their own models to explain the data. From the detergent box model-building activity, through the visit with Mendel, to the work with computer simulations, almost all IGC work involved some hands-on activity.

Other researchers have documented that girls' interest and participation in science coursework is improved by cooperative group work and open-ended learning situations, as well as by hands-on opportunities (American Association of University Women 1992; Mason and Kahle 1989). These opportunities were not only available in IGC, but they were sustained and actively engaged in by most of the girls. Once the computer simulation was introduced, all work in IGC was done in small groups. As the excerpts from the Franklin group show, those girls used the group setting to try out ideas, practice scientific terminology, pursue issues that intrigued them, and help each other understand the scientific concepts with which they were working. While boys used the groups in similar ways, previous research has suggested that such cooperative group work is particularly important to girls' success in science. In summary, then, our findings about the way science content was actually used in IGC and how one scientific process (model revision) was actively engaged by the students are consistent with what others have found about the characteristics of successful school science experiences, especially for girls.

Unfortunately, not everyone in IGC was successful. For students who had previous difficulty with science courses, about one-third also had difficulty with IGC.

Activity and Meaning in the Watson Group

Unlike their peers, the Watson group of previously unsuccessful girls did not regularly participate in the work of IGC. They did not identify themselves as doing work like that done by scientists and expressed little interest in doing so. The Watson girls never constructed a final model, and they attempted considerably fewer models than students in the other three groups: the Watson girls averaged 1.7 attempts over three different problems, compared to 5.5 in each of the other groups.

During the first few days of model revision, the teacher tried to motivate the girls. For example, after three days of work on the second problem, the girls told the teacher that they had not yet developed a final model. When she responded that scientists might take as long as fourteen years to develop working models, the girls replied that if it took them that long they would commit suicide:

Teacher: What's happening today?
Mandy: Nothing.
Jan: We know what's happening, but we don't get it.
Teacher: You mean you know, you can predict?
Mandy: We can predict [but] we still can't [figure it out], yeah like that's three days [of work].
Teacher: Well, let's go back to [Dr.] Temmin [Nobel prize winner in biology] again. He knew that if he put these certain viruses in specific organisms, that organism would get cancer. He knew that for fourteen years, and he didn't find out why for fourteen years. At the end of fourteen years he found out why. And they gave him a Nobel prize.
Jan: I think I'd kill myself, though.

After this exchange, the teacher left the girls to continue on their own.

These girls also worked hard to *avoid* practicing science. Unlike other students, they expended most of their energy on discussions of nonscience topics and went out of their way to avoid conversations with the teacher about their practice. For example, when the girls began work on the first day of model revision, the first observation they recorded was the date; it was Valentine's Day, and one commented that all of them were "wearing red or pink." Talk about appearance—what they and others look like, feel like, or smell like—was very important to the girls in the Watson group. During group work, their conversations regularly ranged from such things as spilling perfume on a book (a book the teacher assigned them to read outside of class), to the smell of the classroom, the ugliness of feet, being ticklish, and having bad eyesight. In-class discussions of such topics were rare in the other groups.

In addition to their discussions about physical attributes, the Watson girls had at least one conversation a day about arrangements for dates, anniversaries with boyfriends, weddings, friends' pregnancies, difficulties in their current relationships, and becoming engaged, as the following excerpt illustrates.

Jan: [It's the] three-month anniversary for me and Tom.
Deb: Oh yeah? Are you doing anything?
Jan: No.
Deb: Good.
Jan: I don't want to, he pissed me off last night.

Deb: What?
Jan: He pissed me off last night.
Deb: Yeah why?
Jan: Because.

Other students did not discuss marriage and relationships in class.

In the following excerpt, the girls make clear their dislike of "talking about science," and they actively silence the one girl (Deb) who wanted to do so.

Mandy: I don't like talking about science; let's talk about . . .
Deb: [Let's] talk about science.
Jan: [sarcastically, making fun of Deb] Science is fun.
Deb: Science *is* fun.
Jan: [inaudible but another sarcastic comment]
Deb: OK [resigned].
Jan: Watch this! Watch this! Hey! Watch this! Guess what I'm do-
          ing? Dada [singing], look at this! Dada . . . dada dada dada
          dada dada. [singing] You know what it is?
Mandy: I don't know.
Jan: It's *Jaws*! [She laughs.]

On several occasions, the teacher tried to redirect and inspire the girls by using the example of a different group of girls who came to IGC (in a previous year) after having been in B-track science classes (as had two of the three girls in Watson). The Watson girls continued their habit of diverting the conversation.

Teacher: You know, that was interesting how many of you guys [*sic*]
            have come up through 2B [the lower-track science classes].
Jan: Yeah?
Teacher: Well, one of the best models I've ever gotten was from
            Molly Brown [pseudonym] . . . She was a 2[B] too.
Jan: She woulda married him, [and] she wouldn't a had to change
            her last name.
Teacher: What?
Jan: My brother dated her. [Jan and Molly were unrelated but
            had the same last name.]
Teacher: Oh. [Laughs] But they came up with a model for this one
            [problem] that a Nobel prize winner had come up with. [But
            the Nobel Prize winner] changed his mind later on, and
            there's no way they could have found [that model] any place
            'cuz none of the textbooks have it at all. They figured it out
            themselves. I was terribly impressed.

The Watson girls did not respond and did not seem interested. After this and other similar exchanges, the teacher left them and moved on to other groups.

Clearly, the Watson girls were not engaged in the activities of IGC, and their interest in science was not piqued by them. In addition, it is especially interesting that the group received very limited attention from the teacher or the researcher during the course. As the dialogue illustrates, when the teacher did not find appropriate behavior among the Watson girls, she tried at first to raise their interest, as she did with other groups. When this approach did not work, she moved on to other groups. She presumably expected that the Watson girls would eventually get down to business, as had students in other groups, but as the data about their modeling activities suggest, they rarely did. So, while the teacher attempted strategies with the Watson group that had been successful with other students, the strategies did not work well, and the girls in the Watson group never did succeed. Our review of past performance in IGC revealed that previously unsuccessful girls, like the Watson girls, were somewhat less likely to succeed in IGC than were previously unsuccessful boys (see table 3.2), although this difference was not statistically significant. Among students who had been successful in previous science classes, IGC helped relatively more girls than boys (87 percent vs. 75 percent), but among students who had been unsuccessful in previous science classes, IGC appears to have helped relatively more boys than girls (75 percent vs. 50 percent).

Without more data on classes in previous years and a more rigorous experimental design, we cannot explain why all of the previously successful boys were successful during the course we observed, or why none of the previously unsuccessful girls were able to succeed. We do not know of any differences between the course offered during the semester we studied it and the courses offered during other semesters that could account for this result.[3] We do have some ideas about why the girls in the Watson group did not succeed.

What Might Account for the Watson Group's Lack of Success?

Several explanations are possible for the Watson group's lack of success. Some center on the fact that neither the teacher nor the researcher was aware of how little the Watson girls were accomplishing and thus did not give them special help or attention. How could two conscientious adults—the teacher and researcher—miss the group's difficulties?

The teacher and researcher may not have recognized the Watson girls' lack of interest and success for reasons connected to the classroom situation and to the behaviors and responses of the girls. Although the teacher and researcher interacted with them in ways that were similar to their interactions with students in other groups, the strategies that were successful with other students (both male and female) did not work with the girls in the Watson group. The teacher used a variety of strategies in interacting with students, all designed to engage them in the process of developing working genetic models: she compared students' work to that of professional scientists (e.g., a Nobel prize winner or scientists employed at biotech firms); she asked questions to encourage students to describe their work (e.g., "How are you doing?" "What's happening today?"); and she offered suggestions to help students when they told her they were stuck (e.g., hints on when to apply and how to use "Mendel's bible," or suggestions about new crosses to try). These strategies worked to encourage and support students in the Crick, Sutton, and Franklin groups; they did not encourage the Watson girls. Since the organization of the class did not require students to document their participation in any formal way (student groups could volunteer to present their working models to the rest of the class, but were never required to do so), and since the strategies the teacher used were clearly successful with a majority of students, the teacher and researcher were not alerted to the Watson girls' lack of engagement and progress.

Moreover, the Watson girls behaved quite differently from students in the other three groups in yet another way. During a typical class period, the teacher was kept busy responding to questions and other requests from students in the other three groups. Girls in the Franklin group, for example, frequently called the teacher over to show her what they were doing and to confirm that they were on the right track. Similarly, boys in the Sutton and Crick groups called the teacher over to ask for help and describe for her what they were doing. Students in all three groups responded eagerly to questions from the teacher when she stopped to talk with them. Girls in the Watson group did not ask for assistance from the teacher, and worked hard to end or avoid conversations about science by responding with brief answers or by changing the subject. The constant demand for attention from other groups and the lack of similar demands from the Watson girls worked to limit the teacher's and researcher's awareness of the slow progress and disinterest of the Watson girls.

These explanations for the Watson group's lack of success focus on why the teacher and researcher in the IGC classroom did not recognize their difficulties and work to ameliorate them. Another set of explanations may be given from the standpoint of the Watson girls themselves. Why weren't the Watson girls intrigued by activities in the IGC as other students were?

One answer may lie in the particular view of being a scientist that was promoted in the classroom. In order to find IGC engaging, students needed to see the identity of research scientist as one worth adopting, at least temporarily. In all three of the successful groups (Crick, Sutton, and Franklin), students seemed to be motivated by the image presented of acting like a scientist. Boys in the Sutton group eagerly worked to create their own versions of Mendel's bible to illustrate their models; girls in the Franklin group worked hard to act in ways that their teacher promoted as appropriate (in this case acting like a scientist); and boys in Crick enjoyed the idea that their spying was "science-like." Girls in the Watson group worked equally hard to *avoid* appearing as scientists (remember their reaction to the idea that they might have to work as long as fourteen years to develop a model, as well as their concerted efforts to avoid talking about science). Was there something about the scientist identity promoted in IGC that made it appealing to most of the students but not to the girls in Watson?

Connections to Scientific Power in IGC

The students in IGC were expected to work with established, taken-for-granted tools of the classroom setting (the teacher and the organization of classroom life) and of science (the genetics concepts, the process of developing and revising models, and the computer simulation). In ways similar to those described by Nespor (1994) for physics undergraduates (see chapter 2), as IGC students proceeded through the curriculum, they were being encouraged to commit to procedures leading to increasingly abstract, mathematical, and invariant models and ideas. According to Nespor, when ideas are abstract and mathematized, they facilitate consensus and network building because people in distant and varied situations, regardless of local circumstances, can use them consistently and communicate intelligently with each other. When inquiry procedures result in the formulation of invariant models and theories, such as the laws of physics, they facilitate social control; that is, they become principles with widespread applicability that are virtually impervious to local variations, needs, or contingencies. As Connell suggests in the quotation that begins the introduction to part 2, herein lies the power of the "dry" sciences: Abstract, invariant concepts, like (or modeled after) those of the dry sciences, are easily and effectively used as the basis for making large-scale social or global decisions such as those made in contemporary U.S. society by industries, companies, nations, or schools. Such decisions regarding policies and the distribution of resources are nearly impossible for individuals or local groups to resist or change. Acquiring proficiency with the abstract and mathematized concepts of genetics is a step toward enabling students to connect to a far-flung network of genetic scientists, the representations they depend on, and the kind of power these representations entail.

For the students in IGC, however, such concepts are currently meaningful only within the confines of this classroom or (later, potentially) in the laboratory settings of genetic science. They are not transportable, usable, and may not even be intelligible in the students' current social lives outside the classroom, as the example of the Watson group hints. As students in IGC develop their models in small groups, talk with the teacher, and present their findings to the class, they are encouraged to use the vocabulary and forms of scientific argument—the technical language of model revision and the routine of proposing an idea (model) for scrutiny and debate by others. The way the boys in the Sutton group developed their model for codominance is a good illustration of this process. At the same time, the students are being disconnected from real-world phenomena as they develop proficiency in the work of IGC. As the genetics problems become more difficult, their solutions become more hypothetical and abstract. As the problems become more difficult, real-world analogs become harder or impossible to conceive. Correspondingly, the discourse for interpreting genetics problems and solutions becomes more formal and mathematized. In consequence, other students who have not proceeded as far, who have not taken the class, parents at home, and many others are no longer able to participate in this part of the students' world.

Nespor (1994) has suggested that the trade-off of immediate real-world concerns and connections to gain scientific disciplinary power can be especially troublesome for girls and young women. In his study of undergraduate physics majors, the trade-off is very pronounced, because the program encourages students to spend almost all their time with other physics students, working on physics problems. Space and time for other coursework, leisure time, and social relationships are forced to the edges of the daily routines of undergraduate physics students. According to Nespor, college women are more likely than men to resist this pressure, and thus they are less likely to continue in or to do well in physics.

Although Nespor reports that women are less likely than men to accept the constraints of a "physicist's life," he does not make clear why this might be so. Holland and Eisenhart's study of college women (1990) does suggest why. According to their results, college women must depend on their social relationships, especially their romantic relationships with men, in order to gain prestige and status among their peers. Further, beginning at least in middle school and extending through college, women's dependence on social relationships for status and prestige increases with age (see also Eckert 1993). In contrast, high school and college men can gain prestige and status among their peers by succeeding in athletic, fraternity, extracurricular, and academic accomplishments, as well as in social relationships. If young women's prestige and status come to depend almost completely on their social relationships, while men's do not, then it makes sense that women would be less likely than men to risk the consequences of pursuing a "greedy" major like physics.

In the IGC class we studied, we found some evidence of this pattern and its differential effects. The classroom transcripts suggested that previously successful girls and boys, as well as previously unsuccessful boys, were willing to give up small-group talk about sports, girls and other interests to engage in IGC-related tasks, while the previously unsuccessful girls in Watson were not. In the Franklin group of successful girls, topics concerning social life, romance, or appearances rarely came up. In the Sutton and Crick groups of successful and unsuccessful boys, attempts to turn the conversation to social matters were discouraged. In the following example, the boys from the Sutton group are visited by a member (Aaron) of another group who is interested in social plans for that evening. After a brief exchange, a Sutton group member asks him to leave.

Aaron: So that means he's buying tickets to the concert tonight.
John: OK.
Aaron: Good. We'll have to get going.

Andy: Leave Aaron, we don't want you disturbing us. Leave! You
        fiendish [person]. [laughs]
John: OK, [the] fat [variation] looks purebred. If I'm right on this
        one [cross] we'll get . . .
Andy: What are you guessing?
John: We'll get all three [variations].

In contrast, it was rare for the girls in the Watson group to stop
talking about nonscience topics and do science. Instead, they were far
more likely to pursue social topics at length and to be diverted from
science to other discussions, as the earlier excerpts from their talk indicate. This suggests that the high school girls in the Watson group may
already be focusing their attention on the social relationships that were
so important to the college women Holland and Eisenhart studied. In
the Holland and Eisenhart (1990) study, decreasing interest in academic
work among women was associated with increasing interest in social
relationships and romance. Girls with previously weak academic records, such as the Watson girls, appear especially vulnerable to this
trend. For students such as these girls, the constructivist-oriented activities of IGC and the identity IGC promised was apparently not powerful
enough to overcome the allure of social affairs and romantic relationships. From the evidence we have, the previously successful girls in the
Franklin group were not (yet) demonstrating a declining interest in
schoolwork. This is not to suggest that they were not somehow participating in romantic relationships but that romantic relationships had not
become so salient a source of prestige for them. Perhaps, as was true
for a few of the women in Holland and Eisenhart's study, the Franklin
girls' success in school has so far protected them by giving them a valuable source of personal pride that can balance the allure of romance.
However, as they get older, the social pressures to participate in the
"culture of romance" are likely to increase, and as they do, the girls in
Franklin would seem to be much more likely than the boys in Sutton
or Crick to turn away from "greedy" activities (including those anticipated by IGC) that limit opportunities to pursue the social activities
that bring girls status and prestige.

In summary, then, the development of technical discourse in the
form of abstract concepts and scientific argument increased the IGC
students' connections to other scientists, particularly geneticists. Students in IGC learned to use the kinds of tools that geneticists use, in-

cluding technical language and models of inheritance, and, even more important, they learned to solve the kinds of problems geneticists solve. Unlike typical textbook genetics problems, in which students are expected to reason from causes (What genetic mechanism is operating here?) to effects (What results would be expected, given that genetic mechanism?), the problems encountered by students in IGC required them to reason inductively from effects (What are the offspring of this cross?) to causes (What model can explain the patterns generated by this cross?). This "effect-to-cause reasoning" (as one of IGC's designers calls it) is characteristic of the work of geneticists (and many other scientists) and gives students an opportunity to engage in practices that are much more closely tied to "real science" than are the practices in traditional genetics classes.

For girls and young women interested in science, this is good news. Their level of participation, development of scientific concepts, and success at model revision in IGC are impressive accomplishments and on a par with or better than those of boys. Compared to the many young women who never have, or never take, such an opportunity to learn advanced science, the girls who were successful in IGC will have a significant advantage if they decide to pursue scientific studies or careers.

Yet to gain this advantage, students must invest time and energy in developing habits of mind that, at least temporarily, distance them from the concerns of their friends, families, and their everyday lives. For the successful girls in the Franklin group, and for the boys in both the Sutton and Crick groups, this effort was apparently worthwhile; for the Watson girls, who seemed to have more compelling interests outside of class, the effort was apparently not worthwhile.

Unfortunately, IGC did not address the possibility that girls' circumstances outside of class might influence their participation in a different way than do boys' circumstances. No aspect of the IGC curriculum design took seriously the possibility that girls' social situation outside of class, well-documented by ethnographic researchers, might affect their participation in what was, in other ways, an innovative curriculum. No part of the curriculum focused on things that might have been of special interest to girls; no part of it helped girls to recognize or understand the socially constructed obstacles to their continued participation in the hard sciences; no part of it allowed girls to express genetics-related interests that may have led them to enroll in the course in the first place, or that might have piqued their curiosity more than fruit flies or eye color. Thus, while IGC is to be applauded for its appeal to and its success with girls, it seems that IGC's success depends on assuming that girls can or should be just like existing "real scientists" and just like boys. To the extent that IGC and similar curricula succeed by ignoring the social realities of girls' lives, we would expect their success with girls to be small-scale and short-lived.

Chapter Four

Learning to Be an Engineer

Programs for women which seek to address attrition solely by reconciling the relatively few women who use them to a learning environment which is inherently opposed to the needs of female [science, mathematics, and engineering, or "S.M.E."] students as a whole, are doomed from their inception. Those S.M.E. faculty who are serious about making the education they offer as available to their daughters as to their sons are, we posit, facing the prospect of dismantling a large part of its traditional pedagogical structure, along with the assumptions and practice which support it. (Seymour and Hewitt 1997, 314)

The Engineering Design Internship (EDI) is a school-to-work experience for prospective engineers attending a highly-ranked engineering college. The course is devoted to accomplishing "real engineering work" contracted to it by clients in industry or the public sector. The problems students are asked to solve in this course are contingent on local circumstances, often ill-defined, and open-ended. Thus EDI is unlike the traditional engineering coursework that constitutes the majority of the curriculum at this and other engineering schools, in which most of the work involves solving sterile textbook problems that have only one "correct" solution.

The EDI program is located at a state-supported engineering college of 2,700 students (two-thirds undergraduates) in the Rocky Mountain region. Admissions criteria are selective and typical of engineering colleges across the United States: all entering students have high school grade point averages above 3.0 and rank in the top one-third of their high-school graduating classes (College Entrance Examination Board

Primary data about EDI were collected and analyzed by Karen Tonso.

1992). The college has a tradition of academic excellence and a reputation for producing capable engineers.

EDI is the fourth course in a series of courses required of all students during their first four semesters at the engineering college. The first three semesters of the sequence provide introductions to word processing, computer spreadsheets, computer-aided design, FORTRAN programming, descriptive geometry (three-dimensional technical drafting), and technical writing, as well as oral communication, teamwork, and professional ethics.

Students in EDI are assigned a project in which they work for a client to solve an actual engineering problem. The project is described as follows in the College Bulletin: "All writing, oral communication, and group work is integrated with the project. Project work strongly emphasizes self-education, integration of graphics, computing, and subjects taught outside of [EDI], teamwork, professional ethics, and effective use of evidence." To deal with this wide-ranging content, EDI was always taught by a team of professors, including at least one from engineering or the sciences and one from the humanities (where technical writing and oral communication had historically been taught).

Karen Tonso collected most of the data for this study, using primarily ethnographic methods. Data collected included participant observations and in-depth interviews with students in one class section of forty-five students, the researcher's personal journal, documents describing the course, and written materials and other tangible artifacts used or produced by the students and professors. Tonso's semester-long participation included conversations with students about their plans; providing descriptions, when asked, about her past experiences as a practicing engineer and an engineering student (see the preface); and (rarely) assisting students as they interpreted the remarks of their professors. Most of her field notes were taken during regularly scheduled classes.

A survey administered near the end of the semester provides some information about the gender and ethnic makeup of the section of 45 students. Of the 39 respondents, 29 (74 percent) were male, and 10 (26 percent) were female. This corresponds roughly with the proportion of female students enrolled in the engineering college as a whole (21 percent in 1993); both are somewhat higher than the national average of 15 percent (Mason 1991; Vetter 1992). This proportion contrasts markedly with the number of women in engineering professions; in the world of engineering outside this college, males comprise 93 percent of practicing engineers and 85 percent of new engineering graduates (Mason 1991). Of the 36 students who responded to the item regarding ethnicity, 32 were white (not Hispanic), 3 were Asian, and 1 was African-American.

During the semester of our study, the section was directed by three professors, Dr. Jarrett and Dr. Smythe, humanities professors with Ph.D.'s, and Professor Mason, an engineering professor with a B.S. degree.[1] Students met with their professors for regularly-scheduled classes two hours twice a week for fifteen weeks. In the first part of each class (usually about forty-five minutes), one or more of the professors lectured; the remainder of the class period was used for meetings of student teams.

The section was divided into teams of five or six students; each team had responsibility for fulfilling a specific client's contract. Once a team was assigned a client, its first task was to contact the client and figure out what needed to be done to address the client's problem. Students spent classroom time, in teams and with the professors, figuring out what they needed to know in order to address the client's problem, discussing issues related to the problem, reviewing professional writing, and discussing professional etiquette. Students spent additional time at their client's site, discussing the problem they were contracted to solve and collecting data relevant to it.

Students' projects during the semester of study included, for example, assisting the Historical Society of a nearby mountain town by surveying the commercial buildings in its historic district so that the town could comply with the Americans with Disabilities Act (ADA); assisting an engineering firm working for a private school by inventorying drainage patterns and suggesting erosion-control measures; and helping a diagnostic equipment manufacturer to identify and solve packaging and marketing problems for a diagnostic test that detects yeast. Table 4.1 lists all the class projects during the semester of study. Professors identified projects prior to the start of the semester by working with their network of contacts in industry and government. The descriptions in table 4.1 were taken from the client letters requesting assistance from the class.

The semester opened with an introductory session in which students received an overview of the projects and were asked to indicate their first three preferences. At the second class meeting, professors assigned students to project teams on which they would work for the remainder

Table 4.1   **Clients and projects for the second-semester sophomore class**

Client	Project Description
Nearby mountain town	Conduct a compliance and liability assessment of an abandoned mill site and advise the town about the possible acquisition of the mill site.
Nearby mountain town	Develop and assist in the implementation of the Community Rating System—Flood Damage Protection Program to make a recommendation concerning the optimal participation level and develop the program components.
Historical society Nearby mountain town	Help the Historical Society by surveying the commercial buildings in the town's National Historic District so that the town can comply with the Americans with Disabilities Act.
The college town	Provide a design and probable cost of construction for an ADA-accessible pedestrian walkway between a dormitory and the student center.
Engineering firm working for a private school in the foothills	Inventory drainage ways, develop a rating system, suggest possible ways to treat the gullies, select erosion control projects for construction by students at the experimental school.
Same client as previous team	Develop a monitoring system and telemetry for the school's water pumping system, storage tanks, waste water pumping system, access road, and other facilities at the school.
Diagnostic equipment manufacturer	Identify and solve packaging and marketing questions for a diagnostic test for detecting yeast organisms.
Nearby mountain camp	Make an environmental sustainability evaluation of the various components and infrastructure of the camp, which provides recreational opportunities for people with disabilities. The evaluation should include an analysis of the year-round population, animal population and profile, water source, sewer disposal, existing air conditions, noise pollution, wildfire hazards, the site's historical significance, as well as how to preserve, maintain, and improve it.

of the semester. Team assignments were based on students' preferences but tempered with the professors' decisions to balance the makeup of each team with respect to representation of different engineering majors, and to ensure that female students were assigned at least in pairs. In this typical class of forty-five students, eight teams, each with five to six students, pursued eight different projects.

Within the class, two teams (referred to as Team A and Team B) were chosen for detailed study. These particular teams were chosen because they were working on similar projects and because they had different gender compositions. Team A started the semester with three men

(Chuck, Doug, and Paul) and three women (Amy, Franci, and Jennifer), although Paul dropped the course early in the semester. Team B consisted of four men (Eduardo, Fred, Jeff, and Louis) and one woman (Robin). The professors who assigned Robin to this team assumed that Robin was a male's name; when they recognized their error, they decided it was too late to alter the teams. Because Teams A and B met simultaneously in class, Tonso tried to split her time between them. However, she became more interested in Team A's activity because there were more women on this team. Ultimately, Team A seemed to emerge as a context in which female students were particularly effective.[2] In this chapter, we focus on the experiences of the members of Team A as they progressed through the EDI program.

Engineering in Practice: The Case of Team A

In EDI, "engineering" was practiced as a form of teamwork in which individual team members first became "expert" in a topic area and then coordinated each area of "expertise" with the others, in order to present viable solutions to a real-world problem that a client thought engineers could solve. Team A's activity illustrates how this form of engineering developed during the semester.

Activity in Class

At the second class meeting, the professors distributed to each team a letter from its client, describing the project and identifying a contact person within the client's organization. The following is an excerpt from the letter from Team A's client.

> [We request a] group [to] help us survey our commercial buildings in our National Historic District of [the town]. Most of the structures were constructed during the 1880s and present unique problems when it comes to compliance with the new ADA [Americans with Disabilities Act] regulations. Although we are, of course, concerned with the cost of compliance, the historical integrity of our buildings is also extremely important to us.

By the third week, the project was divided into different areas of expertise. Each team member was individually responsible for researching and reporting the technical information in his or her area of expertise. At midterm, each student was expected to prepare an "area report" that described what had been learned about his or her area of expertise. Students submitted drafts of the area reports for ungraded feedback two weeks before the area report was due. Similarly, a draft of the team's final project report was to be submitted for feedback two weeks before the final project was due at the end of the semester. The project report detailed the team's recommendations to the client and reasons for those recommendations. Unlike the area reports, in which each student wrote about his or her own area of expertise, the project report was a collaborative team effort to produce a coherent document in which inconsistencies and conflicts among the various areas of expertise were resolved. The final project report was the only piece of graded student work for which a common grade was given.

Both the area reports and the project reports were structured to follow established guidelines for technical writing that had been taught in earlier classes in the course sequence of which EDI was the fourth semester. The EDI professors reviewed these guidelines during class time.

Oral presentations were also required throughout the semester: three meetings with clients, a "staff" meeting, and oral cross-examinations. One or more professors attended each of these oral presentations and provided feedback to the students on their public-speaking skills. The first meeting with the client, at the beginning of the semester, allowed the students and client to become acquainted and to begin delineating the project. At the second, midterm meeting with the client, students informed the client of the team's progress, and the client's feedback provided any mid-course corrections that were warranted. At the final meeting with the client and in conjunction with the final report, the team had to present its findings and recommendations.

The "staff" meeting, sometimes called the first oral presentation, was a role-playing exercise held during the fourth week of the semester. One of the EDI professors played the part of the team's engineering supervisor, listening to a status report on each area of expertise and then giving feedback on each team member's public-speaking skills. The oral cross-examination was another role-playing exercise in which one team performed a "dry run" of its upcoming final meeting with the client, while a second team and the professors pretended to be members of the client's community. This "audience" asked questions of the presenters to simulate the final meeting with the client. The teams then exchanged roles, with the second team presenting to the new "audience," now composed of the first team and the professors. Each of the team members received an individual grade on oral presentations. Table 4.2

summarizes the work (written and oral) that the student teams were required to present during the semester.

The majority of class time and considerable time outside of class was spent working on these projects. The following vignette describes a "typical" class session.[3] We use it here to illustrate how the class was organized for instruction, the activities that participants engaged in, and how gender distinctions were made in the class.

I [Tonso] arrive ten minutes before class and slide into a desk on the left side of the room about halfway back. The room is large enough to hold sixty students, with desks arranged in six rows of ten desks per row. Two of the three professors, Dr. Smythe and Dr. Jarrett [both female humanities professors], wait in the hall to go over last-minute details with their colleague, Professor Mason [male engineering professor]. Five minutes before class Professor Mason has not arrived, so Dr. Smythe and Dr. Jarrett come into the classroom. Professor Mason arrives moments later. As the students arrive and sit close to their teammates, the three professors gather around a movable lab table that is in the front of the classroom.

Professor Mason writes today's agenda on the board:

> Client meetings
> Oral reports
> Divide-and-conquer
> Team meetings

Professor Mason tells Dr. Smythe to give the teams feedback on their client meetings.

> Professor Mason: I've talked to a few clients and they were impressed. . . .

At this point, Professor Mason reminds Dr. Smythe that he will return to class after he attends to another matter. He leaves.

The bell rings, signaling the start of class, and it can be heard faintly above the noise of the students' talking. Dr. Smythe begins class by asking the student teams how their first client meetings went. The students continue to chat with each other, which creates more buzzing than is usually heard when Professor Mason is the lead-off speaker. No student responds to Dr. Smythe's query, so she tries another approach—telling the students to remember to write their client a letter

Table 4.2 Summary of the required student and team products (column heads are week nos.)

	1	2	3	4	5	6	7	8	9	10	11	12	13	14	15
Written															
Meeting minutes	A	B	C		D	E		A	B	C		D	E		
Draft area report						I									
Area report								I							
Draft project report													G		
Project report															G
Oral															
Client meetings		G						G							G
Staff meeting				G											
Cross-examination											G				

Note: *A* indicates that student A writes the minutes the first week, student B, the next week, etc. *I* indicates this task was done by each student individually and graded individually. *G* indicates that this task was a group effort requiring fitting the work of individuals together. However, except for the final project report, each student was graded individually.

summarizing their meeting, reminding their client of future meetings, and keeping the client informed. In the middle of her reminder, an unidentified student in the back of the room calls out, "How long should the client letter be?" Dr. Smythe does not miss a beat, but goes ahead with what she was saying. Then, as if on some unknown cue, she responds to the questioner, saying, "One or two pages."

She returns to her earlier efforts to elicit feedback from the teams on the first client meetings, asking, "What were the good points of your client meetings?" One team member responds that their client was thorough. Dr. Smythe asks, "What about [the] questions [you asked]?" To which the student replies, "The client covered it all, and there was nothing to ask about."

Dr. Smythe tries yet one more approach, "What did your team do well?" A second group answers, "We asked the right questions." A third group answers, "Our group will develop questions as we work on the problem, but our client went over the [client] letter and there was nothing new, so we didn't ask any questions." Dr. Smythe asks about the way the teams organized the questioning, "Did all [of the team members] ask questions, or just some?" Both approaches were tried by different teams. The team that had all members asking questions on different facets of the project felt they "covered more [information] with their approach."

Now Dr. Smythe returns to the first agenda item—to give the teams feedback on their client meetings—saying, "The clients were impressed, so the team members have a lot to live up to. Be sure to watch your body language." She singles out one student who is currently slouched down in his chair: "Sitting like that is OK here, but not at a professional meeting." (As an aside to me before class, Dr. Smythe remarked that in one of the client meetings she attended, the women were incredibly professional, but the men were rocking their chairs back or slouching, and generally not acting at all as she would expect in the situation.) Meanwhile, she asks, "Are there any questions?" When none arise, she walks to the lab table.

Dr. Jarrett takes over for the second agenda item. She turns on the overhead projector to show a slide about the upcoming first oral presentation, when students will participate in a role-playing activity with one of the professors. The oral presentation being discussed is modeled on an industry staff meeting where the professor plays the part of an engineering supervisor, and the students play staff engineers giving status reports. The overhead slide Dr. Jarrett uses to inform the student teams contains an incredible amount of writing and, with the ambient light from the wall of windows, the print is too small for me to read. Luckily, she reads some of it: "The purpose of the oral meeting is to provide an outline of the body of knowledge. Each team should select one team member to be the group spokesperson." The spokesperson will "give the lay of the land telling who is in the group and what each will cover. Next, each member will give a three-to-five minute oral report, using one graphic per speaker." One student raises her arms in an abject and frustrated gesture. Dr. Jarrett asks, "Is there a question there?" The student, embarrassed to be called on, turns red and manages to say, "I just can't think of a graphic." Dr. Jarrett responds that the graphic will be covered later; there will be no problem after it is explained. Dr. Jarrett continues with her explanation: "Each speaker should state their name, the sources used, and those constraints" already known. "You should tell about your anticipated results, options, or hypotheses; how your area ties into the group's problem and goals."

Dr. Jarrett is continuing her lecture on the oral presentations when Professor Mason arrives about twenty minutes into the class. Though Dr. Jarrett was in the middle of her presentation, there were many spontaneous comments from students, such as "Hi, Professor Mason" and "He's late." His arrival completely interrupts (and ends) Dr. Jarrett's presentation. He says he is late due to a deposition he was giving and advises the students about these situations saying, "This lawyer crap is really for serious." He jumps into a description of what the teams should be trying to do in finding and assigning areas for each team member. Dr. Jarrett takes a seat near the door at the front of the classroom. I am caught off guard by the sudden change in the faculty presentations. After a few minutes, I realize that Professor Mason has moved on to the next agenda item, "Divide-and-conquer," which I did not initially equate with "assigning technical areas" to each team member.

To illustrate his lecture, Professor Mason draws a sketch on the front board, and the students begin to fidget and chatter as he describes it (see figure 4.1). He marks off a small interior section between 1 o'clock and 3 o'clock with an irregular boundary (labeled A in figure 4.1), which he called "What we know about the problem so far." From this area, he draws five arrows radiating away from the known information and pointing toward the other side of the circle. These arrows represent questions, "intelligent questions," and have subquestions from each arrow. He tells the team members to "commit to the team what you're going to do" in each area of technical expertise.

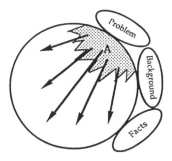

Figure 4.1 Professor Mason's sketch of the information to be gathered

I do not completely understand Professor Mason's sketch, but he leaves it to reminisce about his engineering career, so I expect his story will illuminate his sketch. "I was a district engineer in [a large Midwestern town] with 720 people on the professional staff I supervised. These people were divided into sections for engineering, planning, regulatory and social issues, accounting, and so on. We divided projects into major, those over $10 million, and minor, those about $1 million. Altogether we had about $60 million a year in projects." (It becomes very quiet in the room for the first time today.) "I'd call project meetings, and each team leader would present a five-minute update every month telling me where they were, what they were doing, and where they were headed. This way the management could guide or redirect the work as needed. This is called a project meeting." As I listen to his story, I realize that my initial guess of its purpose was only partly correct. It is not only about his sketch and how to understand his "arrows," but also anticipates the upcoming oral presentations. His lack of explicit connecting statements makes the lecture difficult to follow.

At the end of his story, Professor Mason returns to the board; as he does so, chatter returns. He continues: "A typical new-bee [inexperienced engineer] mistake is to jump to a plausible answer and work backwards. This is to be avoided, because synergism comes in as you guys recognize where each guy's area influences another guy's. What you want to do is find these intelligent questions [gesturing to the arrows on his diagram]. Each person makes blind thrusts of the bayonet, probes around until you find something that says, 'Ouch!' "

Dr. Jarrett interrupts, saying, "Mr. CEO" to Professor Mason, "Are these [thrusts of the bayonet] the hypotheses?" He answers, "Yes. In the oral report on your area, include facts and possible solutions. Pay attention to the 'so what' aspect, how it [your area] bears on the problem. You will be graded on how well you can do the investigation and how well your reports back up, and relate to, the ongoing process of what you and your team are trying to do. You are putting together a body of knowledge [which he emphasized by speaking very loudly]. The final [project] report will not be a composite, and you will still have more to do." He closes giving two pieces of advice: "Number 1: Don't follow in a line, and number 2: Don't do anything that's dependent on others. I want five to six good thrusts into the project, three to five minutes in each oral report. The time's yours." The teams now are free to meet as a group.

Several aspects of the class described in the vignette make it "typical" of the EDI. One is its structure: it began with an agenda written by Professor Mason, was followed by lecture(s), and ended with time for the teams to meet. Another is that most of the professor-delivered information was of the "how-to" variety: how to write meeting minutes, how to write a letter to the client, how to divide the team work among individuals, how to make an oral report, how to use graphics (view graphs, charts, maps, etc.) in an oral presentation, how to write reports, how to document resources, how to behave in a professional meeting, and how to dress for a professional meeting. Whole-class lecture was used almost exclusively. Rarely, professors spoke with individual teams and offered advice about ways to proceed, saying, "Have you tried . . . ?" and "You should. . . ." Finally, the vignette is typical in the way it depicts the relationships among Professor Mason and the two women professors. His actions and statements commanded everyone's attention; theirs did not.

Activity in Team Meetings

Within the context of EDI, each team worked on its own individual project. What the teams needed to do varied from week to week and from team to team. The following vignette of Team A's activity reveals how the team gave meaning to their project.

Team A's project was to assist the Historic Society of a nearby mountain community by investigating the implementation of the Americans with Disabilities Act (ADA) in a National Historic District. They have not been able to contact the client yet, so they have not had the required client meeting.

While the team members are catching up on their lack of progress in contacting the client, Dr. Smythe comes over to the team, which consists of three men and three women: Amy, Chuck, Doug, Franci, Jennifer, and Paul. All but Paul are sophomores.

Dr. Smythe attempts to return this team to the target schedule by telling them what to do. "You should try and call [the client]. At least you should write your client letter anyway, but phrase it differently. Say something like 'We hope to meet with you soon, and these dates are when our next meetings are scheduled.' Go to the site and nose around; see what you can find out." She leaves, and the team members grouse about how unfair it is that they haven't been able to get hold of anyone from [the town].

Group members begin to pull out their resource materials. Amy has a copy of the Federal Register containing the Americans with Disabilities Act that Doug received after calling the ADA Regional Office. Doug has a walking-tour news sheet, which the client sent with the letter describing the project. The students pass both of these resources around. Most of the team members merely glance at the pictures in the news sheet and pass it on to the next team member. In contrast, Paul looks at each page carefully. He reads the captions and a few paragraphs. He asks if all of the buildings they must consider are included in the newspaper and how they will get information on the ones not in the paper. No one gives answers to either of his questions.

They decide to visit the town as soon as possible, which will be Friday at the earliest (two days away). Transportation is their first concern. Each member tells about how her or his car is not OK. Paul's is a "heap"; Doug's is a pickup truck; Chuck's is a four-seater. There is some good-natured kidding about having to go in a small car with six people. Franci says, "We'll be sitting on laps." Amy adds, "It will be bonding between groups." They decide to take Amy's car, which can accommodate all six people. Next they discuss where to meet. There are many suggestions—the dormitory where Amy lives, in front of the building where the class meets, and the games room in the student center. They decide to meet in the student center.

In the context of this activity, students were expected to come to see the value of teamwork for solving real-world engineering problems. The assumption made, both when the college faculty designed the course several years ago and in this course, was that the project activities and the procedures modeled and suggested in the first part of the each class period would provide a model of actual engineering practice.

The structure of student teams was modeled on engineering project teams in industry, in which engineers or scientists, each with expertise in a different area, form a project team. Student teams could not function in precisely this way, because the engineering students were not yet technical experts. Instead, each student on a team was expected to become knowledgeable about one topic relevant to the team's project. In the student projects, topics were not assigned by a project leader, but were negotiated by the team in a process that the engineering professor, Professor Mason, called "divide-and-conquer." On January 25 (the beginning of the third week of classes), Team A agreed to these areas of coverage.

> Amy: ADA rules and regulations
> Chuck: Buildings covered
> Doug: Attitudes of the townspeople
> Franci: Renovation expenses
> Jennifer: History of the town and National Historic District policy
> Paul: Previous renovations in National Historic District buildings

Paul dropped the course after two weeks, and his area of knowledge left with him; none of the remaining team members pursued information in Paul's area.

Of the five students left on the team, each was responsible for locating resources and assimilating information that would provide the background for his or her area. Locating resources to answer an open-ended problem was a new challenge for most of these students. First, there was no textbook; second, the information needed to solve these open-ended problems was not the sort found in engineering texts. Students had to turn to other sources of information.

Alternative sources of information used by students on Team A included the letter from the client (distributed to the teams during the second week of class); a walking-tour news sheet from the town's tourism office; the *ADA Handbook* (both hard-cover and disk versions); a toll-free telephone number in the handbook that gave the team access to information from the ADA Regional Center; information gathered at the town's library; a copy of the *Federal Register* containing the text of the ADA legislation as passed by Congress; and ADA newsletters with information about grants and tax incentives for complying, as well as other telephone numbers for agencies providing services related to the ADA.

Students also contacted "basically everyone who would know anything" (Jennifer, interview, February 22). Those contacted included the professors, the client(s), business owners in the town, other people in the town, and an architect experienced in ADA compliance. Eventually, the team traveled to the town, where the client contact, a local business owner and long-time resident who writes about the history of the town, gave the students a tour of the historic district and introduced them to a few business owners. Doug spent one Saturday in the town interviewing business owners and residents to determine their attitudes toward the ADA. He also read a book about the handicapped to better understand their needs and attitudes. The architect provided the construction industry's standard cost-estimating manual *(The Means Guide to Construction Prices)*, which Franci used to determine prices for specific renovations, such as ramps, chair lifts, and automatic door openers.

Thus, working alone or in pairs, the students developed the resource base for their project. The sources they used and their means of obtaining information drew them into activity and relationships with clients, federal regulators, service providers, and industrial suppliers who are far removed from the university classroom and for whom technical problems must be solved within the parameters set by constraints such as cost, legal obligations, and available supplies.

The Meaning of *Being an Engineer* in Team A

In order to advise the client successfully, Team A had to develop a plan for remodeling historic buildings so that they met the ADA regulations and National Historic District policies and also accommodated the varying abilities of building owners to invest in remodeling. Although the technical knowledge required for this task is not the stuff of advanced courses in mathematics, science, or engineering, it did require students to become knowledgeable about regulations the client did not understand, and to fit those regulations into the particular circumstances of the town. And although details about the ADA were new to the client, students had to learn other things that the client already knew. The students had to become at least as knowledgeable as the client about the town's way of doing things if they were to convince the client of the feasibility of their remodeling suggestions. In particular, this team needed to answer the following questions:

1. What does the ADA require?
2. What limits does the National Historic District place on changes to historic buildings?
3. In what ways are the historic buildings deficient in light of the ADA?
4. What remodeling needs to be done, and how must that be scheduled to meet ADA-imposed priorities?
5. What will different remodeling jobs cost?

As time passed, each team member began to focus on a particular set of issues within his or her area of responsibility. Amy realized that the ADA not only mandates what "accessible" means—specific, measurable features such as door widths, ramp sizes, and numbers of public (accessible) restrooms—but also sets priorities on different kinds of access: entrances; goods and services; restrooms; and additional access. In addition, the ADA provides limits to the amount of money that building owners must spend each year, capping required remodeling expenses at a small portion of total revenues.

Chuck realized that individual buildings often had one owner, but several tenants, each fearful that modifications would impair his or her business and each imposing a variety of pressures on the building's owner. In addition, different buildings not only failed to meet the ADA regulations for different reasons, but also were at different stages in their historic renovation cycles. ADA requires that if any historic renovation is done, then ADA-required modifications also must be done. This meant that a building owner undertaking renovations for reasons other than the ADA regulations must attend to ADA-required modifications, while a competitor could delay complying with the ADA. This situation placed building owners on an unequal footing and created concerns about being competitive in attracting new tenants.

Franci focused on the fact that each potential renovation had several possible solutions. She estimated these situation costs, knowing that building owners would want to select a solution that made economic sense to them. She decided to include a range of solutions with widely varying costs, so building owners could see that they had plausible options for complying with various requirements of the ADA.

Doug discovered that building owners were reluctant to invest in modifications for a clientele they currently did not serve. In support of their past practices, building owners told about the one person in a wheelchair "ever" to visit their town. As the story goes, the wheelchair fit through an existing entrance door that was narrower than required by the ADA regulations. Building owners did not understand why they had to spend money to renovate the entrance and ruin a fine, historic doorway. Understanding the community's resistance to federal regulations, the team would have to defend the ADA regulations, show that they were reasonable, and give building owners choices. They could also remind building owners of penalties for noncompliance—usually larger sums than needed modifications would cost.

Jennifer's work focused on the fact that regulations governing National Historic Districts require that original, valued features of historic buildings be preserved, including architectural features that were central not only to the historic value of individual buildings, but to the district as a whole. Moreover, strict guidelines must be met before beginning work on historic buildings. Thus the team treated individual buildings in the context of the entire district when decisions were made about planned renovations or modifications.

The case of one building provides an example of how the team worked to combine their knowledge in several areas and respond to these complex, interacting issues. This building had a narrow oak door with beveled-glass inserts, all set into an ornate framework with turn-of-the-century woodworking embellishments. The door was a premier example of entryways common to its architectural period, but it was more than an inch narrower than required by regulations, so it violated the ADA's highest priority—entrances. The student team knew that something had be done to improve access and comply with the ADA, but that changing the doorway itself would violate National Historic District requirements. The team suggested to the building owner that he place a call bell near the door so that shopkeepers could provide personal assistance to customers who could not fit through the entrance. This simple option met all the relevant, although conflicting, criteria—ADA, National Historic District, economics, and handicapped access.

By the time of the final presentation, the team could advise the client about the scope of the work needed, its cost, and how best to schedule modifications. This advice protected business owners from lawsuits and penalties for noncompliance, and it reaffirmed owners' desires to maintain control over their assets, without damaging the historic value of the buildings. In the larger scheme of things, the students' suggestions also removed barriers that handicapped persons in the town faced to participating in the full range of available activities—the ultimate goal of the ADA.

Although the kinds of technical information needed for this project were only precursors to the advanced technical coursework the engineering students were beginning to study, they began to see themselves as people who could figure things out using a wide variety of resources, make decisions that took into account the needs of diverse groups of people, and defend their decisions in light of competing demands from a variety of sources. In this sense, they experienced first-hand some of the processes in which many actual engineers engage. These changes in the students over time are detailed in the next section.

The Trajectory of Changing Participation in Team A

In contrast to the vague conversations typical of team meetings in the early part of the semester, the conversations during team meetings in the last few weeks were unusually rich in detailed information necessary to complete the team's project. These late-semester conversations were filled with appropriate technical language used in explanations that crossed the boundaries among areas of knowledge. The excerpts from fieldnotes presented next illustrate the team's progress during the semester. They focus on Team A's discussion of the "building-by-building survey," which entailed evaluating each building in the historic district to determine existing hindrances to accessibility and to decide how best to renovate each building to overcome these impediments. Completing this task became the keystone in the project.

Discussions of the building-by-building survey surfaced periodically throughout the semester. It was first mentioned on January 20 (week 2 of 15) when Paul asked, "Should we use the checklist and go through some buildings [when we make our first site visit in two days]?" There was no response to his query, and no survey was undertaken. Paul dropped the course in mid-February and was not present when the next site visit, and the possibility of a building-by-building survey, was discussed two months later, on March 15 (week 10). As was typical of this team's discourse, discussion of the building-by-building survey was interwoven with other remarks about other topics, about constraints imposed by coursework, and about upcoming presentations. We include a portion of the team conversation on March 15, which highlights the building-by-building survey.

Doug:	What're we going to do on this visit?
Franci:	Go during business hours and tour.
Jennifer:	Building-by-building survey . . . [interrupted by discussion of what to wear]
Amy:	I'll make a copy of the [ADA] checklist, so we can make notes as we go . . . [more discussion and joking about what to wear]
Franci:	Can we do the final [project reference list] in MLA? [A formatting style for references.] Did you like the annotated [bibliography]?
Jennifer:	We have to do annotated.
Doug:	It has to be consistent and annotated.
Amy:	Timeline.
Franci:	Tuesday, building-by-building [survey] . . . [interrupted by discussion of upcoming test and plans for summer school]
Franci:	The timeline, what're we doing Wednesday [in class]?
Doug:	Cross examination is next Monday. Start small, building-by-building, measure doorways.
Jennifer:	Writing, analyzing.
Doug:	Get data to know about the buildings, measuring doorways.
Amy:	Pathways, [can't remember the word], inside pathways?
Doug:	Aisles.
Amy:	Where the people go through, you can't have this big old plant in the way.
Doug:	Doorways, pathways, bathrooms.
Franci:	They have to have one [handicapped-accessible public] restroom for the whole town.
Doug:	They already have one in that little pocket park on the south side of the street.

Even though the building-by-building survey was discussed at this March 15 team meeting, it was not conducted when the team made the site visit on March 23. Instead, some members of the team took sparse notes, which they later realized had failed to capture the necessary information on the buildings.

For the survey to meet the requirements of their project, the team needed to follow the ADA checklist, a cumbersome, twenty-page document listing every item to be considered for complying with all requirements of the Act. About forty historic buildings needed to be surveyed, and the team had to inspect every building and evaluate every constraint to access: presence of steps, stairs, and other entryway "bumps," kind of doorknobs, weight of door, sizes of aisles, height of in-store displays, presence of public restrooms and their accessibility (size of stall, width of door, height of toilet, presence and configuration of railings, height and kind of sink, kinds of faucets), presence of handicapped parking spaces, and so on. Because some buildings were not always open during students' site visits, the students had to coordinate their visits with businesses and building owners.

Although the students realized that they could not meet their project goal without the survey, and they knew at least by March 23 (week 11) that completing the survey would be a considerable task, the team procrastinated for more than two weeks. By April 7 (week 13), making the site visit had become urgent. During the class time on April 7, before the team meeting, Dr. Smythe reminded the teams that the first drafts of the project report were due on April 16. Even though this date was printed in the course schedule that students had received in January, the team seemed surprised by the short time remaining to complete their project. The team now had only ten days to make the building-by-building survey, analyze the data, determine the recommended renovations for each of forty buildings, and write their report.

With a sense of urgency on April 7, the team discussed the upcoming site visit. Again, the portions of the conversation that included the building-by-building survey are illustrative.

Doug: I'll write a memo from the last meeting [to client 2] telling him what we did since we saw him, while he was away. I'll give him our phone numbers. I'll try and call him, but he's on vacation and I don't know if I'll get hold of him.

Jennifer: OK.

Franci: I went to the library and got prices for a stair glide and demolishing stairs. I thought I'd write those up . . . [At this point the team is interrupted for several minutes when Dr. Jarrett and then Dr. Smythe stop to talk to them about other matters.]

Amy: What do you guys think of making a chart like this? [Amy, the team's ADA expert, is showing her teammates a two-page draft of the ADA checklist in tabular form. Down the left side, the buildings are listed and across the top are the features of the buildings to be checked. They pass the chart among team members.]

Jennifer: Cool!

Karen: [To Chuck] Did you get together last night?

Chuck: Amy and I did.

Amy: Can we go to the town Friday and Saturday?

Doug: This week? I'm going home for Easter.

Amy: I could be here most of the day Saturday.

Jennifer: [Chuck], do you have class on Friday?

Chuck: I have to get back at 1 o'clock. [He's unusually adamant about needing to be back, and eyebrows rise.] When it's a choice between the [baseball team's] home opener or [this class], what would you do?

Doug: [This chart] looks nice.

Amy: You have to write in the buildings and then the survey results of the inside and outside.

Jennifer: Not really, just concentrate on the outside?

Amy: I think it's better to do just the general [things on the checklist].

Doug: Maybe include drinking fountains, and telephones, restrooms, too. What else is there on there [getting the second sheet back from Franci]? Do we have to do a checklist of all these? We can't rate them unless we do.

Amy: We need to say a little bit about the insides. I don't think too many of those buildings have problems with the insides.

Doug: What we could do [pauses] if we got all of these done, we've gone business to business. [pauses] This is awesome! We can rate them on a scale of 1 to 5, where a 5 is accessible. Then take separate notes [about the deficiencies].

Jennifer: Like take comments?

Doug: Take this and fill it in. I'll get a copy and use it to put it on AutoCAD [a computer-aided design program that he uses to make large charts and other graphics for his reports].

Franci: Going in the building, is that the path of travel? What do we say?

Doug: 5 means really accessible, 1 not at all. Like the clock tower. The path of travel is a 1, ramps are none.

Franci: When we go, take copies of this. What's emergency egress?

Amy: Like lights and stuff. Alarm bells, flashing lights, signals.

Franci: I've got prices for alarm bells and flashing lights.

Amy: These [historic buildings] I think are exempt from this.

Franci: Take the businesses that are open.

Amy: Write down the address so we don't do them twice.

At last, the students have used their technical knowledge about the ADA regulations, National Historic District policies, and specific buildings and owners to develop a matrixlike chart for conducting the building-by-building survey. In addition, Franci can see the full range of access needs and can compile a more comprehensive list of remodeling options. For the first time in the semester, the students can articulate how their technical knowledge guides their activities. In earlier conversations, for instance on March 15, the students talked in very cursory terms about what they would survey in the town, but no one seemed to understand how that influenced what they would tell their clients. By April 7, the students recognized that having a variety of possible renovations (implemented over time to address the ADA's priorities)

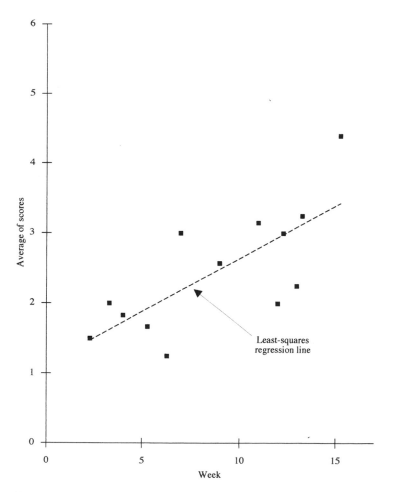

Figure 4.2 Depth-of-explanation graph

would give their clients the kind of information they needed to make wise remodeling decisions. The students also realized that they could gather the information necessary to make engineering decisions about recommended modifications and to defend their decisions.

Figure 4.2 is a graph of depth of explanation versus time (as measured across the observation dates of Tonso's work with Team A). It illustrates the team's increasing sophistication with the technical knowledge relevant to their project. The scale ranges from 1 to 6, with 1 indicting an absence of technical language, and 6 a technically elaborate explanation. Students began the semester at a score of about 1.5 and ended at about 3.5, a practical gain of two full levels on the scale.

Comparing the dialogues at team meetings on March 15 and April 7 illustrates the students' growing skills at demonstrating their engineering prowess. On March 15, the students could only minimally articulate what the building-by-building survey should entail. Phrases such as "use a copy of the ADA checklist and make notes as we go," "start small, building by building, measure doorways," "inside pathways, aisles," and "doorways, pathways, bathroom" were used vaguely to discuss the survey.

Figure 4.2 Continued
Levels Used to Assess the Technical Language and Depth of Explanation in Students' Team Meetings and Oral Presentations[a]

1. Absence of technical language, inarticulate; use of vague descriptors; e.g., *stuff* and *things*.
2. Technical language used, but sparsely, and without evidence of meaning; e.g., *good-faith effort*.
3. Technical language used and connected to isolated facts, but not related to other facts; e.g., *A non-contributing building means too much remodeling and not enough renovation: whatever made the building historical has been remodeled away.*
4. Local integration of facts, especially in one area of technical expertise or in one site or instance; e.g., *[The town] used to be a gold-mining town, but now tourism is a major source of income and it is seasonal. We tried to look at renovations that were relatively cheap—a ramp maybe, or start with good-faith effort.*
5. Networks of related facts indicating a preliminary explanation, especially connecting information from two areas of expertise; e.g., *All restaurants are required to have handicapped-accessible restrooms, but other businesses are required to have a handicapped-accessible restroom only if a restroom is available for the public; signs indicating the location of an off-site handicapped-accessible restroom meet the requirement for nonrestaurant businesses.*
6. Elaborate description or explanatory account; knowledge is extended or applied to a novel situation; e.g., *We use a stress-strain diagram to design supports and predict how a member will fail. For instance, when a concrete member is formed around an I-beam of steel, the design criteria is for the steel to deform elastically—bending, not breaking—because then a bulge in the concrete can be seen and the folks can be evacuated before it falls and crashes. If the concrete fails first, it is catastrophic.*

[a]*Levels adapted from Scardamalia et al. 1992.*

They did not mention how wide a door must be, what kinds of access modifications take precedence, or how the cumbersome ADA checklist in its published form would be used for forty different buildings.

On April 7, Amy showed the team a chart with a comprehensive list of architectural features they needed to evaluate for each building. Each line in the 8 1/2-by-22-inch chart contained all the information for one building. In addition, Amy grouped items related to "entrances" (with the highest priority) together, items related to "goods and services" next, and so on. For the first time, students could see all of the information they needed to check and how it related to the ADA's priorities. Doug became particularly excited about how much easier this chart would make the building-by-building survey. He even volunteered to set up a copy of this chart using a sophisticated software program (Auto-CAD), learned in another course required of all students during their freshman year, and one of the few direct applications of technical coursework we observed. Finally, Franci saw that the information she gathered on remodeling costs would actually be used in the team's work, something that had not always been clear to her.

We attributed the development of technical language and knowledge to the learning trajectory foreshadowed by the final course requirement that each student take responsibility for writing and then orally presenting one section of a final report to the contracting agency. The nature of the EDI's culminating course activity and its meaning as defined by the students gave purpose and direction to their developing skills and identities as engineers. As they worked to explain their efforts to each other and their professors, and thus to display their knowledge, students learned how to "talk like engineers"—that is, to use a technical vocabulary correctly, to say how technical information from different areas fits together and constrains engineering choices, and to defend their choices by citing their sources. Guided by an emergent identity of a practicing engineer as someone who could hold his or her own in a client-oriented discussion of engineering principles in the context of other considerations, students were motivated to develop the expertise they needed for this identity. However, this did not happen until the very end of the semester.

Becoming a "Practicing Engineer"

Although professors emphasized the development of the students' identities as professional engineers, students in Team A continued, throughout the semester, to see themselves as students, despite their increased knowledge and technical skills. They seemed genuinely surprised, and sometimes intimidated, to be considered "experts" whose work would be used by their client(s). Even when a client explicitly mentioned how the report would be used, students only recognized the possibility that it might be. Amy's remarks, coming late in the semester, were typical of students' feelings:

> It's so real. Especially this semester. When we talked [with our client], he talked about how he was looking forward to seeing our paper because he wants to see what we have to say. It's so much pressure. We're only college students who are only trying to do this for a grade, and they want to use this as their back-up to what they're going to do for these buildings. It's scary. In a way, we kind of feel like we don't know what we're doing. (interview, April 21)

Chuck, too, expressed his skepticism that the report would be used:

> I think our client's going to use parts of it [the report], the part that's about what's wrong with the buildings. I don't know how much they'll take into regard of our recommendations. I don't know how much I would have faith in a bunch of college kids, who were just out doing this for a grade. I would have more faith in an actual engineer who has had twenty years experience doing things like this. (interview, April 22)

On the day of their final presentation to their contracting client, however, the students did exhibit analytical skills like those used by practicing engineers, and performed well. Several features of the presentation combined to produce a setting in which students were more likely to act as engineers than as students. First, the final meeting with the client was the last official action taken by the EDI team. After leaving the meeting, most students would go on to finish their work in other classes, or to take final exams; no other work was required in the EDI program. Because of the course requirements, students arrived at the meeting (which was held off campus in a professional setting) with their final report in hand—a copy or two for the client and a copy for the professor to grade. As a result, after the meeting, students could do no more to affect their grades. The oral presentation itself could only influence, at most, 5 percent of the semester's grade. In fact, since there was a semester-long requirement that students receive a maximum of only three grades for oral presentations, students might arrive at this presentation, the fifth of the semester, with enough good grades at oral presentations to make this final assignment meaningless with regard to grades. Thus, for all intents and purposes, the "good grade" fixation, which occupied students during much of the rest of the course, no longer existed.

Second, this presentation was the first time that students met with a group of clients, rather than with the single representative with whom they had worked throughout the semester. For this meeting, Professor Mason asked that the team gather as many of the people representing the client together as possible. Three additional representatives, including the town mayor, a town administrator, and a local business owner, were present at the final presentation, which increased the importance of the meeting. Further, the client's representative made a point of mentioning that he was sorry more people had not been able to attend the meeting, but emphasized that he was "going to pass the information on to the business community . . . in town and also to the interested parties" who were not present. The mayor, who joined the meeting late, also expressed his confidence in the work that the students had done, commenting to Professor Mason (in front of the students) that their report "is the most professional looking report that I've seen out of the groups that have worked for us. . . . Since I've got forty years as a professional engineer and having written a few of these, I think I'm a good judge of it, this is the best one I've seen." All of this, in addition to the authentic setting of the meeting (as opposed to the more commonly experienced classroom setting), added to the students' sense that what happened at this meeting was important, and provided assurance that the work they had done was going to be used, something many students had expressed skepticism about prior to this meeting.

Finally, at this meeting students were expected to know the material they had prepared, and to be able to answer any questions that arose in the course of the presentation. Students who a few weeks before had been uncomfortable responding to questions from Professor Mason, exhibited far more confidence during the final client meeting—a confidence that was supported by members of the client's team, including the mayor:

Mason: We were talking about issuing a certificate of appropriateness and also building certificates. Where, Amy, does that fit in to the ADA review? Is it in both cases that the historical society ought to do an ADA review of appropriateness as well in the process of issuing a certificate? Or is it in the process of issuing the building certificate?

Amy: I'm not sure what your question is. I'm not understanding
           what your question is.
Jennifer: I think that I may understand it. The ordinance, the review
           commission, it's really not their task to see if the buildings
           are going to comply with ADA. It's the individual business
           owner's. They're just established there to make sure that any
           suggested changes will conform with the historical integrity
           of the buildings and they'll [the changes] not cause any harm-
           ful ramifications. So I don't know that it's exactly the com-
           mission's view to look at the ADA regulations.
Mayor: No that's not their position. She's right. She's 100 percent
           correct, that position [responsibility for determining compli-
           ance with the ADA] belongs to the building owners.

Note that oral presentations had been given at each of the three
meetings with clients and at the two meetings between each student
team and the professors—the staff meeting and the oral cross-examination. At the time of the staff meeting (the fourth week of classes), Jennifer, who knew virtually nothing about the history of the town and its
National Historic District policy, became nervous when Professor Mason asked her a question about the organization of the mountain town's
city administration. By the time of the final presentation eleven weeks
later, she was assertive and was not rattled by Professor Mason's questioning. Jennifer, the team's expert on how the town deals with building
permits in the context of the National Historic District requirements,
came to Amy's rescue at the meeting. Jennifer understood thoroughly
how this process worked in the town. In fact, her explanation was so
well done that the mayor intervened to agree vigorously with her.

Like the instructor in the genetics course (IGC) in chapter 3, the
EDI professors continually espoused a particular identity for the students—in this case, the identity of practicing engineer, defined as a
team player who brings one area of relevant information to a discussion
of real-world client problems. As in IGC, the identity of practicing engineer was portrayed as a more "lifelike" alternative to the conventional
identity of student expected in traditional (engineering) courses. However, the EDI students, for the most part, continued to be rewarded
and to identify themselves as students, rather than as practicing engineers, until the very end of the semester. Nonetheless, by semester's
end, and when faced with the need to act like practicing engineers, who
can bring relevant information to bear on an outsider's problem, the
students we followed were up to the task. Despite their beliefs about

themselves, they seemed to have learned what they needed to know to act as if they were practicing engineers. Our data suggest that the improvements in what students could accomplish came about in the context of the activities EDI required. Even though they may have engaged in those activities to be "good students," EDI created conditions in which they could gain and use the resource information they would need to act as if they were practicing engineers.

Connections to Engineering Power

In their regular engineering course work, EDI students were constrained by demands about using time and space that are almost identical to those Nespor describes for undergraduate physics majors. Most of the students' engineering courses focused time and attention on abstract problem-solving conducted by small groups of students who vigorously debated the approaches and solutions to problems (see Tonso 1997). EDI organized space, time, and resources quite differently. Despite the fact that grading procedures and some other conventional features of classroom life persisted in EDI, the class content was not organized around abstract problem-solving. Suddenly, the students in EDI had to figure out how to fit the "real-world" into their work. In particular, they had to learn how to serve a client as a technical resource expert.

The importance of serving the client was repeatedly made clear to the students in EDI. Student-engineers had to contact the client, travel to the client, collect the data needed by the client, and provide a report that the client could understand and use. Further, the student-engineers had to establish themselves as the authority figures with respect to the problem and its solutions, that is, they had to anticipate and be ready to address objections or questions raised by the client (non-engineers but other professionals) to their analysis and solutions (final report). In these ways, student-engineers were learning to work in ways that connect technical resource information and themselves as "experts" to the local concerns of non-engineer clients.

A wide variety of tasks contributed to students' developing skills. Students worked alone and in teams to gather information specific to their client's problem. They used written resources and conversations with experts to compile relevant information. Then, in team-meeting conversations, students worked on seemingly disparate bits of information to construct meanings that could guide development of solutions to the client's problem. This meaning-making activity—applying knowledge about the ADA, for instance, to a specific building—required fitting the federal rules, together with technical possibilities (e.g., the doorbell), to the specific situation. Surveying the historic buildings, developing renovations for each building, writing the final report, and making the final presentation to the clients all encouraged students to synthesize and integrate information across disparate areas. In explaining the ADA regulations during conversations with their clients, other townspeople, and business owners, students received feedback that allowed them to develop contextually appropriate renovations. Here, unlike in IGC or traditional engineering classes in which knowledge moves from the specific to the generalizable, solving the client's problem required localizing knowledge. Rather than moving from the concrete to the abstract, the students' uses of information and knowledge moved away from the abstract, general rules of engineering problem-solving or even the ADA and toward concrete, specific buildings and the actual demands and constraints of renovating them.

In summary, with their increasing proficiency at localizing disparate information, the EDI students' connections to the world as technical resource persons were strengthened. Unlike the disciplinary power of IGC or traditional classroom engineering (which is constructed when practitioners distance themselves from nonspecialists and work on abstract, general problems), the power of the technical resource person is established when practitioners find ways to make themselves valuable authorities to nonspecialists facing local problems.

Although this kind of power is valuable, it is not as potent in contemporary U.S. society as the kind of power that derives from general, invariant principles like those formulated in academic physics or genetics. A good technical resource person is in a position to suggest control by invariant principles as, for example, when principles of cost-effectiveness might be used to set renovation priorities, or when principles of stress might be used to determine the kind of building material needed for a project, but the resource person (unlike the theorist) must ultimately defer to the client, who may, for situational reasons, not wish to use a cost-effective criterion or pay for material that will withstand great stress. In a society that privileges technical-rational knowledge, "experts" who defer to local circumstances wield less control and receive less prestige than those who do not.

Women and Men in EDI

Over the course of the semester, women and men (in the EDI section we studied) performed similarly as judged by grades in the course (average grade for women was 2.91; for men, 2.97; not significantly different at the .01 level). On Team A, analysis of the students' conversations over the course of the semester revealed that both female and male students became measurably more articulate about engineering. There were no gender differences in these gains. Students whose engineering talk at the beginning of the semester was virtually incomprehensible to a professional engineer developed more precise technical language, expressed themselves in longer, more informative sentences, could connect what they knew about federal rules and regulations for handicapped access and historic renovation to the specific situation in their client's town, and could see how information from each of their areas of expertise could be fit together to inform their recommendations to the city government and business community.

As was true in IGC, however, some gendered features of EDI went unnoticed or unremarked upon by professors and students. For example, there were noticeable gender differences in student attitudes toward EDI. The women were more enthusiastic and energetic about the EDI work than were male students. Men complained that EDI work was time-consuming (for all the meetings, travel, attempts to get in touch with people, etc.), took them away from what they thought was more important work of studying for other engineering classes, and did not help them learn engineering. Women, in contrast, enjoyed the opportunity to work in groups, to talk with other students about their work on the project, and to make contacts with professionals outside of school. In response to an interview question about the value of EDI, one woman said,

> I think it helps you not only in engineering work, but just socially, just to be around other people, period. I mean, in this group, basically everyone's getting the same grade, and you have to be able to put up with other people, you have to be able to work with other people, you have to kind of keep an open mind to other people's ideas, and this can be applied to life as well, not just working.

The men, in contrast, expressed frustration that dealing with people took so much time and the outcome was so uncertain; they preferred to work on their own, with library and technical documents that they could control. One man had this to say:

> I think the library is probably a better source [compared to people, for the EDI work]. It's factual and everything. . . . If you need the information, you can copy it or something. Whereas with people, it's hard to remember everything they say. . . . Sometimes people are better, though . . . I know that. . . . So it's just getting hold of [them] . . . the library, it's easier to go . . . it's always there. . . . [And] trying to find information in the library is a lot less stressful. You don't have to make appointments, you can deal with whatever you want, try and find whatever you want, so that's always a help.

In addition, in other situations when gender differences or bias came up in EDI, there were few serious discussions of them. When blatantly sexist comments were made, the women and men in EDI brushed them aside as idiosyncratic and irrelevant to their educational experiences. When women wanted to do one thing and men another, such divergences were not interpreted in gender terms. We will return to this issue and others similar to it in more detail in chapter 7.

We were particularly struck by the finding of equal performance gains by men and women on the one hand and disparate, gender-linked differences in attitudes about EDI on the other. We wondered whether women would have performed less well if their attitudes were not as positive, or alternately, would men have performed better if their attitudes had been more positive? Either way, we were impressed that EDI managed to produce equal performance gains, while so many mixed-gender programs in male-dominated fields seem to spread, rather than reduce, academic differences by gender (Downey, Hegg, and Lucena 1993; Nespor 1994; Seymour and Hewitt 1994). EDI did not appear to harm men academically (i.e., they made impressive gains), even though they did not particularly enjoy or value it. On the other hand, EDI seemed to enliven the women in a way their other coursework did not.

Based on Nespor's analysis of physics and our earlier analysis of the innovative genetics class, we can speculate that experiences such as those in EDI may be especially appealing to women in "greedy" fields like physics, genetics, and engineering (Tonso, 1997, found the engineering curriculum as a whole to be even more "greedy," i.e., to monopolize an even greater share of students' time, than Nespor's physics curriculum). This is because EDI offers a "time" and "space" for participants in a greedy practice to connect their knowledge to the needs and concerns of people outside of engineering. While people outside of engineering may not be conversant with specialized engineering knowledge, they are likely to understand something about the kinds of problems and competing solutions the EDI student-engineers were faced with. Although EDI student-engineers may not find it easy to share with outsiders some of the dilemmas associated with advanced engineering, they may still develop meaningful social relationships with clients and other non-engineers that depend, in part, on the use of technical expertise. For women and others who do not want to distance work life from other aspects of their lives, conditions such as those in EDI would seem to offer one promising alternative.

However, it is crucial to note here that, although EDI did not distinguish women and men by academic performance (which is good), and it may hold special appeal for women, it also seems to have differentiated the orientations and preferences of women and men within engineering. Women, it seems, were identifying aspects of an engineering career which include work with others and the ability to localize knowledge as more satisfying and valuable to them, whereas men were identifying the theoretical aspects of an engineering career as more satisfying and valuable to them. In this sense, women and men in EDI were learning to fill two different niches of engineering work. In university settings of engineering, as well as in contemporary society, the highest academic prestige is awarded to those who concentrate on research and theory (McIlwee and Robinson 1992; Tonso 1997), while those who work in applied, technical capacities for clients command considerably less. In the case of EDI, it appears that men are more oriented to activities that will bring them high status in the eyes of professors and society; women, in comparison, are learning to enjoy activities that, although necessary and important, will bring them less status and prestige in the university and beyond. Thus, although it can be argued that the requirements of the EDI curriculum allow a larger "space" for women to do well than is normally the case in traditional engineering curricula, EDI's success with women may also be contributing to reproducing their subordinate status in engineering.

Chapter Five

Science and Politics in an Environmental Action Group

If this introduction to science has made you a more critical reader, a more careful observer, and a sharper thinker, your work during the year was worthwhile. (Haber-Schaim et al. 1982, 237)

Science education should help students to develop the understanding and habits of mind they need to become compassionate human beings able to think for themselves and to face life head on. It should equip them to participate thoughtfully with fellow citizens in building and protecting a society that is open, decent, and vital. (Rutherford and Ahlgren 1990, v)

The work of the Environmental Legislation Action Coalition (ELAC) is to develop public awareness about environmental problems, influence legislative action, and solicit money to support itself and its causes. Founded in the 1970s on several college campuses, today ELAC exists in thirty-nine states in two forms: college campus organizations (which promote student activism on environmental issues) and citizen organizations (which work at both state and national levels on legislative issues involving the environment, including bills for clean air, pollution prevention, and water quality).

The study of ELAC described here was conducted at two sites in a large urban area. Data were collected during the spring of 1992 from a group located on a metropolitan college campus, and during the summer of 1992 from a group located at a downtown office which housed state-level ELAC administrators and a citizen's canvassing branch of ELAC. Most of the data were collected from the canvassing branch between mid-May, when college students were hired for the summer

Primary data from ELAC were collected and analyzed by Linda Behm.

canvass, and mid-August, when most of these students returned to school.

During this time Linda Behm took part in all of the activities of the downtown office as a participant-observer. She observed new employee interview and hiring sessions, daily announcements, political action "power" hours, press conferences, briefings, car rides to canvass sites, daily lunch breaks prior to canvassing, advanced training sessions, social events, and day-to-day office functions. She also participated in training sessions and canvassing at least once each week.

Behm conducted interviews with all the members of the permanent staff, including the executive director, a legislative director, an administrative director, a regional director, two telephone outreach directors and three canvass directors, as well as one campus organizer. Formal interviews were conducted with fifteen members of the summer canvass staff, and informal interviews were conducted with most of the approximately forty other canvassers who worked through the summer.

Over one hundred canvassers came and went during the 1992 spring-summer canvassing season. Most were college students, and they considered their jobs at ELAC temporary or short-term. Over the summer, the percentage of women was consistently about 50 percent; more than 90 percent of canvassers were white. Although a few were science majors (17 percent) or said that they had studied science in college, most had not. In fact, many said that they had not been at all interested in science at school—a rather inauspicious beginning to a study of a place where science-related activity might occur, and an apparent vindication of those university scientists who tried to discourage Behm and Eisenhart from looking for science-related activities in political action groups.

Nonetheless, we soon learned that these temporary employees came to ELAC not only in search of jobs, but also in search of opportunities to "help the environment" by promoting and learning more about the scientific background of conservation issues. Although not particularly interested in *school* science, they expressed considerable interest in learning more about science if it would help the environment.

When newcomers were interviewed for canvassing jobs at ELAC, they heard that they were expected to become knowledgeable about the science behind the legislation supported by the organization. One of the organization's directors described the canvass this way to newcomers:

The way an organization like ELAC gets the job done is by communicating information at the right place, to the right people, at the right time. And so developing that information and making sure that it has a sound scientific basis is a very important part of what we do because, if we were to have information that was not credible, that would give us a real problem. (interview, July 8, 1992)

Statements like these made new employees eager and excited to begin. One woman, an art major, gave the following reason for taking the job: "I really believe in what they're doing [to help] the environment" (interview, July 15, 1992). Another student majoring in theater said, "I like helping out the environment" (interview, July 1992). A writing/ literature major joined because "I care deeply about the environment" (interview, June 7, 1992). Almost every new employee had something similar to say.

Although ELAC directors talked convincingly about the importance of "a sound scientific basis" to its work, the organization actually did little to help employees learn about science. Despite the organization's failure in this respect, the young employees struggled to fill the gap. They found ways to learn more about science, and some, especially some of the women, were quite proficient.

Science in ELAC Practice

Canvassing of residences to garner financial and political support for ELAC causes was the organization's primary means of achieving its goals.[1] Each day, the canvassing activity included afternoon training or update sessions in how to handle "doors" (*door* is the canvassers' term for the people they talk to at a residence), evening door-to-door canvassing to solicit financial and political support in designated neighborhoods, recording each night's take and debriefing, and a late-night social event for the canvassers. We will concentrate on the first two parts of the activity, because they involve the use of scientific information.

In these two parts of ELAC's activities, science was practiced as a form of advocacy. Scientific facts were used by canvassers as one means of establishing the credibility of the organization and its causes.

Training at ELAC

During training sessions, newcomers to ELAC were told about the organization, its history, and its legislative agenda for the year. Initial training for canvassing took place in a one-and-one-half-hour afternoon session, followed by a night during which the novice canvasser accompanied and observed an experienced canvasser. After the director provided a brief history of the organization, canvassers were instructed about the three parts of the summer's recycling campaign, which, for 1992, focused on three national bills: a bottle bill, a bill to encourage recycled-content standards for packaging and newspaper, and a moratorium on building new municipal solid-waste incinerators until the year 2000. To understand the issues in this recycling campaign seemed, to Behm, to require knowing something about what happens in landfills, how incineration works, and what technologies are available to recycle products.

References to scientific ideas and facts were a prominent part of the presentations that oldtimers gave—in the style of instructors—to newcomers during these sessions, as in this explanation of the moratorium bill given by one director:

> Incineration at first doesn't seem too bad, but if you know any physics, you can change what it is, but you can't get rid of mass, so lead, mercury and dioxin are airfilling. Then there is the problem of concentrated ash, how to dispose of it. (fieldnotes, May 15, 1992)

Trainees were told that a billion pounds of garbage are produced each day in the United States, and only ten percent of it is recycled. They were told that passage of a national bottle bill requiring deposits on containers would increase recycling from 40 percent to around 85 percent, as it had done in the nine states that already require deposits.

Another prominent feature of the training session was "the rap," the basic text that canvassers were supposed to use when talking to a "door." During the 1992 summer campaign, the rap went as follows:

Intro:	Hello, my name is —— and I'm with ——, the statewide environmental and consumer lobby. We're the group that worked to pass the —— Clean Air Act.
Purpose:	Tonight we're on our annual membership drive, campaigning for recycling.
Problem:	We produce a billion pounds of garbage every day, yet we recycle only 10 percent of it. Our land-fills are overflowing, and we're wasting millions of tax dollars.
Solution:	We're working to solve the solid waste crisis by passing laws in Congress to recycle at least 50 percent of our garbage.

Urgency: Key votes are coming up soon. We need your support to win.

Clipboard: This is our statement of support, which outlines our work. (Hand over clipboard, which includes a summary fact sheet about the campaign, four individual fact sheets that explain the issues, and two or three newspaper clippings about the organization.)

Sponsorship: The most effective way you can support the campaign is by becoming a member with a contribution of $35. This gives us the political and financial clout we need to win on this issue.

Closing: You'll be receiving our quarterly newsletter with your membership, and it's best to join with a check.

In training sessions, canvassers were told, in no uncertain terms, that they must memorize the rap and use it faithfully. They were told that the rap had been developed in "a laboratory" over a ten-year period, and that it was the most effective way to reach the public. The director emphasized that in this short, ninety-second presentation, canvassers could explain "who you are, what you're doing, what you want from them, and [it] lets you open a dialogue." Further, it was short enough not to bore people, and it did not misinform the public about the organization.

During practice role-playing during training sessions, one person was assigned to use the rap and another was assigned to be a "door" and respond to the rap. Following each encounter, the trainer or peers in the group were asked to comment on the trainee's skills: making eye contact, using the rap, asking for a contribution of a specific amount, and "clipboard control" (handing the clipboard to the "door" to show the statement of support signed by neighbors).

Trainees who played the role of "door" were asked to offer common excuses for not giving money, such as, "I'm all out of checks," "My husband isn't at home," or "I do my part by recycling." Tips to counter such resistance were given to canvassers during role-playing sessions. In summary, skills practiced in these sessions focused on relating to people and on the best ways to solicit funds; little was said about science except the reporting of a few facts pertinent to the legislative bills under discussion.

However, according to oldtimers at ELAC, skill at canvassing develops as one learns enough science to expand on the rap and answer questions raised by the doors. When one director was asked if having a standardized presentation might limit canvassers' inclination to learn about the science behind ELAC's environmental positions, he replied:

> I don't think so. Because I think that if people are canvassing and canvassing well, and they're to be a good canvasser, they know that the standard presentation is what they say to introduce people to the problem. It's definitely not meant to be, "Here's the problem and I'm going to tell you all about it." It's much more, you know, the whole rap takes a minute and a half, and it's an introduction to the problem. In order to be a good canvasser, you need to know the information for the responses. It doesn't take that much to memorize a rap. But where the knowledge of the canvasser comes in, and what separates a good canvasser from a decent, a great canvasser from an okay canvasser, is that a great canvasser learns more about the issue and is able to more actively answer people's questions and give them the information that they want to know. (interview, July 2, 1992)

It appears, from the directors' statements, the organization's documents, and the training experience, that canvassers should be better educated than the general public about environmental issues of interest to the organization, and that they should be able to provide the public with accurate information about these issues.

The organization made some attempt to provide newcomers with information about the science behind the issues. The two most prominent formats were "fact sheets"—lists of "scientific facts" pertaining to ELAC's current issues—and a "briefing book," which included short newspaper articles, press releases, and informational papers from the national organization. Fact sheets were distributed to each new canvasser; two copies of the briefing book were available in the directors' office and updated regularly. The following examples are from the 1992 fact sheets:

- Our nation's failure to recycle municipal solid waste means decreased landfill space, public health hazards from the disposal of garbage, unsightly litter, depletion of natural resources for future generations, the unnecessary loss of millions of barrels of oil each year, and unparalleled levels of pollution due to the mining and production of virgin material. (Fact Sheet: Bottle Bills)
- Of the top 20 chemicals most hazardous to human health, five are used routinely in plastics production. (Fact Sheet: Packaging)
- Municipal solid waste incinerators are the fastest-growing source of

mercury emissions into our environment. Mercury can cause neuro-
logical damage, blindness, degenerative kidney problems and birth
defects. . . . Suspected to be one of the most carcinogenic substances
known, dioxins bioaccumulate in fatty tissue and milk. Despite this,
several large refuse incinerators have been proposed on sites adjacent
to dairy farms. (Fact Sheet: Municipal Solid Waste Incineration)
• There is little dispute regarding technical feasibility of newsprint recycling at rates of 80 percent. (Fact Sheet: Newspaper Recycling)

These fact sheets, according to the organization's documents, are
intended to provide "a basic sense of what the solid waste problem is
and what our solution entails" ("Campaign Plan," *Briefing Book*). On
the surface, the statements seem simple, and they were presented as
facts, but they could lead to complicated questions requiring considerable knowledge of science.

In fact, the ELAC's list, "Top 10 Questions Commonly Asked at the
Door," indicates that a canvasser is very likely to encounter questions
that cannot be answered with the rap, or with the information contained
on the four fact sheets describing the bills. The list follows:

1. How viable are 50 percent-content standards for packaging, newspaper and writing paper?
2. We already have curbside recycling. Why do we need the Bottle
   Bill?
3. What will the cost of these programs be?
4. What are the specific dangers and costs of incinerators?
5. Shouldn't we focus on reducing the total amount of garbage rather
   than recycling what we create?
6. Who are the major opponents to our campaign and why?
7. How well is the Bottle Bill working in the states which have implemented the law?
8. Why do recycled materials end up in warehouses or landfills?
9. Will government procurement policies for recycled goods end up
   costing the taxpayers money?
10. Won't we always have to incinerate some garbage?

Few explicit discussions took place within the organization about
how canvassers were expected to acquire the scientific background to
answer such questions. When canvassers asked to learn more about the
science behind ELAC's positions—which they frequently did, they

were usually told to "familiarize" themselves with material on the fact sheets and in the briefing book, and to use it and other materials to educate themselves as necessary. When Behm asked one director whether training was ever offered to provide such information, he said that the large turnover of employees made such training too costly.

Thus it appeared that trainees had few real opportunities to learn about the scientific information that supported ELAC's positions. Canvassers were encouraged to make do with the knowledge they already had, to use the fact sheets and rap sheet handed out during training sessions, and to take the initiative, on their own, to learn any additional material they thought they needed.

The Canvass

On the surface, the priorities of the canvass were similar to those of the training. Instead of encouraging canvassers to develop an understanding of the scientific background of ELAC issues that might lead them to develop the identity of activists informed about environmental issues and the related science, the activities of the canvass seemed to support a fund-raiser identity, as illustrated in the following excerpt from Behm's fieldnotes of her first night on the job.

"First Night" (May 28, 1992)

It was to be my first night doing the canvassing work. I was assigned during the announcements to observe Tom, and we were going to canvass in a liberal university town which was described as "good turf." We practiced role-plays and made jokes until we reached the sandwich shop near our turf, the few blocks we were to canvass. We drove to a park where Tom and the other canvassers got a stack of cards from Alex, the field manager. By color, these cards identified people in that turf as active members, inactive members, small contributors, or people who were not to be canvassed. Besides names and addresses, the cards listed all the contributions made over the last few years including those acquired by telephone. Each canvasser sorted his cards and made notes on his tick sheet, the sheet on which the canvassers list every address they've gone to and the result (yes, no, call back, not at home). Each canvasser was also given three types of cover sheets. One contained small contributors [called "small cons" by canvassers] who gave five or ten dollars; another listed twenty-four-dollar memberships, and a third listed larger contributors who gave around thirty-six dollars. People at the doors were supposed to be given the appropriate cover sheet and to write in their name, address, and amount. Which cover sheet they were given to fill out depended upon the amount they agreed to give.

We drove off to a residential neighborhood which was to be our turf. Alex dropped off one canvasser, then Tom and I were left off at our turf while Alex and his observer drove off to theirs. We stopped in a small park while Tom had a cigarette. It was about four o'clock on a sunny June afternoon with a perfect temperature. Then we began our work. I watched as Tom knocked at doors in this large condominium complex. It was pretty early, so many people were not at home. At one door we were told that they were canvassed yesterday. Tom looked over his turf assignment trying to figure out which building he should canvass. Tom moved over to a different building which didn't seem to have any of the house numbers on the previous day's tick sheet. Whenever a person answered the door, he very politely introduced himself and me, and gave the standard presentation. He often added personal comments on the resident's dogs, or cats, or home decorations. He also asked questions like, "How are you doing tonight?" and "Do you recycle?" The job seemed relatively easy. While there were some turn-downs and lots of people not at home, there were several contributors. Some doors were firmly shut on us, but no one was rude. Tom commented that tonight he had a good rate of contributions—about 50 percent of the people he spoke with gave a contribution. However, he felt that we had not knocked on as many doors as we should have.

At 7:30 we separated for the hour I was to canvass alone. I began to knock on doors on my own. I was pretty uncomfortable with the newness of so many things. I worried if I would remember the rap that I never wanted to memorize because it sounded so unnatural. I arrived at some sort of compromise, using the organization of the rap and putting it into my own words. I tried, modeling Tom, to strike up conversations with people at the door. It had always crossed my mind that I might run into a really knowledgeable person who could run circles around my arguments. I envisioned this [person] as a physicist, and ironically I did run into a physics professor. However, that conversation centered on whether ELAC presented both sides of a position, [not on the science involved]. I found myself selling the organization rather than the issues, perhaps because I was not well-versed in them. And in the end, he gave me a small contribution!

I worried a great deal about meeting up with Tom empty-handed until I got that first contribution. I wondered who might be on the other side of that door and what disposition they might be in until it was answered. I wondered if I would get lost, mess up the tick sheet or cover sheets, and where I would go to the bathroom if I needed to. I wondered if this was a safe place after dark and if they would remember where they left me. I unexpectedly ran into a friend who happened to live there, and that proved a great relief. When Tom and I eventually met back up, I had forty dollars for the organization.

He had taken in $145 for the night. We went to the park to await our pickup. When we got back to the office, crews were filing in and filling out cards on the new members and small contributors, turning in money and signing each field manager's sheet, which listed the crew and their amounts for the night. We wrote in our total canvass amount on a map of our turf and colored in the area we had canvassed. Because it was my first night, I had to wait around to be debriefed by a director. He asked me how it went, and I said fine. I felt okay about my first night on the canvass. After all, I had gotten a member (a contributor who gave twenty dollars or more) and two small contributors (those who gave less than twenty dollars). We didn't get struck by lightning or left by our field manager. No one mugged us for the money or ever screamed at us to get off their doorstep. How bad could the job be?

Canvassers were quick to learn how strong the pressure was to raise money in this job. Canvassers were paid a salary and expected to solicit a minimum of $70—the "quota"—at least one of their first three nights on the job in order to remain employed. Thereafter, canvassers were expected to "make quota" most nights. Throughout the summer, many canvassers were fired for not making quota.

Firing was not the only pressure felt by canvassers who did not bring in a lot of money. Each day during announcements (which took place before the daily canvass began), awards were given based on the past day's fund-raising performance. Awards highlighted particular aspects of fund-raising success, including signing the most new memberships, raising $200 in one night, and getting the most small contributions.

Canvassers who came back to the office after not making quota had to be debriefed by a director. While others left the office after checking out, those scheduled for debriefing waited around to speak to a director about what went wrong that night. One canvasser, who had worked for the group for about half the summer and was later fired while on the verge of quitting for not making quota in recent weeks, said this about debriefs:

> The director can treat the canvasser really bad if they want to because, in the end, it's all for the best. Debriefing, to me, seems really dumb, you know. I mean, I can see if you miss quota a couple of nights in a row they maybe want to talk to you and see if there's something wrong with your technique, but to me, it just seems like a humiliation thing. Every canvasser I've talked to, they say the number one reason they want to make quota is because they do not want

to have to go through a debriefing at 11 P.M. and have that be the end of the day. (interview, July 23, 1992)

In addition to the pressure to make quota and the humiliation of debriefings, canvassing itself is demanding work. The canvassers began their workday shortly after lunch when they came into the office for training, briefings, or announcements. Then they drove to the canvass sites and got ready to begin the canvass around 4 P.M. Canvassing continued until about 9 P.M., after which the canvassers returned to the office, accounted for their night's work, underwent debriefing if necessary, and headed off to a nightly social event, sponsored by the organization. It was rare for them to be home before 1 A.M. Yet many canvassers seemed to like the job a great deal.

> "A Good Night on the Canvass" (excerpt from Behm's fieldnotes, June 12, 1992)
>
> Yet another hot evening, and tonight we find ourselves at a Burger King. Our field manager hands out the turf assignments and preprinted cards [with the names of active and inactive ELAC members living in that turf]. I set out to just observe someone else and not risk canvassing myself, but no one much likes having an observer with them. The field manager says she has an extra turf for a no-show and invites me to take it. Okay, I'll give it a try. I don't even have a clipboard with me, but suddenly the atmosphere changes and everyone is helping me out, digging through bags and backpacks to come up with extra clipboard materials, giving me tips and encouragement. Since I'm only a volunteer, I get the last turf with the least number of active and inactive members.
>
> I am let out in an area of small homes, an older, established neighborhood with plenty of trees. When I arrive at my first house, I notice a dummy seated on the porch and balloons adorning the entryway. It's obviously Andy's birthday. The doorbell plays "Happy Birthday" when I ring it, and a large banner across the door wishes him a happy birthday. There is some noise from the back. A woman answers the door, but the phone rings immediately. I say I'll drop back later.
>
> Halfway down the block, I run into two elderly women who each give one-dollar contributions. I am consciously thinking of Alex's advice to keep it simple. The safest thing to mention from the three [ELAC-sponsored] bills is the bottle bill. Many people remember a time when there were deposits on bottles, and they liked that. I will stress the organization, a citizen lobby, nonprofit, supported by neighborhoods like yours. Few people have heard of the organiza-

tion. I receive a five-dollar contribution from a woman. A man gives me a dollar after telling me about his battle with cancer. I have trouble with this, except I think the organization would say that people like the chance to get involved regardless of their financial situation. One woman talks about her problems with the IRS, another says she just got a loan that day but hopes someday to get involved and do what I'm doing. A couple of small contributions later, I'm watching dark thunderstorm clouds gather and planning an escape to a business area not too far from here. The storm is short and doesn't interrupt my work. Suddenly it's 8:15 and getting dark. I walk around the corner to the birthday boy's house. This time, Andy answers the door. He tells me to talk to his mom, who is very supportive of environmental groups but isn't home at the moment. I ask Andy if I can wait on his step for my pickup. He invites me inside, but instead I wait by the dummy. The red car arrives and I get in. I didn't get a large amount, but I feel good. I decided to go for small cons, and I did get those. I run down my night's work: total—thirty-two dollars, number of doors—seventy-three, number of completes [completed rap and received an answer from the door]—thirty-eight, number of new members—zero; number of small contributors—twelve. "That's incredible," the field manager remarks. When I leave the office that night, the director thanks me for canvassing and invites me to go along with her one night. I leave peacefully, feeling like one of the group.

Thus it appears that the ability to raise money and support for ELAC is what received recognition and reward both from the organization's directors and from other members of the canvass. The canvassers became committed to working long, hard hours to raise the money needed to support the organization and its causes. While the directors expressed some concern about canvassers having knowledge of the science "behind" ELAC's issues, this concern was given little attention during training and was rarely brought up by directors when they talked to the canvassers. But, despite the organization's emphasis on fund-raising and the hard work, many of the canvassers liked the job, and in order to do it better, they wanted to know more about the science behind the issues.

The Meaning of *Science* to Canvassers

Canvassers, to a person, considered scientific background knowledge to be a valuable asset. One canvasser summed up a widely stated belief that they needed to know more science than what was in the rap and gave this reason:

> If you . . . in your rap, you could throw in something to back up
> what you're saying, it makes a big difference. And then, if you can
> answer their questions in more, in a real make-sense way but still
> have the basic information in it as opposed to just a clichéd answer
> that you've picked up at the office, you know what I mean? (inter-
> view, July 23, 1992)

Some canvassers recognized that the organization did not really care
how much scientific background they knew, but they were personally
interested—for various reasons—in knowing more. One said,

> I think it [the organization] holds us responsible for just knowing
> the figures and facts that you have to relay to people. But as far as
> the in-depth things go, you don't need to know them. . . . [But]
> personally? I'd like to know it. And I try to learn as much as I can
> about it. (interview, July 6, 1992)

Another said,

> You've gotta have a basic understanding of the problem and of some
> environmental science to be able to become passionate about the
> issue and to just be coherent at the door. (interview, July 23, 1992)

Most canvassers shared the feeling that they would be more comfortable if they had enough knowledge to converse about the issues raised
by the "doors." Behm's concern about knowing more was reflected in
her journal entry about encountering the physicist:

> He asked me whether the organization might present only one side
> of the story to the public. I was not sure but suspected it might. He
> noted that a water-use study done by an environmental organization
> gave statistics of water use at the governor's mansion but did not
> take into account the size of the property nor the number of people
> using the water. He said they had not considered "scaling." He felt
> things like this were misleading and organizations should be more
> responsible in informing the public.

In general, canvassers recognized that they were receiving limited
information or only one viewpoint, and they wanted information that
would help them counter opposing viewpoints. One expressed his frustration with not having enough knowledge about the opposing arguments in this way:

> What's it going to cost the industry? Is the consumer going to be
> picking up the extra cost? Is it just going to be another law that's

just going to cost more government dollars to afford? Yeah, there's a lot of questions, a lot of things people are curious about and if all you do is study the standard rap and learn what these bills are and what they say, you really don't know all sides to it. (interview, June 17, 1992)

When someone suggested that opposing information might be biased, another canvasser reacted, "Biased or not, I want it [to sort out my position]." Thus, in addition to worrying about simply having answers for the doors, canvassers also were concerned that they not mislead the people they talked to.

When canvassers felt a need for more information, they used a number of strategies, some more successful than others. One strategy was simply to ask a director. For example, at a community fair, one visitor asked Behm why the bottle bill was being pursued at the national level instead of the state level. Behm was not sure and asked the director. The director replied that the state legislature had already adjourned and that a national bill would cover *all* the states. This answer was not entirely satisfactory to Behm, given that there is a new legislative session each year and it would appear to be easier to pass such a bill at the state level, since nine states have already done so. On other occasions, directors glossed over questions with fund-raising suggestions (like "repoliticize" the argument), or they stressed the urgency of an upcoming vote.

Another not entirely successful strategy was to ask "experts" at briefings. At one briefing, a canvasser asked a U.S. Representative to tell why there was opposition to the proposed national bottle bill. The following exchange took place:

Canvasser:	I have a question on the bottle bill. Why are the people in the [Congressional] committee so opposed to it, besides being paid by the industry?
Rep.:	Because when they go to mark up the bill, there's about 500 guys in Gucci shoes standing outside the door. . . .
Canvasser:	What are they using as their excuse for being opposed to it?
Rep.:	A whole series of things. Mainly, it's a hassle, and they're tired of government regulation. I mean they don't really argue on the issues. They argue more on, we're being regulated out of business, and this is a hassle for everybody, and it will keep people from buying ours, and they'll go to cans or they'll go to something else or they'll go to cartons, or they'll, you know.

Canvasser: But they passed, they were in favor of the 50 percent content which seems to be more regulations than the bottle bill.

Rep.:   Well, they still see this as something, I guess, that they think will affect them. I think part of the problem has been their main experience with bottle bills has been by locality and you know, some localities have put in bottle bills and then people drive over state lines and all that, and, of course, sometimes you'll just have a downturn because peoples' tastes change or the economy's bad, but they blame it all on the bottle bill and so the folks who've had to live with it and different things and the industry . . . hollers about "this is the worst thing that ever happened and don't let it transpire." And I must say, there's also a real industry in making all these things sound twenty times worse than they ever are because they collect dues from all the bottlers, and they have themselves a little job. You know, it's much harder to collect dues from all the citizens than it is from the bottlers, right? That's one of the problems. (fieldnotes, July 10, 1992)

Although the canvasser appeared to be looking for substantive information about the opposing view, the representative, instead of providing that, focused on the workings of the political system.

Another strategy among the canvassers was to pick up information from their "doors" that might be useful in promoting the position of the organization or in learning about opposing arguments. Then they tried to formulate positions of their own. One canvasser, prompted by a "door," became curious about the need for de-inking plants in paper recycling. The need for de-inking plants had come as a surprise to him, but based on what he learned from the "door," he developed his own position this way:

> Yeah, I had a guy—we talked for probably twenty minutes. He didn't give me anything, but he worked for Georgia-Pacific or something. Anyway, it's a paper place, and they're trying to use recycled paper and trying to get or sell government contracts and everything like that. He said the problem is, there's no de-inking plant. Because when you recycle paper, you have to take the ink off. And I didn't know that. I thought you just recycled it. He said there's only a couple of de-inking plants in the whole country. You know, they never told us about de-inking plants or anything like that. I assume that once [the law regarding] recycled-content standards is passed, it will

Table 5.1 **Participation in informal science activities**

Activity	ELAC	Population
Regular viewer of TV news	6%	75%
Watch science TV programs occasionally	66%	60%
Regular reader of science magazines	40%	10%
Occasional reader of science magazines	60%	15%

Source for the population figures: Miller 1991; table adapted from Behm 1994, p. 147.

> stimulate the demand for de-inking plants. That seems logical to me. (interview, July 23, 1992)

For most canvassers, however, the best strategy for obtaining more information was to *read* more about environmental issues, conservation science, and ecology on their own. Every canvasser Behm interviewed mentioned reading at least some magazines, newspaper articles, or books about environmental issues. One canvasser described a book she had read as follows:

> [The book said] when you do recycle you are creating pollution maybe as much or more than with virgin material. It taught me to be careful about what I tell people. If I'm going to tell them something, I'd better know for sure what I'm talking about. That's the hard thing about this campaign: you get so many opposing ideas and never really correct figures. The thing that I am concerned with, though, is that we do use a lot of natural resources that we don't have to use. (interview, August 4, 1992)

Another summed up her "outside" reading experiences as follows:

> You know, they [the directors] provide you with the basic information about the issues, but you go in and read the books and do a lot more, [and] you find out how really important this stuff is. (interview, July 10, 1992)

Some canvassers also relied on television and radio programs to provide them with more information about environmental issues.

Interestingly, when Behm compared the level of participation in informal science activities among ELAC canvassers to a comparable (college-aged) sample from the general population, she found that canvassers read science magazines considerably more and watched television news considerably less than the general population (see table 5.1).

By the end of the summer, the majority of canvassers we studied were very positive about ELAC's aims and the value of working there, despite the long hours, demands to meet quota, and limited help in learning more about the scientific background of the organization's agenda. Many of the canvassers valued their experience enough to volunteer that they would incorporate what they had learned in ELAC into their careers or lifestyles. One said,

> Personally, I try to recycle more and save energy—turn off lights, don't shower as long, think about what I'm buying. Every time I throw something away now, [I think:] It could be recycled, or I shouldn't have bought it, or it's overpackaged. (interview, August 2, 1992)

Another said,

> I think it's good that there actually are jobs out there that deal in good issues. You don't have to volunteer. You can actually decide to do this and have it be your career and be paid for it. This job, it's totally dignified; it's definitely a fulfilling feeling at the end of the day. (interview, July 31, 1992)

Two others said, "Everybody [here] has really good hearts" (July 9, 1992), and "You mean well for a person [here.] You have their best interests at heart. It's not so petty here" (July 23, 1992).

The most significant reward, and one mentioned by all the canvassers, was talking to the "doors" and having some success at "getting people involved." One canvasser said, "I like it because I get to talk to people about things that actually concern me and concern them" (July 15, 1992). Another said, "Well, it's not the money, I'll tell you that. . . . I like the people a lot, and [I like] helping to spread social change and open people's eyes to what's going on; [it] gives me a good feeling" (July 23, 1992). While money was something they got for the organization, they got a sense of satisfaction from advancing the organization's goals and encouraging citizens to become more active politically. One described the job as "planting a little seed of activism in everybody" (July 9, 1992), and another summed up his feelings as follows:

> I never worked with a greater bunch of people. I used to think the American Republic would not survive my generation, but now I see the kind of people that are out there, and you know, we might do okay. . . . People really got concerned about the issues. (interview, July 23, 1992)

Women's and Men's Proficiency in Science at ELAC

As one indication of how proficient ELAC employees actually were in science, we decided to administer Jon Miller's (1991) survey of scientific literacy[2] to a small sample of ELAC canvassers (seven women and eight men). The survey was administered near the end of the 1992 canvassing season. Respondents were blindly selected (controlling for gender) from the forty people who had worked the entire summer or longer at ELAC.

Miller defines scientific literacy as "the level of understanding of science and technology needed to function minimally as citizens and consumers in our society." Miller's test of scientific literacy contains three sections: (1) understanding of basic scientific and technical terms and constructs; (2) understanding of the process of science, or the nature of the scientific approach; and (3) understanding of the impact of science and technology on society broadly and on the daily life of individuals as consumers, parents, and citizens (1991, 5).

Miller's criterion for an understanding of scientific terms and concepts is based on nine questions. Respondents receive one point each for identifying the following statements as true:

- The oxygen we breathe comes from plants.
- Electrons are smaller than atoms.
- The continents on which we live have been moving their locations for millions of years and will continue to move in the future.
- Human beings, as we know them today, developed from earlier species of animals.
- The universe began with a huge explosion.

Respondents receive one point each for identifying the following statements as false:

- Lasers work by focusing sound waves.
- The earliest human beings lived at the same time as the dinosaurs.

Respondents also receive one point each for correctly answering that light travels faster than sound, and for a pair of answers indicating that the earth orbits the sun once a year. A score of six or more points meets the criterion.

To demonstrate "an understanding of the process of science," Miller's survey requires a respondent to provide a satisfactory open-ended explanation of what it means to study something scientifically and to recognize that astrology is not scientific. The final part of

Table 5.2 **Scientific literacy in ELAC and the general population**

Component	ELAC	Population
Understanding scientific terms and concepts	93%	36%
Understanding scientific process	47%	13%
Understanding the impact of science on society	73%	26%
OVERALL		
Demonstrating scientific literacy[a]	33%	7%

Source: Behm 1994, 150
[a]This figure is considerably lower than the others because the overall score required literacy in all three components.

Miller's measure of scientific literacy, understanding the impact of science and technology on society, requires a score of three or more points on four items. Respondents receive one point each for the following:

- Recognizing that antibiotics are ineffective against viruses
- Understanding a one-in-four probability
- Indicating that all radioactivity is not man-made
- Indicating that they have a clear understanding of the term *computer software*

Table 5.2 summarizes the scientific literacy of the ELAC group and the general population as measured by Miller's survey.

For the entire questionnaire instrument, only 7 percent of Miller's national sample met the minimal criterion for scientific literacy, while 33 percent of the ELAC sample did so. The ELAC group, most of whom had taken three or more high school science courses, also outscored their equivalently educated counterparts in Miller's national sample for the instrument as a whole (33 percent in ELAC versus 19 percent in Miller's study). On the individual components of Miller's instrument, the threshold criteria were met by a higher proportion of the ELAC group than of the national sample (see table 5.2).

Some interesting gender differences also emerged from the comparisons. In Miller's national sample, more men than women qualified as scientifically literate: 9.2 percent vs. 4.9 percent. A disparity existed even when Miller controlled for education in mathematics and science: among Miller's college-educated subgroup, 23 percent of men and 17 percent of women qualified as scientifically literate. In the ELAC group, about the same proportion of men (25 percent) and a higher proportion of women (43 percent) qualified as scientifically literate compared with

Miller's college-educated sample, even though only a few of the ELAC employees held college degrees. Although the number of people sampled in ELAC ($n = 15$ in total) is too small to serve as a basis for firm statements, note that while no statistically significant difference in scientific literacy exists between men in ELAC and men in Miller's national sample (25 percent vs. 9.2 percent), significantly more women in the ELAC group than in the national sample were scientifically literate (43 percent vs. 4.9 percent; $\chi^2 = 20.72$; $d.f. = 1$; $p < .001$).

What might account for the higher levels of scientific literacy in the ELAC sample, especially among women, compared to the general population sampled by Miller? Our data do not permit a definite answer to this question. However, given the fact that ELAC employees had not pursued much college science, that little overlap exists between the items on Miller's test and the domain of science relevant to ELAC's activities, and that ELAC itself did little to educate employees about science, we can speculate that ELAC attracts women whose interests are not piqued by school science but who have some interest in and knowledge of science and its social uses. Although ELAC's female employees were apparently not excited by school science, they did seem to have a "scientific bent" more pronounced than that of the general population, and they seemed to find it worthwhile to participate in science-related activities while working with others on issues of public concern.

In some ways, ELAC encouraged individuals to develop such interests. Canvassers daily found themselves in situations where science knowledge could be useful and was sometimes expected—for example, during canvassing, when they asked people to support ELAC's causes. In terms of identity, what seemed to be at stake for the canvassers was their personal credibility with the "door," on the spot, and the status they gained from co-workers when they provided scientific information that could be used effectively in the canvass. Because canvassers believed they were likely to be asked science-based questions by the "doors," they were motivated to obtain some scientific background, regardless of what ELAC's training stressed (the "rap") and neglected (providing relevant science-based information). Because, among themselves, canvassers defined their inability to answer science-related questions as "personally embarrassing" and as an important reason why "doors" might not give money, they were further motivated to learn. Finally, because the canvassing cohort often defined the most successful canvassers as those with the ability to discuss environmental science, individual staff members were encouraged to develop their own identities as people with some scientific background knowledge.

The question remains, however, why women in relatively large numbers and with a scientific bent were attracted to ELAC. Our answer derives from positions we have developed in earlier chapters. As we argued in explaining Nespor's finding of few women in majors that demand abstract problem-solving distanced from real-world issues and social relationships (chapter 3), and our finding that women were especially enthusiastic about the engineering design internship, EDI, which encouraged them to develop their engineering practice in the context of working with others to solve technical problems (chapter 4), women with a scientific bent may be especially inclined toward opportunities that give time, space, and important identities to people who want to engage in scientific or technical practices that are socially or publicly meaningful. In contrast to the "greediness" of most school science (e.g., physics and the innovative genetics course, IGC), which narrows the organization of time, space, and identity to be meaningful primarily within the discipline, ELAC's organization widens the possibilities for people with a scientific bent, allowing them to develop their interests in science without sacrificing social interests. Thus, like the engineering internship, ELAC broadened, rather than compressed, the social spaces to which its participants were connected. Compared to the innovative genetics class, IGC, or Nespor's physics program, the activities in ELAC (as well as in EDI) seem to support the inclusion of a wider social variety of people, especially women, and encourage learning about a wider set of skills (e.g., fund-raising, public speaking, political action) than is available in settings of elite science.

Connections to Networks of Power

Yet, as in our other two sites, we find grounds for being guarded about these indicators of success. The quality and quantity of the science these women and men have available to them in the context of their work at ELAC is disturbing. Analyzed through the lens of Nespor's theory (1994), the tools of science developed in ELAC are not (and are not likely to become) powerful. Science as constructed in ELAC is a body of facts and a few ideas about environmental processes that can be used to lend credibility to the organization's activities. The networks (links among people) that ELAC fosters are sporadic and temporary compared to those developed in academic disciplines (physics, genetics) or professional occupations (engineering). Thus, although ELAC widens the opportunities for practicing science and seems to stimulate involvement in science-related activities among people who have not pursued college science, it does not enable participants to access the power (control) of academic science or even that of the technical expert. Instead, ELAC activities encourage a kind of power or control that comes from being instantly personable and quickly able to retrieve relevant facts in a brief encounter. For canvassers to be successful, they must immediately engage a "door's" attention, quickly establish a bond with the person, convince that person of the worth of ELAC's causes, obtain the contribution, and move on to the next house. Information about science can be a valuable asset for success, but ELAC does little to support employees' development of their science interests in ways that might enable them to participate knowledgeably and effectively in public debate about science-related issues. Employees learn to rely on personal-interaction skills, quick talk, and isolated facts about science for their success. This is a weak form of power because it is based on superficial bonds between people and a kind of knowledge that cannot inform debate involving competing claims.

Chapter Six

Science and Scientists in a Conservation Corporation

When I started, . . . saving land was a relatively simple business. We'd look around, find some land that we liked, and buy it. Once we had acquired an area, I really believed that it would be protected in perpetuity. I, like most people, had never heard of acid rain, the greenhouse effect, or holes in the ozone layer. We didn't deal in doom and gloom. We bought land. Today, things are different . . . there are no simple solutions. What good does it do, for example, to buy a forest unless you can protect it from acid rain? . . . Who can worry about a piece of tallgrass prairie when we are destroying the atmosphere? (Morine 1990, ix–x)

"Where else could you find an environmental agency that is interested in operating a working ranch?" By keeping the ranch in production, the [Conservation Corporation] hopes to learn how conservation and agriculture can best work together. Research and restoration projects will test new conservation strategies and provide valuable information for land stewards around the country. An educational center will be established to showcase the history and operations of the ranch and the ecological significance of the . . . River. [CC] is raising $3.5 million to cover the acquisition, the educational center and a stewardship endowment for the overall . . . effort. (CC national magazine, May/June 1996, 30)

The Conservation Corporation

The conservation corporation (CC) we studied is a nonprofit organization devoted to preserving one state's biodiversity by protecting land where species, habitats, and ecological processes are threatened. Relying on conservation science, business acumen, and sensitivity to local con-

Primary data were collected and analyzed by Margaret Eisenhart.

cerns and interests, CC has quietly contributed to protection efforts on more than one-third of the state's land.

Data about CC come from an eighteen-month ethnographic study Eisenhart conducted there from October 1992 until March 1994. During that time, she spent an average of four days each month participating in and observing CC's activities. She participated as a volunteer who worked on reseeding projects, seed collection, and monitoring at preserves; stuffed envelopes in the office; distributed materials at fundraising activities; contributed to conversations; and became friends with many staff members. After approximately nine months, she conducted formal interviews with most of the staff and began to follow closely the experiences and learning trajectories of five new scientists who joined the organization at that time. All of the new scientists were making the transition from full-time school to full-time work.

During the study, twenty-two people, mostly scientists and lawyers, worked for CC. Not surprisingly, most of the employees were white; more surprising for an organization known for giving serious attention to principles of conservation science, the numbers of women and men were about equal.

CC divides its work into eight program areas: Site Ranking, Site Design, Site Management, Reserve (i.e., special) Sites, Fund-Raising, Legal Affairs, Public Relations, and Administration. The first four areas are referred to by CC employees as the "scientific" aspects of CC's work. Thirteen people were employed in the four "science" program areas during the study. Figures 6.1 and 6.2 show organizational charts of the "scientific" and "nonscientific" program areas.

Women hold important positions at CC. At the time the study began in October 1992, four of the eight program directors and the executive director were women. In the four science programs, one of the directors and six of the nine staff members (all nonclerical) were women. Everyone working in the science areas, (except two men), had college degrees in a science field. All of the science program directors held doctorates, and all of the staff members in the science programs held or were working on master's degrees in science.

CC is a place with a sense of crowded-in intensity, purpose, and urgency. Just walking in the door of the stately house that is the main office, one immediately notices open office doors; casual dress; spaces made cramped by room dividers, furniture, machines, books, office supplies, and shopping bags of plant clippings. There is always a bustle of

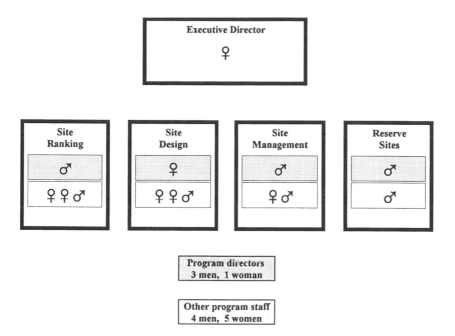

Figure 6.1 CC organizational chart: Science program areas

activity as people squeeze around and over one another and the office "furnishings." On the walls are beautiful and sometimes haunting nature photographs and posters. Staff members seem extremely busy, perennially "behind," and warmly appreciative of each other's work. They speak supportively of each other as people who "work their tails off" to manage all the aspects of their work load. They accept long hours, weekend work, all-nighters, and few opportunities for advancement or high salaries. They are the kind of people who carry their own plates when they walk downtown to pick up take-out lunches, order new office carpeting made from recycled ketchup and soda containers, and "recycle" their friends' apple cores in compost heaps. They are also driven by an abiding sense that time is running out in the effort to save what remains of pristine environments and priceless natural resources in this country.

Despite the heavy workload, limited rewards, and the sense of urgency, people genuinely seemed to like working at CC. It was widely described as a "good place to work." When a position as program director in one area was advertised, three hundred people applied. In the

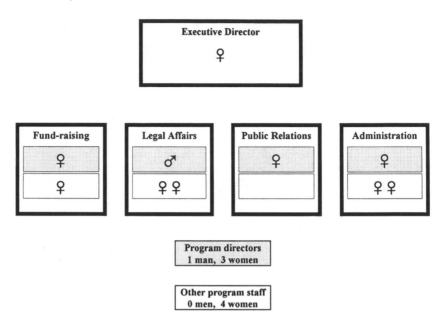

Figure 6.2 CC organizational chart: Nonscience program areas

larger environmental community and in nearby university communities, CC was highly regarded as a good place to do "serious science."

Science in CC Practice

CC's activities can be divided into two areas: (1) the scientific work, which CC defines as inventorying, collecting, mapping, and analyzing data about plant and wildlife species; analyzing ecological processes; and designing means for protecting and conserving parcels of land; and (2) the administrative work, which CC defines as raising money to run CC and pay for acquiring and protecting land, and negotiating with landowners and the public for access to land.[1] Although work responsibilities are clearly divided between the two areas, everyone is involved in some way in both. The organizational context of CC's work creates a kind of "tightness," wherein a large portion of the work to be done is required of everyone. To accomplish the myriad and pressing demands of CC's work, everyone on the small staff invests long hours and considerable work in the evenings and on weekends.

The following excerpt suggests the kind and range of issues of which CC's employees must have command. The speaker is an old-timer at

CC but a nonscientist. She is talking to Eisenhart about her efforts to close a deal on a property containing a threatened wetland area.

> It's a very high-quality, ephemeral wetlands site, probably the best in the Valley. In general in the Valley, the wetlands have been drastically altered. What were once shallow wetlands have been drained for agricultural uses, and there's been a lot of deep water added (by Fish and Wildlife) to make duck habitat. This has disturbed the shallow playa lakes that serve as habitat for many shorebirds, such as sandhill cranes.
>
> We knew from the beginning that the Bureau of Land Reclamation's pumping project was right next door. And there are a lot of water issues in the Valley—arguments between farmers and developers—that have been ongoing for a long time. In a sense "water" is *the* issue in the Valley. And especially around the ephemeral wetlands, which hardly exist at all there any more.
>
> Then the serious water questions came up. There were questions about whether the deep and shallow aquifers were connected, what the effects of the Bureau's project would be; these were complicated hydrologic questions. We had hired a hydrologist to do a literature study—examine the existing data—and interviews with various people and agencies in the Valley. Her report was due in January. I had talked to the landowners in December; I wanted to be honest. I said, "Here are our concerns, and we're getting a hydrologist to do a study. Let me get back to you in January when the report is done."
>
> They said fine, but it wasn't quite that simple. They didn't have other buyers, so that was not a problem. But there was the threat that I was gonna make them mad, that I would lose their confidence.
>
> Then the report was inconclusive, and I think we probably knew that it would be before it was in. I was honest with them; I'm not the kind of person who can work by hiding things from landowners. The report wasn't going to tell us definitively whether we should buy the land. CC would have to estimate the risks . . . and then just make a decision. I couldn't keep them waiting forever. Finally we decided just to go with it. They had been so understanding; they expected us to buy. (fieldnotes, October 14, 1993)

This way of talking about science evokes a very different image from that of the dispassionate, laboratory scientist, free of political, social, or local concerns. The excerpt reveals an attempt to accommodate scientific rigor, environmental applications, public interests, and business practice that is daily enacted at CC. Work practices in CC produce a way of talking and thinking that deeply interweaves political, economic, and personal concerns with science.

We can gain further insight into the nature of CC's practices by examining four organizational components: its organizing values, work activities, constituencies, and workforce characteristics.[2] The focus is on the way scientific knowledge is embedded in these four components, and what we learn sheds light on the opportunities for learning science in CC.

Values

Two sets of values seem to organize CC's work. One set includes the liberal values of the environmental movement: the value of saving environmental resources; the belief that knowledge of ecological processes supports the need for conservation; and the urgency of protecting global biodiversity, which is being rapidly depleted. The other set includes the conservative values of good business practice: product distinctiveness; cost-effectiveness; economic "compatibility;" investment for the future; protection of privacy; and assurance of access to private property, leisure, recreation, and quality of life. These two sets of values are linked and repeated throughout CC's promotional literature, its appeals for support, its strategic plans, and the conversations of its employees. The following excerpt, taken from an appeal for support, is typical:

> You see, we have pioneered highly successful ways to protect wildlife and habitat—ways that make us unique. . . . And our success comes from the fact that we talk business, not confrontation. We work in cooperation with farmers, corporations, government and private land owners. And we do not single out an "enemy" and launch an orchestrated attack. Does all this compromise our position? Not in the least! . . . If all else fails, we simply buy up and manage the land that the plants and animals need in order to survive!

A national magazine author, writing about CC, notes that

> [a]lthough many purchases turn into public lands, recreation and aesthetics are by-products, not the primary goal. "We're in the science business, not the pretty business," says [a national official of CC]. . . . "Our mission is very focused. We are preserving biotic diversity in the world."

This dual system of values permits CC's employees to discuss and support such divergent projects as launching a three-million-dollar campaign to save an ordinary forest from residential development, and constructing low-cost housing on scarce open space. In this value system, scientists and scientific information are important because they provide the rationale and arguments for CC's activities. In this sense, the ability of staff to use scientific knowledge accurately, meaningfully, and effectively is an important aspect of CC's value system. However, scientific priorities are explicitly negotiable; they can be compromised or modified by other priorities, such as business or private interests. In this sense, the value of scientific knowledge is restricted or circumscribed by business demands. This is a pattern that reappears throughout the data on CC.

Work Activities

CC's work activities are also organized in two parts. One part includes the activities necessary to make CC's case in terms of environmental-protection arguments; the other includes the activities necessary to make a case that appeals to middle- and upper-class sensibilities and concerns. As described earlier, CC refers to the first kind of activity as "science" and distinguishes it from the organization's other work.

Work in the Science Program Areas

Four of the eight program areas at CC (Site Ranking, Design, Management, and Reserve Sites) do natural-science work. This work is both in-depth and far-ranging. To illustrate, a management plan for one year of only one of CC's twenty-one (statewide) conservation sites includes the following:

> Map the distribution of the two highly ranked plant associations; identify and map other plant communities; initiate inventory of vascular plants; initiate inventories of butterflies and moths, reptiles, and amphibians; inventory . . . for spotted owls; locate and map raptor nests; initiate breeding bird atlas program; continue mammal inventory; . . . [Determine] how much public visitation can be conducted without affecting wildlife. [Determine] how much grazing (if any) should be allowed. [Determine whether] controlled burns [are] a good idea. (*Canyon Management Plan*, 9–10)

An even more extensive and ambitious management plan identifies the work necessary to conserve riparian forest, shrubland, and wetland communities in areas encompassing a third of the state. This plan, prepared by CC's staffers with the assistance of a few outside experts (such as a water attorney), includes scientific analyses, protection recommendations, and specific tasks regarding river hydrology; geomorphology; forest regeneration; wetland restoration; water quality; endangered species protection; migratory bird corridors; threats from dams, reservoirs, agriculture, mining, tourism, highways, and residences; nonnative species introductions; and changing plant, animal, and water dynamics (*River Strategic Plan*, 3–24).

CC's activities are driven by the work necessary to assess and preserve the state's biodiversity. This work begins with the procedures and "strict criteria" used by the Site Ranking program to give each location a "biodiversity score," a calculation reflecting the presence of endangered species, the quality of the habitat, existing threats to species or habitat, and the urgency of protection. Locations are ranked as CC's protection priorities according to the biodiversity score given by the Site Ranking program. All the other program areas organize their activities around this ranking, although each area defines its own priorities in a distinctive way. Because the Site Ranking program's work is the primary basis for determining the work of the other program areas, we begin by describing it.

The work of the Site Ranking program begins with extensive site surveys and the finding that a rare species lives in a particular place. The steps in the process were described as follows by the program director (a zoologist).

1. The first step is to gather all existing information about the rare species—from academic literature, trade publications, talking to experts, and field work—to develop a picture of its distribution and habitat requirements. This involves extensive research to gather all the information.

2. Based on this information, the species is given a global "rarity" ranking or a state "rarity" ranking. These rarity scores will later contribute to the calculation of the final biodiversity score. (In each state a "ranking authority" is designated for certain species to avoid duplication of effort.) Species that are globally rare get the highest score; those that are rare only in a state get lower scores.

3. Once a global or state rarity score is assigned, a "full natural history" of the species is developed. (The rarity score determines the order in which the natural histories are done.) The natural history includes the species' distribution, status of habitats, use of habitats, threats, genetics, and management issues. This is a very extensive treatment of the species; it "can take a whole semester dogging through literature at the library." Many of these natural histories are new, and thus represent potentially publishable materials for the people who work on them. (CC does not have the staff to complete many natural histories in-house; it relies on volunteers—students, professors, amateur scientists—to do much of the work.)

All of the information collected and analyzed becomes part of a relational database, which links information about the rarity of a species with information about the quality of its habitat, the cultural history of the habitat, potential or existing threats to the species' survival, and the urgency for protection, given existing threats. These elements are then converted to numerical values that are used, together with the rarity score, to compute a location's final biodiversity score. This score is the culmination of the Site Ranking program's work. A high biodiversity score is the single most important criterion for determining what land to preserve; it is considered a measure of what is needed, and when, to prevent the loss of a rare species.

When an area has a significant biodiversity score, a boundary is drawn around it, and it is given a "site name." The biodiversity score is the only criterion for site names. This is a very powerful designation, because it places the site on CC's list of potential "conservation sites." The biodiversity scores of these sites, then, set the scientific priorities for all of the other CC programs. The rest of CC's work—developing preserve and reserve designs, developing site-management plans, coordinating efforts with other agencies, acquiring land, and fund-raising—all follows from the scientific priorities established by the Site Ranking program. Every year, the sites are reviewed, the information about them is updated, and the scientific priorities revised. CC's offices are themselves ranked each year by the number of conservation sites they acquire or protect.

To summarize briefly: the assumptions and procedures of the Site Ranking program determine what kind of scientific work must be done, in what order, and with what urgency. Once the Site Ranking program has completed its work, the other program areas use its list of scientific priorities to establish their own (more specific) priorities and time lines. Conducting environmental protection work according to the assumptions and procedures of the Site Ranking program is the linchpin of CC's science-related activities.

The three other programs of the CC that involve science are Site Design, Site Management, and Reserve Sites. Site Design and Site Management work relies heavily on the biodiversity information provided by the Site Ranking program, but includes other information as well. Design, for example, is responsible for collecting and analyzing new, up-to-date, and comprehensive information about each of the Site Ranking program's top-ranked sites, and for developing an integrated proposal for how to protect each site. Site Management is responsible for determining the cost and feasibility of implementing Design's plans. Reserve Sites' work focuses on similar issues but considers larger land areas than Design or Management have traditionally addressed. Reserve Sites links sites together through a mixture of protection strategies and implementation plans, and represents a new and emerging program area within CC.

It seems clear that principles of conservation science are actively used and central to the work activities in these four program areas. As a group, the people who work in these areas need to know a lot about conservation biology, natural history, and ecology. They must learn about species and habitats. They must understand ecological processes and ecological modeling. They must be familiar with theories of conservation and population genetics. They need all this knowledge in order to put together the preservation and conservation reports and plans that are required before CC's land-protection and fund-raising activities can proceed. One science program director, Dan, described the work he and his staff did as "unique: it's right between science and applied science; if you're collecting data and statistically analyzing it, you're definitely doing science" (interview, December 23, 1992). We can see from this introduction to CC's work practices that knowledge of conservation science is valued as a central feature of doing one's job, doing it well, and making a positive contribution to the wider community, society, and the world.

Work Activities in the Other Program Areas at CC

Despite the centrality of conservation science and its value in the work practices of the four science programs at CC, the importance of science changes when one looks beyond the science programs to the entire corporation. In his book, *Strange Weather*, a cultural critique of claims made for science and technology, Andrew Ross writes,

> While the politics of global warming [for example] is almost wholly dependent on the word of experts, . . . other networks of authority and sponsorship are a powerful shaping influence on the way in which the story gets told. (1991, 198)

Scientists at CC would understand what Ross is talking about. They provide "the word of experts," but their story gets told in a particular context of authority and sponsorship. Although CC relies on conservation science and the scientists on its staff for proof of its claims and the basis of its work activities, the corporation must also appeal directly to the well-to-do public for money, for land to protect, and for volunteer services. Widespread public understanding, financial support, and volunteer initiative are fundamental to their activities and crucial to their survival and success. Accordingly, CC must tell its story to the people, most of whom are not scientists.

Thinking about science in this broader institutional context, the business potential in scientific information becomes more prominent. In contrast to the science-program areas, the Fund-Raising, Legal Affairs, Public Relations, and Administration programs are committed to raising money from public and private foundations, to making purchases and other arrangements for preserving land, and to educating the public about the importance and significance of CC's work. Although CC's activities proceed according to the scientific work (the other program areas would not be working on fund-raising, acquisitions, or education unless scientific significance was already established), the second set of activities seems more important to the day-to-day functioning and success of CC as a whole. For example, when Eisenhart approached CC for permission to conduct a study, she was told that it would be fine to spend time observing and interviewing the people working in the science areas; however, it was important that she did not disturb or take time away from people in the other areas. They were, she was told, "behind," and the organization could not afford the cost of any delays in their work.

This was true for several reasons. First, because CC is a nonprofit organization, it depends on money raised from outside sources to remain in business. Every dollar spent on operating expenses, as well as most of the money for land purchases, must be raised by the local CC staff. Because fund-raising is so crucial to the organization's survival and success, scientific information must be used in ways that contribute to revenues and do not create a need for extraordinary expenditures.

Second, as indicated earlier, the local CC branch receives recognition and status from its national organization according to the *number* of land acquisitions (regardless of their size) completed each year. For this reason, the organization's science must be used (along with other incentives) in ways that support land purchases: for example, to persuade a landowner of the value of the long-term conservation benefit compared to the value of other possible uses for his or her land. Thus, although knowledge of science is a fundamental aspect of the organization's work, and its scientists work long, hard, and diligently at their jobs, scientific knowledge tends to play a supporting, rather than a leading, role in CC's day-to-day business priorities.

CC's Constituencies

CC's constituencies are the rich, the middle-class, mostly white "establishment"—who can be called upon for financial and volunteer support—as well as other organizations and agencies, governmental and nongovernmental, including colleges and universities, that are involved in or committed to environmental protection. These two sets of constituencies reflect and reinforce the duality already described within CC. They form a context of sponsorship in which it is more important for CC to impress the establishment than to impress other environmental groups. Thus, Ann, the director of Design, finds herself intrigued by the possibilities of directing a state-of-the-art workshop for representatives of an environmental agency on the changing conservation priorities in the western states, yet pressured to complete preserve designs that are a prerequisite for developing site-acquisition packages. Bill, the Management director, finds himself making numerous out-of-town trips, not primarily to maintain or monitor sites, but to talk to community leaders and wealthy individuals about the need to support site conservation.

The talks that Bill gives on such occasions are intended to make CC's science interesting and understandable to its constituencies. Bill's talk on a fund-raising hike, revealed in the following vignette, is illustrative.[3]

As the group hiked up the old road, Bill stopped every few feet to point out interesting or important plants ("This big-eyed bluestem once covered the tall-grass prairie"), signs of wildlife ("Notice the white stuff on this piece of turkey poop. Birds have developed a form of semisolid urine so they don't have to be hauling around all that liquid when they fly"), and management tasks required at the preserve ("We don't know anything about the butterflies and moths here. Wish we could find someone who wanted to come out and look around at them.").

At almost every stop, he had a story of some kind to tell. One was about how to tell the difference among pines, spruce, and firs. The group huddled around Bill as he began to talk. First, he described the different shapes and locations of the cones; then he continued on to the differences in the needles. Finally he said that if all else fails, you can chew the needles. "If it tastes OK, it's a Douglas fir; if it tastes *really* good, it's a white fir." Everyone laughed.

As the trip continued, Bill discussed his plans to control-burn some areas and to chop down some trees. Some of the group objected. "Why set a fire; why not let nature take its course?" "I thought you were here to preserve the trees!" Some questioners sounded curious; others sounded alarmed. Bill calmly explained that he wanted to preserve the meadow, and without the burn and some tree removal, it would develop into forest. He also explained how the meadow, as a transitional zone between the plains and the mountains, was a favorite place for many animals. The group seemed satisfied—they nodded and smiled—and then trudged on.

Later a question came from the group about what to do about a dilapidated cabin on the preserve land. Bill said CC was concerned about its liability if someone should fall through the rotted floor boards and get hurt. Someone suggested restoring the cabin. Bill said he wasn't sure if it had any historical significance and expressed concern about whether restoration would be worthwhile; he suggested he might burn it. Many in the group were openly aghast. Someone suggested dismantling it and carrying it out. Bill thought that might be possible but a lot of work. Maybe a fence could be placed around it. Bill didn't think that would look very good or be very effective in the long run. After about fifteen minutes of this kind of talk and no clear resolution, the group left the cabin behind.

Bill's formula for talks like this one seems to be to "make them interesting"; to interject some information about CC's plans, reasons, and needs; and never to mention money (explicitly) unless directly asked. On this hike, the formula seemed to work. The group seemed interested in what Bill had to say and, after hearing his stories and reasons, they expressed support for CC's activities—except in the case of the cabin. Many turned away from Bill's discussion of the cabin unpersuaded. Eisenhart's journal contained the following entry about this:

> Thinking back on it, I thought this was one occasion when Bill could have been more successful if he had discussed money. It did not seem

to me that the group was thinking seriously about how costly this broken-down cabin might turn out to be for CC, e.g., the financial costs of insurance, to restore it properly, or to maintain and protect it once restored, as well as both the financial and forest-degradation costs of either hauling in renovation supplies or hauling the cabin away from its remote location. The group wanted the cabin preserved because it was there, and it was apparently old. They thought Bill was unenlightened for wanting to burn it. In this particular case, the middle-class sensibilities of the group were not fully satisfied.

This glimpse into CC's constituencies and ways of handling them reveals more about the fine line that CC's employees must tread. They must find ways to act and to argue that both satisfy the scientific requirements of environmental protection, as CC defines them, and enlist the public support upon which CC depends.

CC's Workforce

CC's workforce is (for the most part) young, bright, energetic, idealistic, and committed. In an organization of slightly more than twenty people charged with conservation in a large state, they probably would have to be. But for all their hard work, intelligence, and commitment, they are at the mercy of larger corporate and public interests. Without the financial support of the well-to-do and private foundations, the contributions of volunteers, and the good will of the public, they would not be able to pursue environmental science or environmental protection. This explains why Bill, for example, feels he must craft his talks to the public in the way that he does.

The duality of CC's values, work practices, and constituencies is clearly communicated to newcomers. In one example, Bill, a five-year employee and a director, explained to Ted, a relative newcomer who had been working in Site Design for less than a year, why one piece of land was better than another to serve as the centerpiece of CC's next capital campaign (major fund-raising initiative to involve the public, raise money, and provide visibility for CC). This conversation took place in the car, as we were returning from a field trip to Canyon Preserve.

> Bill threw out the question, "In our new budget, we've designated $1.4 million as the target for our next capital campaign, but we haven't got a site yet; what should it be?" Ted said he liked Border site. He named the rare species there and said the land was in good

shape and beautiful. Bill said there were a lot of problems with Border: It is completely surrounded by private land; it's a long ways from a population center; it's a three-day trip to get down there, do something, and come back; it would be hard to manage. Bill said the fund-raising director would "have a fit" because it would be so costly to go down there—it would take three days of staff's time, they would have to spend the night, provide food—and so few people [members of the public] were close enough to visit. Ted persisted, saying he really thought Border was important to protect, that its ranking [from the Site Ranking program] was very high.

Bill didn't disagree with what Ted said but countered that the Sandhills site would be better, because "a lot of things come together there." Bill said the site was very large—a draw for the public. He went on to explain that part of the site was "fantastic prairie . . . the best example in the state [although he specified no ranking]." The rest of the site was in good condition. Sandhills was within an easy commute of three population centers, and for that reason it would be easy to get the public out there and to find a preserve manager [often these are part-time workers]. (fieldnotes, March 6, 1993)

In this conversation, Bill, the old-timer, was giving Ted, the newcomer, a lesson in how CC's priorities work. Although scientific significance is basic, business-related practical and logistical considerations, such as how to involve the public, how to raise money, and how to assure proper management, can (and often do) take precedence over even the highest scientific ranking. In fact, the tension between science and business turned out to be the central problem of the transformation from newcomer to old-timer in the CC.

Becoming a "Good Scientist" in CC

CC's orientation to science is similar to that described for the environmental biology degree program discussed in chapter 2: CC and the environmental biology program stress the application of conservation-science principles to real-world environmental issues. Like the practices of environmental biology, CC's applied practices preclude using the experimental conditions of laboratory science, but CC does not challenge the value or importance of "real science." CC is committed, as is the environmental biology program, to using science to address complex, contemporary environmental problems. For these reasons, CC seems to be a workplace in which graduates of programs like environmental biology would be able to express the applied-scientist identity they learn in school.

In fact, CC employees expect that students from programs such as environmental biology will want to work at CC. In its job announcements, CC makes clear that a bachelor's or master's degree in science or applied science is required. In interviews with prospective employees, CC old-timers tell newcomers that they will be expected to build upon their academic science as they develop proficiency in CC.

On the other hand, old-timers at CC also make clear to newcomers that even "good" (applied) degree programs do not fully prepare students for CC's work. Three of four science-program directors commented on the lack of preparedness among newcomers. One said, "We use science, we apply it. [But] we have to train people in what's really needed [here]. For example, natural history is no longer taught at the university, so we need to train the experts [we need]." This CC scientist was concerned that recent graduates did not possess the knowledge of regional natural and cultural history necessary to make decisions that could be accepted and supported by environmentalists as well as local landowners. Another scientist said, "[Recent graduates] come to us knowing statistical procedures for ecological modeling; they have to be willing to learn how to join what they already know about science and statistics with the kinds of things we deal with." What CC deals with are such things as landowners reluctant to allow biologists in search of threatened species or habitats onto their property; oil companies and cattle cooperatives who question CC's motives; ranchers who object to removing land from production; community pressure on elderly farmers not to sell or bequeath land to CC; and inconsistent scientific findings. Although programs such as environmental biology may try to turn out conservation scientists who are prepared to handle some real-world issues, old-timers at CC do not think that schools are completely successful at this. Thus, CC itself, in the way it organizes activities and presents information to newcomers, must do the job.

Eisenhart closely followed the trajectories of five new employees who were making the transition from school to work in CC; she also monitored her own and others' experiences as new volunteers. Two themes emerged from the analysis of these experiences. Around newcomers with academic backgrounds in science, CC old-timers behaved as if they believed that newcomers must be convinced of the value of the business or practical side of CC's work. Bill's "lesson" for Ted (recounted earlier) is one example of this theme. When newcomers lacked science backgrounds (e.g., Eisenhart), old-timers worked to convince them of the nature and importance of science in CC.

The learning (or participation) trajectories of those in the first group can be divided into four phases. Phase 1 encompassed the job interview and period of work immediately after someone was hired. When newcomer-scientists joined CC, they were collectively identified as "people who know the science." The actions of both old-timers and newcomers were consistent with this shared sense of their identity. For example, old-timers repeatedly asked newcomers to display their knowledge of academic science—during interviews with various staff members before being hired, at staff meetings shortly after being hired, and at training sessions devoted to the technical aspects (e.g., the site-ranking procedures) of CC's work. Newcomers complied with old-timers' requests and also found their own ways of demonstrating their academic prowess. These displays were remarked upon and celebrated within the organization.

After a short time, old-timers began to "correct" newcomers' scientific contributions; at first, newcomers did not respond. This is phase 2. Old-timers' corrections pointed out that "pure" or academic science was not always sufficient to make decisions about actions within CC. Bill's lesson to Ted occurred during this phase. Ted had been demonstrating his familiarity with CC's procedures for site ranking; Bill tacitly accepted Ted's knowledge, but at the same time, he was pointing out what *else* Ted needed to take into account. The appearance of corrections suggested that old-timers were thinking differently about newcomers: In this phase, old-timers began to call newcomers "naive" scientists—people who still had to learn about CC's business and practical priorities. As Bill liked to put it, "You [have to learn that you] can't say the same thing about conservation to a rancher and to a farmer. Ranchers don't care if rivers move; farmers do." For some time after the corrections began, newcomers—including Ted—continued to display their academic scientist's identity, apparently uncertain how to interpret the corrections. Thus, during this phase, newcomers worked at being seen as beginning scientists in the familiar way (phase 1), while old-timers worked at demonstrating ways that newcomers should also take nonscience concerns into account.

Although old-timers' corrections during this phase seemed to go unheeded at first, they eventually shaped a problem for the newcomers.

Newcomers began to talk about the need to reassess their own views of science within the context of CC. One newcomer, Marty, had this to say:

> CC doesn't have the emotion of other environmental organizations. It's not an advocacy organization, and that affects how I talk about things now that I'm a staff member. I'm not quite comfortable with that yet. Take for example the [proposed] airport [near Creek Preserve]. Bill talks about this a lot. We [CC] have a concern because the airport might pollute the ground water, but otherwise we don't care. And then there's peat: I wouldn't buy [local] peat because it's such a rare resource [peat was mined at Creek Preserve before the land was protected], but that's not the CC position. A lot of people will give money to CC for Creek Preserve so they can mine peat somewhere else. That's a problem for me, but not for the organization. . . . We [CC] never tell agencies what to do; we help them with things they can't do. I don't know of any other environmental group that can say this. I'm trying to come to terms with this: my personal stance versus my stance as a CC employee. (interview, July 10, 1993)

As they reflected on this conflict, newcomers looked to the tools available in CC for this reflection. In this example, Marty listened carefully to the way old-timers like Bill talked to the public and to members of other agencies about CC's priorities. In other cases, she made appointments to talk with senior staff in the business-program areas. At one point she expressed her reservations about talking to one wealthy gentleman as follows:

> I was nervous, because he's such an important person . . . and he hasn't contributed to CC for awhile. I thought [the fund-raising staff or the executive director] would be nervous about my meeting with him. They gave me some tips. . . . They told me some things to mention if I had a chance. (fieldnotes, September 7, 1993)

By talking and acting in these ways, she announced her lack of knowledge about how to represent CC to the public, as well as her desire to learn more about how to do it.

Old-timers responded in two ways once newcomers got to the phase when they began to view themselves as naive. First, old-timers began to plan occasions for newcomers to publicly display their knowledge of science and the CC. As soon as newcomers entered the "naive phase" (phase 2), old-timers almost immediately began to schedule opportunities for newcomers to make public presentations. Old-timers often described this as throwing newcomers "into the lion's den," and although old-timers worried about its effects on newcomers, they continued to do it:

> We throw people right into the lion's den. We expect the world; we expect them to do everything. And we don't take the time to bring them along. We're in such a hurry to do conservation work . . . we sometimes just ask too much of people. I know it and so [do others]. But that's what we do. (interview, September 24, 1993)

Newcomers almost always saw these public appearances as coming too fast, before they were ready to display the identities they envisioned were expected. Their expressions of anxiety about getting the science right, and getting CC right, and getting the two aligned increased. During this time, newcomers tried to make clear what they didn't know and to figure out how to get the information they needed quickly.

Second, old-timers began to differentiate newcomers by labeling them, that is, to identify each of them as a *certain kind of CC member* (e.g., "self-starter"; "promising but needs support"; "shy in public"). This was the point at which newcomers' personal identities began to diverge within the organization: In the way newcomers asked for help, they were given personal labels; in the way old-timers provided help, newcomers were further differentiated; thus their distinctiveness as individuals within CC came to be identified. These personal identities have their own, somewhat separate trajectories, which Eisenhart has described in more detail elsewhere (Eisenhart 1995a).

In phase 3, newcomers aggressively pursued means of resolving the problem but did so with virtually no direct help from old-timers. Like the young people in ELAC, the environmental action group discussed in chapter 5, CC newcomers in this phase were on their own to figure out what they needed to know and what, specifically, they would say at the public events to which old-timers assigned them. Whereas ELAC did not have scientific expertise readily available for canvassers, the resident experts at CC indicated that they were simply too busy with their own jobs to set aside time specifically to instruct newcomers. Old-timers assumed that newcomers would "pick it up" as they spent time in the organization. As happened in ELAC, CC newcomers searched in their immediate environment for ways to resolve the problem. In the case of CC, public meetings at which old-timers described CC's work to potential supporters and long car trips to conservation sites were both commonplace; there the old-timers themselves and their ways of talking about CC and its work were easily accessible. Like those in ELAC, CC's employees had little extra time in their lives; they worked long, hard hours, often at night and on weekends, for a cause in which they deeply believed. If they were going to get better at becoming "good scientists" in CC, they had to do it during the time and with the tools available at work. Discussions about how to talk to the public about CC—as in Ted's talk about Border and Sandhills—were the principal way in which newcomers practiced their knowledge and ideas and tried to develop their own styles. Old ways of speaking about environmental commitments, as illustrated in Marty's deliberations about peat, were reassessed, and CC's version of how to speak effectively in public about its priorities was close at hand. Of all the things in the CC environment that *might* be learned, newcomers in this phase had time and space to learn ways of speaking in public about how CC *used* scientific knowledge.

Finally, newcomers began to feel comfortable with taking advantage of opportunities to talk to the public about CC's work. Both they and the old-timers said they were willing to do so and comfortable in doing it. This is the fourth and final phase. By phase 4, the newcomers' problem had been resolved, generally in line with the scientist identity accorded highest status in the organization: the ability to "speak" effectively to the public about CC's priorities. Whether in oral or written form, "good scientists" at CC can convincingly present the organization's scientific *and* business priorities to a diverse array of potential supporters and challengers. During Eisenhart's study, all of the new employees she followed reached phase 4 within two to three months. Certainly some became more proficient than others, but everyone learned enough for old-timers to feel comfortable having them speak directly to the public about CC.

Further, no major difference was detected in the level of participation or the success rates of women and men (as groups) within CC. Although women and men, as well as newcomers in different job categories, sometimes became more proficient at different things (see Eisenhart 1995a for further elaboration), they got better at the same pace, they advanced in the organization, they felt satisfied with their work, and they were praised for their efforts in roughly equal numbers.

Old-timers assumed that newcomers without backgrounds in science were already committed to CC's cause. In this case, old-timers worked hard to demonstrate the scientific grounding of CC's work, and for this reason, spent more time explicitly instructing nonscientist newcomers. For example, old-timers were explicit with newcomers about their professional connections to the larger community of conservation scientists who work in environmental protection. They frequently mentioned articles they had read in environmental journals and conferences they attended with other scientists. The following is one example, taken from Eisenhart's fieldnotes of a conversation with Bill, the Site Management director.

> We went back to the office, where Bill ate his lunch and we talked. He told me about reading a recent journal article written by a biologist about a small preserve in New Jersey, near where the author grew up. His years of watching the preserve and its surroundings, along with his scientific training, had led him to the conclusion that small preserves whose surroundings were not protected from development and whose characteristics could be radically altered by some natural event (e.g., a hurricane) were not (no longer) good candidates for conservation or a good way to think about conservation. The author's point was that conservation efforts needed to focus on larger areas and more expansive ways of maintaining the integrity of large tracts (i.e., more was needed than just buying a piece of land, putting a fence around it, and throwing away the key). Bill had been really excited to see this article, because it confirmed the direction that CC was going in thinking about conservation. The article's author had no connection to CC; he just happened to grow up near a preserve. To Bill, this made the confirmation all the more exciting. (fieldnotes, February 22, 1993)

Ann, the Site Design director, was also deeply involved in organizing a western regional meeting of about twelve people to talk about how preserve designs would have to change if larger conservation sites became the priority. Bill called the work on larger preserve designs "cutting-edge stuff" for the field of conservation ecology.

Old-timers also make clear how their work contributes to areas of basic field science and thereby connects them to university scientists. During a field trip to restore a portion of recently preserved wetland, one of the tasks was to nip branches from two kinds of willows and then plant the branches in a disturbed patch.

> Bill told us that the willow project was an experiment. There was no literature about propagating willows this way, but [a university professor] and his graduate students (who had a small experimental

> plot at the site) had tried it with limited success. Bill planned to ob-
> serve what happened in the larger patch in which we were working.
> When I asked about the research on wetlands and their restoration,
> Bill said there was little applicable research. [The professor's and
> Bill's] plots would test out some ideas on a small scale, and if [they
> were] successful, Bill would use them more extensively at this site
> and elsewhere. (fieldnotes, October 24, 1992)

In general then, CC defined a good scientist as someone who is able
to combine scientific expertise and commitment with good business
practices in ways that make sense to the public and to other organizations involved in conservation and protection. This identity depends on
establishing one's scientific legitimacy with the public and with other
scientists outside of the organization. It relies in large part on ways of
speaking about CC that weave its scientific and business priorities into
interesting and compelling stories, and it seems to be motivated, as in
the engineering course and the environmental action group we studied,
by a desire and need to appear competent and knowledgeable in public
settings and among both scientists and nonscientists.

The burden for this learning is carried not so much by the physical
tools of the environment (e.g., see Hutchins [1993], who explains how
the tools and charts of navigation contain most of the knowledge necessary for novice navigators to learn how to pilot a ship), nor is it carried
by instructors and pupils cordoned off from the organization's normal
routine. Rather, it is carried by the organization's social and cultural
tools—the socially salient demands, categories of participants, ways of
talking, and their implications—that direct the actions of individuals
within the organization (see also McDermott 1993; Mehan 1993;
Mehan, Hertweck, and Meihls 1986). By these means, taken up sporadi-
cally by old-timers and newcomers as they address current issues within
a program group, attend a staff meeting, work on projects, travel together to a distant site, or speak to the public, newcomers, women and
men alike, are moved closer to the meanings of *science* and *good scientist*
that are celebrated in CC.

Connections to Power

The nature of CC's activities and the relationships among people that
are formed through them establish conditions in which principles of
conservation science are used to inform and support land-protection
efforts that make good business sense to the organization. Like the

student-engineers in EDI, CC employees had to learn how to use technical information in ways that were business-sensitive and locally appropriate. But whereas the student-engineers used their skills to formulate solutions to a problem given to them by their clients, CC employees were in the position of defining the problem (more land should be protected), developing solutions, and convincing others (mostly nonscientists) of the value and appropriateness of CC's preferred solutions. In this sense, their activities were larger in scope and more similar to those of the environmental group, ELAC, than to those of the student-engineers in EDI. Yet CC's activities placed greater demands on individuals to rely on scientific knowledge and principles to guide and inform the organization's work, and they connected staff members with others (local residents, business leaders, employees of other conservation agencies) in more stable and enduring relationships than did ELAC. Unlike the activities of academic physics or genetics, however, CC's activities required staff members to use science in ways that were not only scientifically credible but also involved good business sense and were locally compelling. These characteristics appeared to make the kind of control that CC fostered especially potent. In CC's attempt to define a problem, identify the solutions, and argue for certain solutions by relying on *both* science and situational demands, the organization established a context in which the power of academic science and the requirements of local circumstances could be linked. This power might be referred to as a kind of civic power, that is, the power to educate and persuade in the public interest, as defined by conservation science.

In addition, CC seemed to enable both women and men to take up high-status identities and their power almost equally. Recall (see figure 6.1) that women and men were nearly equally represented in the high-status positions of the organization, and that 46 percent of environmental biologists at CC were women. For many years, CC's executive director was a woman. This changed near the end of Eisenhart's study, when CC's employees agreed that a male candidate was the best qualified. More informally, two CC employees enjoyed particularly high-status identities by virtue of their skills at talking to the public about CC—one was a woman; the other, a man. These findings compare very favorably to national figures showing women's participation in environmental science: women are only 24 percent of employed life scientists and only 14 percent of employed environmental scientists with master's or doctoral degrees (National Science Foundation 1996).

The kind of power embedded in CC's work may contribute to CC's reputation and record with respect to women. Like the power of the technical expert in the engineering class, and even the power of the itinerant advocate in the environmental action group, the kind of civic power represented in CC depends on activities that give time, space, and important identities to people who engage in publicly meaningful, science-related work. As in the engineering design internship, EDI, technical expertise in CC must be situated in the concrete contexts of real people, as well as in the parcels of land they own and use. Even more than in EDI—because CC's mandate is larger than EDI's and its public considerably more diverse than EDI's clients, technical expertise in CC must be context-sensitive, generally accessible, and locally compelling. In all of our sites where such proficiency is prized, but especially in CC, women are well represented, and they participate and succeed in much the same way as men.

In summary, the connections of CC staff members to the world as civic voices or leaders are strengthened as they become increasingly proficient at using conservation science to educate and persuade the public. Their power as civic leaders grows as they find credible, sustainable ways of directing the thinking and actions of the public in accord with the principles that inform the organization's priorities. In this case, scientific principles of conservation are integral to the process, and women are key participants.

Considering the positive dimensions of CC's work, especially the motivational context it provides for women and men to put credible science to public use, it is sobering, but necessary, to note that CC is a small organization with tenuous financial support, where smart, well-trained individuals work extremely hard for very little pay or other tangible benefits. For these reasons, few people can take advantage of the learning opportunities CC provides, and those who do incur high costs in terms of their financial well-being and security. CC and similar organizations may offer compelling, credible sites for the development of scientific literacy and social responsibility, but few know about these organizations, support them, or seem to care.

Patterns across the Four Sites

In chapter 2, we reviewed previous findings about women's experiences in high- and low-status sites of science and engineering as well as in other professional fields. Whatever characteristics are associated with status, we found that more men than women work in high-status sites, while more women than men work in low-status sites.

At the end of chapter 2, we wondered whether our low-status sites— where women are relatively well represented and well rewarded compared to the men who work with them—would turn out to be better places for women to participate in or learn science. While we had some reason to hope they would be better (e.g., Rossiter's 1995 findings about the success of women scientists in nonprofit organizations), the literature we reviewed also clearly indicated the possibility that they would not. We hoped to find evidence that different science practices, different meanings of *science* and *scientist*, and different relations of power in our "marginal" sites would create organizational contexts where women could shine. However, we were not so sanguine as to think that women could do so unfettered by larger social or cultural forces. Our findings regarding science practice, its meanings, and the networks of power developed in our four sites reveal a more complicated picture than we expected.

In all four sites, we found women engaged in some form of science or engineering practice. Across a set of diverse sites, we found women who were interested in scientific or technical information, wanted to learn more of it, and were succeeding in work practices related to it. Notably, three of the four places where women were numerous and did well are characterized by more socially relevant activities; more expansive definitions of *science* and *scientist*; more public involvement and exposure; more limited financial rewards; and less academic power than is found at high-status sites of science or engineering.

These results call into question the familiar assumptions that ineffective school science, long years of gender-appropriate socialization, or innate gendered tendencies discourage girls and young women from pursuing science or engineering. The women we studied continue to be interested in science, despite (in some cases) discouraging school and personal experiences. They remain interested even though it means competing with men in the classroom or at work. They continue to be interested even when the pay is low and the other tangible rewards few. Compared to women's low participation in elite sites, including many school programs, and the discouraging findings of researchers who have studied women's experiences in elite sites, the women and places we studied are impressive counterexamples.

Our findings also call into question familiar assumptions about how to increase women's interest and participation in science. Women are especially successful in places where science or engineering is practiced and can be learned in purposeful, public activity, with all the inevitable messiness, compromises, and scrutiny from many quarters that attend such activity. Our findings contrast sharply with statements made by some proponents of reform in current science education about how science should be taught. They suggest, for example, that

> [r]elevance [i.e., connections to real-world phenomena] may well be a key component of good motivation, but practical problems are often very complex, and variables identified are almost impossible to isolate or control. Student interest in personal or societal problems is highly individual, and group learning in a classroom setting appears very difficult. The range of problems, issues, and concerns could easily spread into areas beyond the natural sciences, leading to a blurring of distinctions in areas where such distinctions are very important, such as between science and technology, or between science and philosophy and religion. (Aldridge 1992, 18)

In our cases, women's interests were engaged in places where "blurred distinctions" were common.

In contrast, other studies have found that women rarely participate or succeed in the more narrowly controlled and more private spaces of conventional classrooms, laboratories, or university research teams. Significantly, participants in IGC, the innovative genetics class—our most controlled and conventional site—came to use knowledge and develop identities in ways that most clearly reproduce the hegemony of elite science, including the exclusion of girls' distinctive interests or concerns. This was less true in the other three sites.

In the other three sites, we found evidence that science-related information was being debated and acted upon more expansively (i.e., with respect to competing social, economic, or political interests) than in IGC. We found evidence that opportunities to use science in relationships with other nonscientists—particularly to convince nonscientists of the value of a specific position on a public issue—seemed to be more compelling contexts in motivating women to develop science-related interests than are conventional academic opportunities. We also found evidence that opportunities to use expertise in publicly meaningful ways were appreciated more by women than by men. Finally, we discovered that even women not previously interested in science (e.g., the nonscientists in CC) could be motivated to learn more about it when the conditions of their work required public performances to convince others of the value of a scientific position.

Thus it appears that women are well-represented and do relatively well in places where the meanings of *science* and *being a scientist* oppose, in specific ways, the meanings characteristic of elite science. Although each of our less-conventional sites relies in some way on findings or evidence from elite science (thus each site can be viewed as "within" hard science, like the environmental biology program discussed in chapter 2), each one is also characterized by activities, meanings, and relations of power that are distinctly counter to ("against") those in elite science. In elite sites and the genetics classroom, *science* means controlled, experimental, rational problem-solving performed by dispassionate and apolitical scientists. These scientists exercise power through networks of other scientists, many of which are supported by large, well-financed corporate, national, or global interests. In our three less-conventional sites, science may be a form of teamwork in which technical information is organized, a form of advocacy in which academic facts are used as background information, or a form of surveying, analyzing, and talking about real-time data. Scientists may be people who devote time and attention to using science in immediate, politically and socially meaningful ways. Power is exercised through networks that include many nonscientists and are supported by smaller, more financially precarious, and more local concerns. Although the three less-conventional sites differ in their specific activities, understandings of the terms *science* and *scientist*, and networks of power, each one gives time, space, and important identities to people who engage in immediate, politically contingent, and socially relevant science-related activities. In this shared characteristic, they differ substantially from elite science sites and the genetics classroom we studied.

On the other hand, success in our sites entailed some troubling oversights and compromises for women. In the innovative genetics class (IGC), successful girls, like successful boys, were those who conformed to the expectations of the curriculum and the classroom. In this case, conforming meant participation in practicing (i.e., learning) the forms of knowledge, the set of tools, and the way of being a scientist that could connect a person to the widely dispersed, relatively impersonal, but intellectually powerful world of the hard sciences. Although many of the girls in IGC participated in genetics in this way, some consistently did not—a fact that the teacher and researcher missed. In addition, no attention was given to the social realities that may present obstacles to girls' continued participation in the hard sciences.

Yet, the kind of power afforded by the academic genetics practiced in IGC is not the kind that brings prestige to many young American women. In fact, when young women demonstrate such academic power, they are often denigrated for "acting (too much) like men." Further, the power that does bring prestige to young women—the power to attract an attractive romantic partner (Holland and Eisenhart 1990)—requires attention to social activities in ways that are made virtually impossible by the tight, greedy demands of intellectually powerful disciplines like genetics (or physics).

In the engineering design internship (EDI), female student engineers enjoyed an engineering niche that was much less interesting to men. This niche, which included proficiency in group facilitation, interpersonal communication, and public presentations, connected those who developed it to engineering experts and clients in important but less-prestigious relationships. While female engineering students appreciated the opportunity that EDI provided and worked hard to do well, male students eschewed it and gave more of their attention to the abstract and technical problem-solving work that characterized their other engineering courses and gained them more prestige at the university. In this manner, women and men could develop similar basic proficiency in engineering, yet come to view it and develop it in distinctly different ways, with different implications for their prestige and status in college and beyond. In this particular case, women (more than men) seemed to be orienting themselves to a lower-status form of engineering practice.

In the environmental action group (ELAC), women and men were motivated to learn more about science, and women in particular came to the organization already primed with a scientific bent. Unfortunately, the quality and quantity of the scientific information they found available and had time to use was poor. Any science interest or aptitude the women exhibited was squandered by the organization, which did not have the time, commitment, or means to further develop it.

Finally, in the conservation corporation, both women and men struggled with the sometimes competing demands of science and business that defined CC's practice. Yet, this context seemed to provide the strongest and most equal connection of women and men to science. Unfortunately, because of CC's small size and the precarious state of its financial base, very few men or women can have the opportunity for using and learning science there.

Thus, although our sites are, in some ways, impressive illustrations of women's success in science, and although our experiences at the sites challenge some conventional wisdom about how to promote interest in science among women, women's opportunities there are compromised in various ways. These compromises are built into our cultural-historical understandings of the organizational activities in which the women excel: Classrooms are for subject matter, not social issues; engineering and other disciplines depend on having both theoretical and applied workers; political action and advocacy groups must exist by public favor and privately financed support, and must do their best with whatever resources they can muster. But the effects of these organizational arrangements and understandings seem consistently, although differently, to limit the potential of women's contributions in science.

Our look inside the four sites allowed us to see how women come to participate in and grow better at forms of science practice that either reproduce the hegemony of academic science or differ substantially from it. We have seen, in the way academic science is "made" hard for women by the scope of its demands, how the organization of academic science can force women either to conform or to leave altogether. We have seen, in the way the engineering internship differentiated the orientations and preferences of women and men, how women can end up in low-status sectors of a high-status field. In the environmental action group, we have seen how, in a place that attracts women with relatively strong backgrounds in science, no one cares very much whether anyone learns more science. Only in the conservation corporation   a small, financially precarious place—did we find something approaching serious science *and* gender equity. Thus, regardless of the practices or meanings of science, the actual opportunities for women to engage in science in ways similar to men seem to be limited indeed.

Nonetheless, we hoped that a closer look at women's experiences in nonacademic science, especially as it was represented in the conservation corporation, might provide some clues about how to develop potentially powerful, science-related opportunities for other women. Unfortunately, as we looked more closely at the experiences of women in our sites, we discovered that, as in the genetics classroom, women's success and rewards at the other three sites came only insofar as they con-

tributed to the way work activities were already being and had historically been practiced. That is, the customary ways of doing *work* were
not up for grabs or open to debate. Women could participate in and
learn various ways of practicing science and do it well, but this success
came at a price, as the next chapters will show.

Part Three

Discourses and Struggles

For the staff women, then, participating at Renewal [an alternative health clinic], whether as a volunteer or an employee, meant they were working for a good cause with friends. . . . By doing work that had significance that went beyond the specific tasks themselves, the women felt they were doing good for others, outside of Renewal. They believed they had found a community of sentiment—like-minded people with whom they could work hard and have fun. . . . They valued their attachment to others, the feeling that they were one with a community of special people. From that perspective, the structure of Renewal was a superficial matter, something necessary for the outside world rather than something that had consequences for relationships on the inside. (Kleinman 1996, 98, 103)

However, communitarian philosophy as a whole is a perilous ally for feminist theory. Communitarians invoke a model of community which is focused particularly on families, neighborhoods, and nations. These sorts of communities have harbored social roles and structures which have been highly oppressive for women, as recent feminist critiques have shown. (Friedman 1991, 305)

Our work in the sites described in the preceding three chapters suggested that many of the women we studied had the same feelings as the women in Kleinman's study. They appreciated the opportunity to do what they perceived to be socially valuable work, in communities of like-minded individuals. It is interesting, therefore, to consider Kleinman's findings from her study of Renewal, an alternative health clinic (Kleinman 1996). We would have predicted (as did Kleinman) that this clinic, created to be an alternative to (existing within and against) conventional medical care, would offer women better opportunities than they would have in conventional hospitals or clinics. But this was not the case. At Renewal, Kleinman found, men and women reproduced an especially virulent form of the conventional gender hierarchy in medicine. Women who worked there were assumed to have no better career options; thus, their unpaid or underpaid activities on behalf of the struggling clinic were taken for granted and were not considered oppressive or exploitative. Men, in contrast, were assumed to have better career options and to have made a special sacrifice to work at Renewal; thus the extra efforts required of them were minimized and compensated whenever possible.

Kleinman was intrigued that members of Renewal could espouse such a strong commitment to the organization, criticize instances of discrimination elsewhere, and yet regularly enact gender inequality in their own workplace. She argues that in the way men and women in Renewal constructed the meaning of *alternative* ("doing something different" from mainstream practice that is based on a medical model of individual illness) together with the meaning of *legitimate* (having a rightful place in medical practice), they also defined different "gendered moral identities," one for men, and one for women. Men were viewed as people who had sacrificed lucrative medical careers in favor of a commitment to the ideals of alternative medicine; thus their presence and contributions were crucial to establishing the clinic as both "alternative" (the unconventional choice of those who are informed) and "legitimate" (staffed by "real doctors"). Women (including female doctors), in contrast, were viewed as people who did not have other career options and were not "real doctors"; their presence and contributions were valuable but not nearly so crucial to the clinic's legitimacy. Thus, women were viewed as people who made a less substantial sacrifice than men to join Renewal and were less crucial to the organization's success. Consequently, "good" women employees were expected to put up with poorer treatment than the "good" men who worked there. These moral identities masked gender and class distinctions according to which some people (professional men) were treated much better at Renewal than others (professional and staff women). When topics that might unmask these gender or class distinctions came up at Renewal, they were evaluated in terms of "individual expression," individual needs, opportunities to promote individual healing, and the need to maintain legitimacy in the eyes of the medical establishment. In this analytical context, discussion of structural inequality or discrimination was made nearly impossible. Like the lads in Paul Willis's study (1977), the women on Renewal's staff had some insight into how this system worked, but they lacked the authority or status (both as staff and as women) to bring about significant change.

Kleinman reviews other studies of alternative social movements, including the draft resistance, ecological, and animal rights movements. The authors of these studies report that gender inequalities were pervasive inside those movements, as they were at Renewal, despite rhetoric to the contrary. Other researchers have demonstrated that even women with prestigious credentials—lawyers and scientists—are treated as second-class citizens in many organizations (e.g., Pierce 1995; Rossiter 1995; Seager 1993).

In the next two chapters we take up, first, the pervasive "discourse of gender neutrality" that seemed to obscure gendered features of the places we studied (chapter 7) and then women's attempts or "struggles" to deal with workplace features that disadvantaged them (chapter 8). These chapters reveal how women and men together coproduced cultural forms and social practices that often—but not always—served to reproduce the gender *status quo*, even in places where this might not be expected.

Chapter Seven

Women's Status and the Discourse of Gender Neutrality at Work

The condition of Otherness enables women to stand back and criticize norms, values, and practices that the dominant culture (patriarchy) seeks to impose on everyone, including those who live on its periphery—in this case, women. Thus, Otherness, for all of its associations with oppression and inferiority, is much more than an oppressed, inferior condition. Rather, it is a way of being, thinking, and speaking that allows for openness, plurality, diversity, and difference. (Tong 1989, 219)

[E]quality cannot be achieved by allowing men to build social institutions according to their interests, and then ignoring the gender of the candidates when deciding who fills the roles in these institutions. The problem is that the roles may be defined in such a way as to make men more suited to them, even under gender-neutral competition. . . . The difference approach [to gender equality] insists that gender should not be taken into account in deciding who should have a job, but it ignores the fact "that day one of taking gender into account was the day the job was structured with the expectation that its occupant would have no child-care responsibilities." (Kymlicka 1990, 241)

Many of the women in the innovative genetics classroom (IGC), the engineering design internship (EDI), the environmental action group (ELAC), and the conservation corporation (CC) are undoubtedly impressive individuals who challenge some commonplace assumptions about where and how science or engineering is practiced, about women's interest in these fields, and about their ability to succeed in them. Most of the women we studied were doing significant and consequential work. They were included in various networks of scientific or engineering practice. They were listened to, rewarded, and promoted. They felt satisfied, valued, and competent.

On the other hand, women's experiences at these sites were diverse and did not necessarily match those of men. In chapter 3 we touched on this issue in our discussion of the girls who were unsuccessful in the genetics class. In that case, we speculated that commitment to the activities and identities of IGC could be more problematic for girls, especially as they faced pressure to participate in the social world of heterosexual romance that brings special prestige and status to so many young women. Other researchers also have found that the demands of "hard science" coursework and careers—which seem to require an almost single-minded orientation to work, with little time for a social life or other interests—are of greater concern to women than to men and are an important factor in college women's decisions not to pursue careers in science, mathematics, or engineering (Downey, Hegg, and Lucena 1993; Holland and Eisenhart 1990; Nespor 1994; Seymour and Hewitt 1997).

In this chapter we will demonstrate that although EDI, ELAC, and CC were generally known as good places for women, and although many women experienced them that way, women there faced work-related obstacles that men usually did not. This occurred because—to varying degrees—work norms in EDI, ELAC, and CC privileged "prototypical white male behavior." That is, the organizational expectations regarding commitment to work activities and identities favored people who put the priorities and demands defined by high-status work ahead of other social or personal interests, people who could do so because other interests were not salient, were not made pressing, or could be handled by someone else (e.g., a woman, a wife). In addition, these work activities and identities favored people who did not fear harm or scorn in public places. Thus women (and men) regularly succeeded in IGC, EDI, ELAC, and CC only insofar as they acted in ways that were consistent with already-established work norms that favored commitments and behaviors historically, socially, and culturally more available to white men than to women.

At the same time, however, participants in EDI, ELAC, and CC described and acted upon their work activities and identities *as if* they were gender-neutral—as if gender did not matter, or as if no important gender-connected differences were inherent in experiences, successes, or difficulties. Not only were the women (and men) quick to apply the label of gender neutrality to their situations, they strongly resisted suggestions that their work practices might not be gender-neutral (see also

Rhode 1997, for other examples of this denial of gender inequality in the United States). We will argue that in the contexts of our sites, gender neutrality is a socially and culturally constructed discourse, or way of talking and acting that gives meaning to what occurs. This discourse hides prototypically white male features of the work; confers legitimacy on women's professional contribution only when they act like men; makes discussion of women's distinctive issues virtually impossible; and nearly overwhelms the potential that Tong finds in women's otherness.

This, we believe, is an extension of the process by which girls and women acquire subordinate status in contemporary U.S. society. In middle school through college, young women are subjected to a discourse about attractiveness and heterosexual romance that competes with and often overwhelms discourses about schoolwork and careers (Eckert 1993; Holland and Eisenhart 1990). In many workplaces, women face a discourse of femininity that celebrates their contributions when they "act like women"—provide assistance, nurturance, and other forms of support traditionally associated with women (Hochschild 1983; Kleinman 1996; Pierce 1995; Rossiter 1982, 1995). In these contexts, women who try to act "professional" find it difficult if not impossible to measure up to being either a "professional" or a "woman." In our sites, women are diminished, ironically, by a discourse of gender neutrality that renders women's distinctive circumstances invisible, irrelevant, or inappropriate.

The Construction of Women's Status

In *Educated in Romance* (1990), Dorothy Holland and Margaret Eisenhart argued that college women's status was constructed primarily in their college peer groups. In the peer groups they studied, academic capabilities and career plans were virtually ignored, while social activities and heterosexual romantic relationships were emphasized. Especially for a woman, campus peer groups conferred status based upon her physical attractiveness and her ability to attract a male romantic partner. Academic prowess or ambitious career plans might be personally satisfying, but they were not widely noted by peers. Women who wanted to develop academically, or prepare for careers during college, *and* who also wanted to enjoy friends and status had to find ways of reconciling the often competing demands of academic identity and gender identity.

For the most part, the women Holland and Eisenhart studied resolved these competing demands by keeping the two identities separate. On their own, or perhaps with the support of family, faculty, or other older mentors, some women pursued their academic and career identities, but often expressed disinterest in these identities when interacting with campus friends. Among friends, however, women acted as if they were pursuing gender identities. The women did not necessarily approve of this system; in fact, some complained about it. Most of them, however, found it expedient to behave this way because the pressure exerted by the peer system was so strong.

Ethnographic studies of elementary and secondary schools suggest that the college women Holland and Eisenhart studied were enacting a pattern learned much earlier. The separation of academic from social life is institutionalized beginning in elementary school, where academic coursework is cordoned off from nonacademic, "extracurricular" activities; school norms dictate that social business be conducted when schoolwork is not going on (LeCompte 1980; Sieber 1979). By the middle grades, while maintaining that academic work is or should be "gender-blind," schools further elaborate social differences by gender through the organization of numerous extracurricular activities (Eisenhart and Holland 1983). Roles in which girls support boys (e.g., cheerleading, homecoming court, bake sales) or perform in their shadows (e.g., girls' sports) abound, whereas the reverse is rare (Eder and Parker 1987).

Penny Eckert (1993) has suggested that the crux of adolescents' identity crisis is in making the transition from a normatively asexual community to a normatively heterosexual one. In the United States at least, the transition is accomplished by participation in what might be called "the culture of growing up." This culture motivates adolescents to adopt appropriate adult heterosexual discourse and behavior (Eckert 1993; Eisenhart and Holland 1983; McRobbie 1978; Willis 1977). Adolescent girls gain status with their friends by talking about boys and romantic relationships, by making themselves physically attractive to boys, and by doing things with a boyfriend. As Eckert points out, by acquiring status through characteristics associated with grown-up women, girls assume both a gendered (female) identity *and* the gendered subordination that goes with it.

In previous chapters of this book (see especially chapter 2), we reviewed recent literature suggesting various ways in which women in professional workplaces, including those in science and engineering, are pressured to reproduce traditional (and subordinate) gender roles at work. In addition, the popular and scholarly press is replete with articles about sexual harassment and gender discrimination in elite workplaces (Eisenhart and Lawrence 1994; McIlwee and Robinson 1992; Pierce 1995; Rossiter 1982, 1995; Yoder 1991). This body of work demonstrates that being perceived as a female or as a sexual object is consequential for women's status in elite workplaces, almost always to women's detriment.

In contrast, most of the women we studied dismissed such possibilities as irrelevant to them in their present circumstances. Instead, they celebrated their work sites as "good places" for women and steadfastly maintained that women were "equal to men" in the world of their work.

Nonetheless, in this chapter we will argue that the processes that relegate women to subordinate status were still present in the world of work into which women moved at the sites we studied. To do the work well and thus to acquire high status in the engineering design internship (EDI), the environmental action group (ELAC), and the conservation corporation (CC), the women had to behave *as if* they were prototypical men; they had to make work *the* top priority of their lives; they were expected to fit social and personal concerns into their lives as best they could, given the requirements of doing a good job at work; they had to work around the concerns or needs that prototypical men do not have. In pursuing status this way, the women pursued identities that depended on "acting like a man." Thus, to extend Eckert's metaphor of identity crisis, we would say that the crux of the identity crisis for contemporary young adult women is in making the transition from a normatively heterosexual community in which academic or work identities must be hidden or downplayed (as in high school and college) to a normatively egalitarian community (of professional work) in which gender identity is not supposed to matter, but does. In our three less-conventional sites (EDI, ELAC, and CC), practicing, talking about, or insisting upon gender-sameness, gender equality, or gender neutrality was part of the "cultural work" (i.e., construction of meaning) that women and men engaged in as they made the transition into the workplace. For these men and women, and for the institutions of which they were a part, this cultural work effectively masked prototypically male-oriented features of their workplaces, at least for a while.

In the following sections we illustrate how prototypically white male behavior and gender neutrality were manifested in EDI, ELAC, and especially CC. To understand this situation in the case of the engineering design internship (EDI), we must first step back from the immediacy of the design class itself.

Prototypical White Male Behavior and Gender Neutrality in the Engineering Design Internship (EDI) [1]

Recall that EDI integrates numerous features of engineering work that seem to be both valuable and appealing to women students: group work, professional relationships, and real-world applications (see chapter 4). In many ways, EDI is (and was partly designed to be) an alternative to traditional engineering coursework, which (for reasons discussed previously) may be easier for men than women to accept. But EDI is only one of six courses in the semester's curriculum, all the rest of which are traditional. In fact, in a subsequent analysis of degree programs at the school where EDI was taught, Tonso (1997) found that engineering curricula are even more "greedy" than Nespor reported for physics (1990, 1994); that is, they include many required courses, a large percentage of which must be taken in sequence and demand considerable time for solving problems outside of class.

When students were enrolled in EDI (and other design courses), they had to devote even more time after school and on weekends to their coursework. In this context, we found that men, but not women, complained about the extra and unusual demands of EDI, and tried in various ways to limit their involvement. In chapter 4 we heard from a man who used the library rather than trying to make more time-consuming personal contacts with clients or other resource persons. On Team A, both Chuck and Doug complained about how much time it took to call townspeople for appointments and how frustrating it was for them to play "telephone tag" with townspeople.

It also was more common for the men on Team A, especially Doug, to skip the EDI class, miss a group meeting, or fail to complete an assignment. For instance, Doug was on an athletic scholarship, and his commitments to his sport and out-of-season weight training always came ahead of the team's work. Franci was also on one of the athletic teams, but her commitment to sports was balanced with design-team work. Doug also thought nothing of missing a team meeting. He never notified teammates when he missed. In contrast, Franci came to meetings so she would not let down the team, even when she was sick. On one occasion when Doug slept in, Franci became noticeably irritated that he had cut class when the rest of the team had also had little sleep and could have benefited from sleeping in as well. She went into the hall and phoned Doug to insist that he get out of bed and bring photographs to the meeting so the team could decide which photos to include in their final report. Franci suspected that Doug would wait until the last minute to produce the photos and that, ultimately, she would have to drop everything and scramble to complete the photo attachments for their report. Chuck's behavior, too, seemed half-hearted. On several occasions, he offered to make calls or schedule meetings and then failed to do so.

In contrast, when the team faced deadlines, Amy and Jennifer increased the amount of time they spent on the design work. As the deadline approached and the professors asked students to fill in a schedule, Jennifer took over these arrangements, contacted the client, and scheduled the meeting. When the due date for the final report approached, Amy and Jennifer compiled texts from their teammates into one document and pushed teammates to attend a group-editing session at Chuck's apartment. Amy was the one who finally developed a means of surveying the town's architectural features, and Jennifer was the one who had the comprehensive knowledge to answer questions during the team's final presentation to the town. Thus, while Doug and Chuck took a casual approach to EDI work, the women on Team A took charge.

Tonso (1997) also found that the campus prestige system valued success in traditional courses considerably more than in design courses such as EDI. Prestige accrues for academic performance (completing problem-solving homework assignments accurately and on time, attending class, and getting near-perfect scores on exams) and for campus "leadership" (e.g., serving on campus committees related to student life, or being an officer of campus organizations, such as fraternities, sororities, student government, or student chapters of professional associations). Students with the highest grades and those who were visible as leaders in the social spaces occupied by professors and administrators were recognized by the institution and had more status on campus (see also Eckert 1989). In design classes, students motivated by prestige goals focus on acquiring the traditional markers of success. Thus graded products became the work worth doing, which in the case of EDI meant written and oral presentations. EDI's goals of learning teamwork and performing practical engineering fell outside the scope of the prestige system.

Thus, at least in the case of Team A, it apparently became the women's responsibility to see that the team's work was successfully completed, a responsibility which they accepted and which seemed to increase their interest, even as it added to their workload and diminished the workload for men in their group. Further, because of the prestige system on campus, as women devoted more time to design courses like EDI (and correspondingly less to traditional courses) and men did just the opposite, women had the greater opportunity to get better at low-status activities, while men had the greater opportunity to get better at high-status activities.

Despite these differences in work preferences and workload, Team A behaved *as if* each student should be, and was, equally involved in delineating the project, finding the resources to solve the client's problem, using the team's resources to develop a comprehensive remodeling plan for the town's historic buildings, and meeting the course's requirements. At no time did any student ever talk as if one person were doing more than another. They recognized that each student had "specialized" in a different area, but maintained that any one of them could have developed the same understanding had she or he taken on the same topic.

The inclination to consider everyone on the team as being the same extended to the assumption that everyone was equally safe in public places. One vivid example comes from a team visit by Amy, Doug, and Franci, during late January 1993, to the mountain town in which their project work was being conducted. As they prepared to return to campus, they decided that the team needed a map of the town. They drove to the tourist information booth to find one. Doug went into the information booth to get a map, while the others waited in the car. Doug took longer than Franci expected, and she became concerned about his safety. Talking to Amy, she said, "Someone will mess with him." Amy disagreed: "Someone as big as Doug? No one will mess with him." Amy thought Doug's safety was not an issue, because as a large, athletic male, he towered over his classmates. Franci said no more about it but sat in the car carefully watching the building and her watch. After Franci's repeated glances at her watch, Doug reappeared with a map and Franci breathed a noticeable sigh of relief. Doug had taken so long because, much to his surprise, the tourist information center did not have a city map handy. The man helping him went back and forth to a storage area and eventually found a map that served the students' purposes.

When the students talked about Franci's concerns during their team meeting a few days later, Franci received some kidding from the others for being "paranoid" (field notes, January 27, 1993). While Franci tried to argue that something *could* have happened to Doug, her teammates only laughed at her. But Franci's feeling remained, and her own discomfort in the mountain town was evident throughout the semester. Whenever she had to visit the town, she went with another student.

During an interview with Tonso in April, Franci did talk about her sense that she did not "belong" in the mountain town. One day she visited the town to survey some of the buildings. Although she went with a teammate, they surveyed separately. Here is what she said about being on her own during the building-by-building survey:

> Well, when I was first going around and surveying buildings and had the checklist, I kind of just walked in. I wouldn't say anything, I just walked in and kind of looked around, and the people looked at me. I could tell that they knew that I did not belong there. You can kind of sense that they have their regular customers that come in there all the time. They have regular people, [and] they talk to each other on the street. They know that I don't belong there. But I just walked in, and I would just sit there, and I would write notes. Someone would finally come up, and I would say "Well, I'm a student at [this college]." When I said that, they kind of perked up and went "Oh, okay, well she's not that bad; she's an engineer." Then I'd explain what I'm doing. So then it went better. But I don't know, they just don't, they seem like they definitely know what's going on in town, what belongs there and what does not. (interview: Franci, April 15, 1993)

Franci used her affiliation with the engineering college to construct a link between herself and townspeople. Yet, even with this advantage, she felt exposed and vulnerable in the town.

Franci's awareness of vulnerability brings to mind other situations where women's concerns might not match men's. Consider, for example, women's general hesitation to travel alone to unfamiliar areas or walk alone to their cars at night. At no time, however, did the team or the class validate Franci's concerns. Instead, the team, including the other women members, teased her about being "paranoid" and never took her concerns seriously, validating Doug's perspective that if he was safe, then everyone would be safe. The position that Doug and the other team members took reflects a perspective that is considerably more accurate, appropriate, and reasonable for white men than it is for anyone else in contemporary American society. This perspective denies the merit of Franci's circumstances; thus the team felt no need to develop a means of addressing her concerns. Consequently, she was left feeling *more* vulnerable than was necessary and was forced to handle her vulnerability on her own.

Students in EDI also disregarded profanity and blatantly sexist comments made by the male instructor, Professor Mason, or male students. Professor Mason's comments took three forms: mild profanity, semisexual humor, and violent metaphors. For instance, words like *damn, hell, shit, bullshit,* and *ass* liberally sprinkled the discourse, occurring over ten times in each two-hour class. In this setting, *I could not care less* became *Who gives a rat's ass?* and *I will have to invent meeting minutes since I didn't take notes* became *I'll pull some shit out of my ass* (fieldnotes, March 15, 1993). Of the instances of mild profanity attributable to individuals and recorded in the fieldnotes, all but one came from male students or the male professor. When men used this language in class, no one said it was objectionable: no one made any comments about it or had any evident nonverbal reactions.

Likewise, male students, but not female, participated in humor centered around semisexual double entendres. For example, during one of her lectures, Dr. Jarrett had difficulty when she attempted to focus an overhead slide image on the screen at the front of the room. Not only was the screen swaying in the breeze from the open windows, but the projector was too far from the screen—an attempt to make the small print as large as possible for the huge lecture hall. Only moments before, Professor Mason had lectured about creating legible overhead slides and "test-driving" the slides before presentations. This made Dr. Jarrett's fumbling all the more embarrassing. She told the students she was setting a poor example and advised them to "play with your graphics" before using them in a meeting with clients (fieldnotes, February 8, 1993). There was chuckling and eye-rolling among several male students, one of whom asked in a stage whisper, "Is that what you play with?" As the men laughed and made these remarks, the women near Tonso fidgeted in their seats, then sat up straight and tight-lipped, their eyes directly ahead as they actively ignored the men. The use of the words *teammates* and *team members* caused the same kind of classroom twittering among the male students; they found these references humorous. The women did not join these nudge-and-chuckle activities, but no one (except Tonso) seemed to notice or care; no one even mentioned, much less challenged, these comments. By these behaviors, Dr. Mason and the male students manifested a normative assumption that everyone was, or should be, equally comfortable with profanity and sexist humor. The differential use and impact of such behaviors went unremarked upon and unchallenged throughout the semester.

The assumptions that everyone was doing the same or an equal amount of work, that everyone was equally safe in public places, and that everyone was equally comfortable with profanity and sexist humor pervaded EDI. These assumptions of "equality" obscured any general awareness of the fact that women were taking considerably more responsibility for, and becoming more heavily committed to, EDI than men; that women were more vulnerable to harm (or fear of harm) in public places; and that women were silenced and ridiculed by the use of profanity and sexist humor in ways that men were not. In effect, these assumptions of equality allowed the EDI experience to be interpreted as gender-neutral when in fact it was not. The assumptions allowed faculty and students to ignore gender differences that have profound effects on women's experiences both in EDI and beyond.

Prototypical White Male Behavior and Gender Neutrality in the Environmental Action Group (ELAC)[2]

The assumption that prototypically white male behavior *is* gender-neutral had similar invidious effects on work practices in ELAC. The impressive figures for women's scientific literacy there (43 percent) stand alongside another, more sobering figure: 31 percent of women quit the organization before three weeks had elapsed, compared to only 16 percent of men. Thus, many fewer women than men experienced whatever learning opportunity the organization provided. We speculate that an important reason for women's higher drop-out rate was the organization's failure to deal with safety issues: how to handle being in an unfamiliar neighborhood after dark and how to deal with men at the residences being canvassed. These safety issues concerned some of the women but none of the men. When confronted with these problems, ELAC's directors (two of three were women) responded to the women who expressed concern with statements like, "You're probably safer canvassing than driving your car" (interview, July 22, 1992).

Although the canvass director (a woman) repeatedly stated that the canvass was safe, many women disagreed. Of the women who quit, half expressed safety-related concerns to the researcher.[3] Periodically, women canvassers would ask the director if they might canvass in pairs. Ordinarily, the request was refused. The director's reason follows:

> A team can slow each other down because they spend too much time chatting or goofing off. Another thing that happens is there's a lot of communism. Say one person makes quota; they go until they have enough money for both of them to make quota, and then they take the rest of the time off. (interview, July 22, 1992)

The director authorized canvassing in pairs only once during the study period, after hearing from several "doors" that gang activity was occurring in a neighborhood being canvassed.

While on the canvass, which took place from 4 p.m. to 9 p.m. every night, canvassers constantly had to make decisions that might affect their safety: whether to enter a house when invited in; whether to ask to use a bathroom in a private residence; where to take shelter in a summer storm; whether to accept rides, drinks, or food from strangers; and how to handle unpredictable dogs or people. In all these situations, women were fearful of accepting help from strangers but often had little choice if they were canvassing far from the crew car or from public facilities.[4] By late in the canvass period, it was always dark. During the study period, at least one woman canvasser was threatened with a gun, another with a knife, and one was raped.

Men, in contrast, found it easy and fun to spend time with strangers. They might eat something, watch a bit of TV, or play with a dog. As far as we know, no male canvasser felt threatened or harmed during the study; none ever talked about such an experience.

Women's concern about safety is strikingly revealed in the following vignette.[5]

A very bad thunderstorm approached the area in which I was canvassing. This is how the crew dealt with it. One male canvasser went into someone's house and watched TV with them. One female canvasser, the field manager, sat in the crew car with a male trainee. This is a description of what I did.

I looped back to Paragon [Road], and it is thundering, lightning, and hail the size of marbles is falling. I stop at a house on the corner. He won't give any money and will only sign a post card in support of the bottle bill, not the other two issues. He says he's been watching the storm gather and predicts I am going to get wet. Yes, indeed, his prediction came true. As I trudged toward a grocery store three miles away whose location I had earlier confirmed at several doors, I was drenched by rain, pelted with hail, and threatened by the lightning. Pretty soon, a car with a young couple pulls over and asks me if I want a ride. They want to put me in the back seat of a two-door. "No thanks," I say. I just can't ride with a stranger. After walking fifteen minutes further, a man with two children in his car pulls over. Okay, I'll take it. . . . After the storm abates, I decide to hoof it back to my turf. . . . After all, I have taken in only $36 and I need $70. . . . It is 8 P.M. It takes until 8:40 to walk back. I pass Paragon in hopes of finding Barcelona St., which is on [the field manager's] map. Then I discover that the map has been drawn backwards. I canvass three more houses. . . . It's nearly time for my pickup, and I need to get back to Paragon. I stand there with my clipboard, flagging down cars to get directions. They aren't inclined to stop. Two stop who don't know the neighborhood. An older woman and a man stop in a Jeep. They give me directions and offer me a lift. I take it—I am late and exhausted, and wonder why the man is wearing white gloves. They drop me off and seem concerned that no one is there to meet me.

Discussing women's safety concerns was discouraged at ELAC, as was expressing the thoughts revealed in this vignette. When women voiced their concerns, the director (a woman) or field managers (often women) impatiently stated that there was nothing to worry about because statistics were on their side. When a woman was threatened or hurt, she was asked not to talk to others about it, so she would not alarm them. In other words, women were discouraged from even mentioning the possibility of female-oriented safety issues. Although the threatened and abused women we knew did speak out, all but one quickly left ELAC. The influence of their experiences on the organization was therefore limited. No change was made in organizational practices to accommodate the women's concerns.

We do not believe that the authority figures in ELAC acted maliciously. Rather, they were people pressed for time and results in a demanding work environment that is not organized to recognize women's special concerns or to take them seriously. ELAC's directors had been taught canvassing procedures that were demonstrated to be effective in field tests by the national organization; the directors were taught that the success of the organization depended on using these procedures universally. In such an organizational climate, deviations from the norm to accommodate women's safety were made difficult, if not impossible, to justify. Believing that ELAC's established canvassing procedures benefited the organization and thereby its individual employees, that "statistics" were on their side, and that any one who was unhappy was free to leave, ELAC's authorities and others who stayed with the organization learned to be blind to gender differences that could affect women's experiences and opportunities more seriously than men's.

In summary, although ELAC seemed to attract women with a scientific bent, many more women than men left after only a brief time. We attribute women's high dropout rate to their concerns about safety and to the organization's inattention to these concerns. The organization's inattention seemed to derive from its commitment to a gender-neutral work environment; that is, to work-related activities and identities that disregard how women differ from men.

The Meaning of Prototypical White Male Behavior and Gender Neutrality in the Conservation Corporation (CC)

An extended illustration from our study of CC reveals in greater detail how prototypically white male behavior there was miscast as "gender neutral." This illustration is based on an analysis of all recorded instances of men's and women's talk about work and about gender at CC. Special attention was given to interactions of old-timers at CC with newcomers, on the grounds that norms regarding the local meanings of gender and work were most likely to be made explicit in the lore communicated when old and new employees talked together.

Talk about Women and Work at CC[6]

When the topics of women and work came up together in the talk between old-timers and newcomers at CC, the organization was portrayed by the old-timers as a good workplace for female scientists. Four ways of depicting women at CC make this image clear: (1) women are said to *like* working at CC; (2) CC is described as *unusually successful* at hiring and retaining women; (3) CC is said to be *sensitive* to women and their issues; and (4) CC is said to *treat women much better* than do other science-related workplaces. Together, these four tenets convey the impression that CC is a good place for female scientists to work. We consider each in turn.

Women Find CC an Attractive Place to Work

In numerous conversations at job interviews, introductions of new hires, and informal staff get-togethers, old-timers convey the impression that women like working at CC. For example, I overheard one male old-timer tell a female newcomer, "I'm not sure what accounts for it, but women like to work here" (fieldnotes, December 23, 1992). Another male old-timer told me: "This place is very female-oriented" (fieldnotes, September 7, 1993). A female old-timer described her impression of CC as follows:

> I am so impressed at the level of intellect, how dynamic it is, and the creativity in this office. I was *really* impressed with the caliber of people working here . . . and a lot of them are women, you know. I have to tell you that having so many strong women was really inspiring. . . . I *love* working at CC. (interview, November 22, 1993)

CC's Unusual Success at Hiring and Retaining Women

CC's image as a good place for women to work is supported by a reputation for employing many women, a reputation discussed both outside and inside the organization. In the wider conservation community and at nearby universities, CC is well known for hiring, retaining, and promoting women. For example, when I was searching for potential sites for conducting this research project, I was a rank newcomer to the professional domain of women in science and conservation science. I surveyed a number of university scientists and employees at environmental agencies to learn something about the territory I was about to enter. I told them I was interested in a group with a reputation for "serious science" and approximately equal numbers of men and women employees. CC was consistently mentioned as a good choice, because "they have an incredibly high number of women working there."

Once inside CC, I heard many accounts of this record. Insiders confirmed that CC is unusually successful at hiring and retaining women. Early in my study, one old-timer told me, "CC has hired an incredible number of women. At one point, we were two-thirds women" (interview, November 22, 1992). Later, another old-timer told me, "[One woman] was here for seventeen years; [another's] been here almost as long. Ann [a third] has been full-time for more than five years now. . . . It's kind of a surprise to find so many women at a place like this" (interview, November 22, 1993).

CC's Sensitivity to Women

People within CC also represent the organization as particularly sensitive to women's issues. The story of Ann is one example. Ann, an old-timer at CC, a botanist and program director, was portrayed as successfully doing her CC job while she was pregnant, and by taking her newborn daughter to work and out on field trips, she was able to work and be a mother at the same time. In the story, CC is depicted as considerate of Ann's need to be with her daughter and willing to accommodate her special requests. The story of Ann was four years old when I arrived at CC, and it was often told to newcomers as a means of demonstrating CC's sensitivity to women.

CC Treats Women Well

The women working at CC were adamant that the organization treats female scientists much better than other places do. One biologist, also an old-timer, told me the following about another environmental agency in which she had worked:

> I never *felt* my opportunities to advance were affected by my gender; but, you know, there just weren't many opportunities. And there were no role models. There were no women in higher-level positions there. . . . After about five years, I left and went to work for [another agency]. There I really had more male duties: firefighting, search and rescue—I got my EMT—and law enforcement. I was the only female in the department. There my experience was very negative with respect to being a woman.

When asked what was so negative, she responded,

> Mostly it wasn't directed at me, but just comments about women in general that were crude and showed a lack of respect for women. I left after two years. . . . Then [at a third agency], there was a lot more respect for women in public [at least]. But I supervised men who were older than me, and that was difficult. By then, I was older and more used to it, and [their comments] didn't really bother me as much. I felt relatively appreciated for my skills, but there's still that—what do you call it? . . . a glass ceiling. Things didn't look

good there for women. It took me thirteen years to get to a GS7, and that's not that high. And there weren't any women above my level. . . . [In contrast] CC evaluates you on a merit basis. I like that. (interview, November 22, 1993)

A newcomer scientist, talking about her recent experiences in graduate school, said,

I started out in the Ph.D. program. . . . Ph.D. students are expected to do basic research. I had a good relationship with my advisor, but not with the other [faculty] in the department. I was the first person, and first woman, to attempt a Ph.D. there without a basic science background. For the Ph.D.'s they want "only the best" [said derisively] to go out and make a name for themselves and make the department famous.

Eventually, she was asked to take a master's degree—her second—and not to pursue the Ph.D.:

I think there's a gender bias there. Half the women there either dropped out or scaled down their projects like I did; no men graduate students did that. My advisor has been there twenty-five years, and I was only his second female Ph.D. candidate. (interview, July 10, 1993)

Of the ten women I interviewed formally, every one told me that CC differed dramatically—and in a positive direction—from the norm in its treatment of women. In their judgment, the glass ceiling for women exists elsewhere, but not at CC.

The Meaning of *Good Work*

In their ways of talking about women and work at CC, both women and men, both insiders and outsiders, conveyed the impression that CC was a good place for women. However, the phrase *good work* conveyed culturally, or prototypically, white male characteristics. That is, the meaning of *good work* was defined primarily in terms of behaviors that are commonly and often implicitly identified with white men. Examples include being the primary breadwinner or being able to work without the interruptions of child-care responsibilities.

In the next section, we demonstrate that despite CC's reputation as a good place for women to work, its work norms did not take into account culturally female characteristics. Specifically, the "good work" norm disregarded the responsibilities associated with child-rearing and kin-care; it privileged culturally male characteristics instead.

Hard Work Is Expected

In general, when the women and men at CC talked about their work, they talked about how many hours of hard work it takes to do the job well. A norm of hard work and lots of it was clearly articulated. The statements below were made with pride, not as complaints. The first two came from old-timers; the third and fourth from newcomers.

> I'm the kind of person to spend too much time on work. . . . But, that's the way I am. . . . I'll probably make a hundred calls to [potential donors] between now [end of November] and the end of December [the calls are in addition to her regular full-time job]. That's just what you have to do. The way to deal with this [job] is to stay active all the time. (interview, November 22, 1993)

> During the field season, I was doing two field trips per day on the weekends and working five days a week in the office. I was commuting eight hundred miles a week. And I did that for four years. Finally, I asked, could I work a four-day week, with longer hours each day. [My supervisor] agreed. What he cares about is getting the work done; he doesn't care how many days a week I work. (interview, November 22, 1993)

> CC is famous for working people to death. . . . The first six months I was here I was working every Sunday and most Saturdays. Now, I do it less, but I still work at least one day of the weekend, especially during field season. . . . There's always just so much to do. (interview, July 10, 1993)

> For my own self-esteem, given that I'm hired for 60 percent time, I've decided I can't work more than forty hours a week, but I don't mind working those extra hours. There's a lot to learn about doing this job well. (interview, July 10, 1993)

These statements suggest that to command high status in the organization, employees are expected to meet a demanding schedule and to work with exhausting intensity. These expectations fit with the demands of a nonprofit organization dependent on public support: Employees must raise all of CC's operating expenses, and they must ensure the existence of their jobs and their causes by soliciting sustained external support for CC's projects. Thus, CC's employees, in addition to their scientific and other activities, must be continuously involved with the public and accessible at the convenience of potential supporters—often in the evenings or on weekends. These expectations also assume a prototypically male employee—someone who can give most of his time, during normal working hours and beyond, to CC's work and be flexible about it.

The Discourse of Gender Neutrality

Thus, CC's reputation as a good place for women to work seems to conflict with the culturally male characteristics that are embedded in the organization's expectations for good work. Yet CC employees do not see this conflict clearly; it is obscured by a discourse of gender neutrality, a way of speaking and behaving that focuses employees' attention on whether everyone is being treated "equally," and assumes or takes for granted the prototypically male characteristics of CC's workplace. The discourse of gender neutrality leads employees to think that if women and men are treated equally at work, then no gender discrimination can be occurring. This discourse is promulgated in three ways: in talk about hard work being expected of everyone; in talk that denies gender differentiation; and in talk about how well women measure up to CC's work expectations.

Hard Work Is Expected of Everyone; There Are No Gender-Based Distinctions

In the CC context, both women and men are expected to work hard. No one thinks the organization needs to adjust its expectations according to gender. As one woman explained,

> We expect the world [of the people who work here]; we expect them to do everything. We're in such a hurry to do conservation work— and we should be—that we need people who are incredibly self-motivating. It doesn't matter if you are male or female, but you have to be self-motivating. We sometimes ask too much of people. But, that's what we do. (interview, September 24, 1993)

Comments about gender discrimination at CC were routinely dismissed. When I asked about it, the women consistently told me that "gender doesn't matter here," as in the next two excerpts.

> As far as salaries and promotions go, I've never felt discriminated against. The salaries are just plain terrible, but that's not because of gender. (interview, November 22, 1993)

> Let's take a program managers' meeting: It's Donald, Bill, Beth, me, and Kelly [a woman], and Ann at those meetings [these are the program directors]. I'm never reluctant to say anything there. Both Donald and Bill are very open-minded. I can often predict what people are likely to say at the meetings. Donald, for example, is often trying to get everyone's viewpoint and then compile them into some plan or decision. But this is not tied to gender. (interview, July 10, 1993)

One old-timer scientist summarized her positive feelings about the organization's treatment of women by saying, "I forget I'm a woman here" (interview, November 22, 1993).

Women Take Special Pride in Measuring Up

The women at CC actually seem to take special pride in accomplishing tasks that they and others consider traditionally male. One told me in an interview, "In my job, I think it helps me to be a woman, especially a woman who's doing some good stuff in fund-raising, because there aren't very many [of us]" (interview, November 22, 1993). Others spoke as follows:

> As a woman in [this job], I deal with a lot of men, especially rural landowners, real estate people. I think it can be an advantage with rural landowners. I never thought they would take me seriously, [after they had been dealing with my predecessor, Frank]. Frank and I have very different styles. He could talk about male things—castrating bulls or whatever men talk about when they get together—but I can't do that. I don't know how, and it wouldn't be viewed as appropriate by the landowners. But they are very polite to me. I think [my] being a short woman . . . disarms them, disarms any anger they might feel toward CC [i.e., for taking land out of production or off the tax rolls to protect it]. They won't throw me off their land; they're too polite for that. They won't be hostile towards me. (interview, October 14, 1993)

> You know, when I was pregnant and went out to survey sites [for the presence of threatened species], I got onto a lot of properties I might not have otherwise. When those ranchers saw me, they were so nice and willing to let me take samples. Before I was pregnant, it wasn't always so easy. (interview, September 24, 1993)

Another woman, commenting on Ann during her pregnancy (above), said, "It's such a great image: of Ann down on her hands and knees with her stomach out to here [gestures with arms fully extended in front of her], crawling through some brambles to see some plant!" (interview, October 14, 1993)

In these ways of talking and others like them, employees at CC seem to be constructing women in the image of hard-working and successful men. Although the women say that they modify male techniques and exploit some features of their femaleness, the orienting image of good work is prototypically male—including considerable evening and weekend work; extensive travel around the state; fieldwork away from home; and making presentations that appeal to politicians, wealthy individuals, and business leaders at their convenience. At the same time, the model of good scientists and workers portrays everyone as committed to the priorities of the organization, everyone in the fray of conservation work together, and everyone fulfilling his or her share of the work load, *regardless of gender*. In other words, a discourse of gender neutrality pervades CC: although the "curriculum" of CC produces women and men who are *supposed* to be the same and interchangeable with respect to work, it also hides the prototypically male characteristics of the expectations of this workplace under a false veneer of gender neutrality.

Marty's Experiences

Given the track records of most workplaces employing scientists, CC is justifiably proud of its record of hiring, promoting, and retaining female scientists. Similarly, women who have become successful scientists at CC have accomplished something quite extraordinary. But this success comes at a cost to individual women and men who want to be, or must be, culturally female. Marty's experiences suggest how the meanings of gender and work and the discourse of gender neutrality affect individual employees of the organization. In her case at least, the effects were double-edged; the cultural system of gender and work both attracted her to CC and obscured the organization's prototypically male characteristics.

On the one hand, Marty was attracted to CC because she thought the organization was sensitive to women's issues. Marty's construction of this view began even before she interviewed for the job. In my first talk with her, which occurred during her first week on the job, she told the following story:

> The week before my interview I had a miscarriage. I called and told
> them [CC] about it, and they were *so* supportive. I thought right

> then: This is an organization that really cares about a person, that knows that there's more to life than work. I was really impressed with that. . . . When I had the miscarriage, at first I wasn't going to say anything, but then I decided to call them and let them know. (interview, June 7, 1993)

Marty explained that she made the call because she was upset, and she worried that her distress might affect her interview. Bill and Kelly interviewed her. Kelly said she'd had a miscarriage, too, and that was comforting to Marty. Bill told Marty that Ann had taken her baby with her to the field. Marty continued,

> We even discussed child care, and how Ann had taken her baby daughter on some field trips. I couldn't believe that we were talking about child care during the interview! I felt so supported, and I really wanted a supportive environment.

From this introduction to CC's sensitivity, Marty went on to develop a particular view of the relationship between being a career scientist *and* a mother at CC. When I later asked Marty what her family plans were, she said she had not given up her plan to be a mother and thought that she could manage a baby and this job.

> A lot of my work will be writing [reports of what the monitoring projects on CC lands were revealing] . . . and Ann took her baby into the field with her. . . . I'm an ecologist, and there's always a lot of traveling in this type of work. I expect it.

This statement and others made later by Marty suggest that she found appealing the image of herself as both a career scientist and a mother. This image was made real and possible for her by the story of Ann, and by the expressions of support for the image that she felt before, during, and after her interview.

However, Marty's view of CC's sensitivity to balancing motherhood and a career was unduly optimistic. Formal rules concerning maternity leave, together with CC's informal norms of hard work and gender neutrality, worked against any easy way for Marty—or other women—to be both a scientist and a mother.

For one thing, Marty was unaware at the time that CC had no formal child-care provisions, aside from federal requirements that pregnant women be given the same consideration as employees with any short-term "disability," and that child-care leave be granted on the same basis as other nonmedical leave. Thus, although Marty imagined CC permitting her to take at least six months off before and after her pregnancy, CC was not required to provide such leave. While she anticipated arrangements by which she could work at home, travel with her child, and alter her schedule to manage child-care for an even more extended period, CC was under no obligation to help her make such arrangements. Marty's needs were not necessarily beyond the organization's capabilities, as Ann's example suggested, but they also were not part of what the organization was required to do for its employees.[7]

In addition, the nature of CC's work routine, its corresponding norm of hard work, and its small size, left little room for others to take over informally for Marty, if she were absent or part-time for very long. To accommodate Marty, other staff members would have to work extra hours and more weekends, a feat not easy to achieve when everyone was already working so much.

Marty's prestige and status within the organization would also be at risk. As a new scientist at CC, she was trying hard to demonstrate her commitment to CC through long hours of extra work and a lot of travel around the state. Should she decide to take substantial leave, she could not simultaneously uphold the norm of hard work. Further, in expecting CC to support her needs as a mother, Marty could be seen to violate the gender-neutral discourse that everyone be treated the same. Unless the norm of hard work *and* the discourse of gender neutrality could be somehow suspended, resentment toward Marty and her privileges might ensue and threaten her hard-earned status in the organization.

Some might expect that in the case of pregnancy and child care—distinctly female issues—norms that privilege male characteristics would be overlooked or superseded. Such expectations seem reasonable regarding organizations like CC with a reputation for being sensitive to women's issues. But the evidence shows that this was not, in fact, the case. Consider, for example, a discussion of the possibility that men in CC might take time off to raise children. Participants noted that the difficulties confronting men who wished to coordinate the activities of a demanding job at CC with those of raising a child were the same or greater than those of women. Paternity leave is not federally protected,[8] even as a "disability," and of course CC's informal norms applied to men as well as women.

These considerations did not, however, lead to a discussion of how CC might meet the needs of fathers. Instead, employees suggested that because fathers, too, had problems managing work and family, the organization could truly be called "gender-neutral." In other words, they used work/family conflicts experienced by fathers as evidence that—and as a positive example of how—CC acted in gender-neutral ways toward mothers and fathers. From another perspective, however, men have difficulties coordinating work and family for the same reasons that women do: both are experiencing the effects of trying to bring culturally female characteristics into the workplace. But the fact that the employees at CC invoked the gender-neutrality discourse to celebrate the organization, and in so doing made conflicts acceptable, suggests that suspending the norm for Marty or anyone else would be unlikely.

Further evidence that CC's informal norms were not suspended when culturally female characteristics were at issue comes from Ann's own account of her experiences as a scientist and mother. Although Marty did not know it, Ann's own report of her experiences was quite different from the version others volunteered at Marty's interview. Ann told me that CC was *not* generally supportive of family life. For example, Ann thought her requests not to travel out-of-town and not to work on weekends were seen, at least by some, as unreasonable. She expressed dismay that while she tried to care for her newborn and work too, she could no longer stay on the cutting edge of her field. Colleagues stopped calling her for advice or consulting her when a difficult problem arose. Because she traveled less after her daughter's birth, she no longer was as well known around the state. In addition, she did not have time to read the latest articles in the relevant professional journals. She felt that her career suffered considerably more than that of her husband, who also worked at CC.

Ann had not anticipated these difficulties, and neither did Marty, who had never talked to Ann about them. The fact that Ann and Marty never talked together about their different versions of the story meant that they had no opportunity to interrogate the discrepancy or reconstruct a more nuanced alternative. As Marty planned for her future motherhood and career, she was unaware of the pitfalls that Ann had experienced.

How this lack of foresight and communication developed is not precisely clear, but two features of the CC workplace seem to support it. For one, Ann and Marty's different status within a busy organization—Ann was a very senior member; Marty, a newcomer—precluded a close friendship and focused their interactions on work-related, rather than personal, matters. Second, talk about gender distinctions and the possibility of gender discrimination was discouraged by the discourse of gender neutrality. As the illustrations presented earlier suggest, the discourse of gender neutrality was constituted by talk about men and women doing the same work and about women being able to do jobs traditionally held by men. When I asked about gender distinctions, I was told in no uncertain terms that "gender doesn't matter here." Marty had a similar experience. The following exchange between Marty, the newcomer, and a more senior woman at CC occurred during Marty's first month on the job.

> Newcomer: The man I work for is phenomenal [at treating me fairly]. I've gotten some negative impressions from some other people.
>
> Old-timer: Really? I'm surprised. I used to see a lot of things in terms of gender discrimination, but not anymore, not here.
>
> Newcomer: Maybe I'm wrong. (fieldnotes, July 10, 1993)

It appears that the discourse of gender neutrality made it unusual and unacceptable to raise the specter of gender discrimination at CC. By focusing employees' attention on equal treatment of women and men and on the ways women demonstrate that they measure up to male models, the discourse of gender neutrality discourages talk about gender differences and prototypically male characteristics of the workplace. The silence created around these topics leaves individual employees unprepared for what can happen if culturally female characteristics are enacted there.

Implications of the CC Case

In summary, CC is known as a good place for women to work and is proud of hiring, retaining, and promoting female scientists. CC is also committed to what it considers a gender-neutral work place. In addition, CC wants to be sensitive to its women employees and succeeds in creating this impression among newcomers. CC's reputation for treating women well made the organization attractive to prospective employees, particularly to women like Marty. The impression that CC created led Marty and others to believe that they could be successful scientists and at the same time raise a family. Unfortunately for them, CC's reputation was in conflict with demands of the workplace and the norm of hard work that included prototypically white male characteristics. Employees were unlikely to anticipate the conflict because the discourse of gender neutrality obscured the organization's culturally male characteristics behind a curtain of demonstrations that men and women were treated equally and could behave in the same ways. Yet difficulties stemming from the conflict emerged when individual women (or men) actually tried to manage the culturally female parts of their lives. Despite CC's assertions, its organizational lore and norms did not really assist employees to coordinate culturally male and female characteristics.

As Eckert (1993) and Holland and Eisenhart (1990) have suggested with regard to younger women, when women (or men) demonstrate characteristics associated with womanhood, those characteristics can be used to subordinate them. Although Marty and Ann escaped the pressures that divert so many women from pursuing professional careers at all (much less in science), they were being confronted with (and participated in) another assault on a balance delicately struck between work identity and female identity. Although women held identities as esteemed scientists in CC, their status became vulnerable if they decided to act like women.

In the context of CC's commitment to be a good place for women, offers of rewards for hard work, and espousal of gender neutrality, professional women like Marty and Ann were uncomfortably surprised by the vulnerability they experienced when they tried to do something culturally female. Their surprise was heightened in the context of frequent comparisons to more elite sites of scientific practice, including previous workplaces and school sites from which the women came. In contrast to these sites, where women said they were treated "unequally," that is, "poorly," women expected CC to treat them "well."

Just how much of a cultural (interpretive) "accomplishment" the discourse of gender neutrality is at CC was strikingly revealed when pregnancy became an issue. In the standard interpretation in U.S. law, special treatment by gender, or discrimination, is legal *only* when unequal treatment can be justified by reference to a clear and consequential gender difference; child-bearing is usually considered the quintessential example of a potentially justifiable difference (Kymlicka 1990, 240). Absent such a consequential difference, access, opportunities, benefits, and rewards are supposed to be gender-neutral, or gender-blind; that is, a special treatment of men or women is disallowed. At CC, special treatment for pregnancy and child-rearing have been culturally transformed into violations of the gender-neutrality discourse. To allow special treatment for pregnancy or child care for women or men, even though justifiably related to maternal or child health and welfare, has become a form of illicit discrimination. Resistance to *justifiable* special treatment becomes, in turn, acceptable and even championed under a discourse of gender neutrality that hides, and thus leaves untouched, the culturally sanctioned male bias in the workplace.

Although the intent of legislation and norms to assure equal treatment by gender is legitimate—to give women access to what men already have—it is not sufficient to overcome subtle yet invidious forms of gender discrimination. As the CC example suggests, uncritical efforts to achieve gender neutrality, defined as sameness, can work *against* women's interests. At CC, the discourse of gender neutrality—elaborated in the spirit of assisting women and used to support women's accomplishments—also contributed to discrimination against women by hiding the ways in which the CC workplace privileged culturally male characteristics and ignored or penalized culturally female ones. Although none of the women left CC during the period of study, the effects of the discourse of gender neutrality made it difficult for them to pursue their careers and have a family without suffering loss of prestige, forced choices between career and family, and guilt about not being a good colleague.

Discussion

Although EDI, ELAC, and CC can be proud of attracting and supporting women's participation in science and engineering, in all three sites the workplace was constructed as gender-neutral when in fact it was not. The women we studied in ELAC, EDI, and CC appropriated a discourse of gender neutrality by which they positioned themselves as "equal to men" in the world of their workplace. In so doing, features of the workplace that supported gender neutrality were made salient, while those that did not support it were hidden. However, measuring up to gender-neutral discourses was not as easy for women (as a group) as it was for men.

To become and remain successful, women had to engage in work activities in ways that assumed they did not have the traditional responsibilities of womanhood or any special needs for support or personal safety in public places. Thus, while women were "empowered" by access to science, *they were not necessarily enabled to take charge of their own gendered lives or to express culturally female characteristics.* They were not attaining what Nel Noddings (1990) would call a "second-generation" equity achievement. Noddings argues that "first-generation" equity for women enables them to gain the knowledge, credentials, and positions that men already have. Second-generation equity enables women to express their distinctiveness as women without penalty to their knowledge, credentials, or positions.

We believe that the discourse of gender neutrality has become a powerful representational tool in a "politics of prestige and safety" that obscures the need for second-generation equity. It is a politics made necessary by the pervasiveness of work norms that are called "neutral" but favor prototypic men and threaten women's prestige and continued involvement in science, engineering, and other workplaces, whether they try to bring female-based experiences (e.g., fears of physical harm) to the organization's attention, or whether they try to enact culturally female behaviors in the context of work. This politics develops as women and men are encouraged to use, and themselves appropriate, the discourse of gender neutrality to describe their work situations. As they do so, features of the workplace that disadvantage or discriminate against women (e.g., the denial of physical safety; the forms of jeopardy to one's prestige) are obscured, and the needs and understandings they might express or demand because they are *women*, are ignored.

As the women in our sites participate in this discourse, they are supporting and blending with—that is, they are "learning" to reproduce—the gender status quo in which women's issues and concerns are subordinated to men's. Most of the successful women we encountered did not admit to experiencing the threats to their status and prestige, and when confronted with such threats, they often denied that the threats were either gender-related or serious. This situation leaves little or no space for identification, articulation, or activism based on gender-related critiques of science or the workplace. It closes off opportunities or reasons for women to talk or think about their problems as common or shared, to develop a shared critique, or to act in concert for change. In the main, women's involvement in various forms of science- or engineering-related practice, together with a discourse of putative gender neutrality, created the conditions for the women to gain (learn) more about science or engineering, to feel that they were treated well, and, in turn, to accept (reproduce) professional work in its dominant form. However, as we will see in the next chapter, there were a few women who attempted to alter this situation.

Chapter Eight

In the Presence of Women's Power: Women's Struggles at Work

The culturally enmired subject negotiates its constructions, even when those constructions are the very predicates of its own identity.

The injunction *to be* a given gender produces necessary failures, a variety of incoherent configurations that in their multiplicity exceed and defy the injunction by which they are generated. Further, the very injunction to be a given gender takes place through discursive routes: to be a good mother, . . . to be a fit worker. . . . The coexistence or convergence of such discursive injunctions produces the possibility of a complex reconfiguration and redeployment. . . . There is no self that is prior to the convergence or who maintains "integrity" prior to its entrance into this conflicted cultural field. There is only a taking up of the tools where they lie, where the very "taking up" is enabled by the tool lying there. (Butler 1990, 143, 145)

The cost of dissent was high for the women at our sites as they learned "good worker" identities and as they took up the discourse of gender neutrality. For women to argue for special consideration *as women* would threaten their prestige and status as good workers in the organization or group. Further, it would undermine their belief in the legitimacy of what they had accomplished. Like the women in Kleinman's alternative health clinic, a gendered critique of the workplace would have thrown their identity into serious question. If the organizations were not really "better places for women," knowing that this was so would undermine the significance of their decision to join and their success there. Knowing that the organizations were not, in fact, gender-neutral would undermine the women's sense of satisfaction in what they had accomplished and what they might achieve in the future. For many of the women we studied, such analyses were simply unthinkable.

But not all the women in our sites passively took up the practices, identities, or discourses made available to them at work. They did not always simply accept organizational practices, expectations, or norms. Sometimes they voiced complaints and critiques of what was available to them. Occasionally they consciously tried to produce alternatives; at other times, they seemed to act, without clear direction, out of what Henrietta Moore calls simply a "knowledge of how to proceed" (1994, 82), and in so doing, they caused some changes. These actions, whether conscious or not—actions that might alter the status quo—are the focus of this chapter.

The Meaning and Outcomes of Struggle

Since Willis's (1977) study of the lads, it has been common to assume that attempts to oppose dominant structures (e.g., schools) or cultural forms (e.g., the myth of meritocracy; the discourse of gender neutrality) were likely to produce ironic reinventions of them. When the lads brought behaviors such as smoking, drinking, boasting of sexual exploits, and work slowdowns to school, they opposed the efforts of teachers to define and control their behaviors. However, their oppositional behavior also left them unprepared—without the academic background, educational credentials, or normative expectations—to do anything other than join the working class. Thus, their opposition to school, mediated by working-class male identity, eventually led them to reproduce their position in society. Face-to-face use of gender- and class-related identities that oppose or resist a locally oppressive institution (the school) gave the lads alternative subjectivities to take up with pride. At the same time, however, this production of their own valued identities hid from the lads' subjective view their simultaneous enactment of working-class identity and its attendant subordination in a class-based society.

Extending Willis's work, Dorothy Holland and Margaret Eisenhart (1990) found that college women who were bored with or disinterested in academic work often took up participation in a campus "culture of romance" instead. As a consequence of their rejection of academic work, the women learned to value themselves primarily in terms of romantic relationships with men; they learned how to be romantic partners, not career partners. Their pursuit of romantic relationships drained time, energy, and commitment from academics and career, and left the women best prepared to defer to their partner's career plans, to marry,

and to take the kind of low-status, low-paying jobs that support or accommodate men's career needs. In other words, participation in the
culture of romance eventually led women into historically female positions of social and economic subordination. The women's use of romantic identity as a source of pride and status that could compensate for the
day-to-day tedium of schooling hid from their view the simultaneous
reinscription of women's subordination.

Something similar seemed to happen in our genetics classroom, IGC.
The Watson group of previously unsuccessful girls was not interested
in science as presented in school (even when improved in ways consistent with current proposals for reform in science education). Despite
reforms that seemed to work for other kinds of students, the interests
of these previously unsuccessful girls apparently lay elsewhere: in working out details of physical appearance and social and romantic relationships. Like many of the women in Holland and Eisenhart's study, the
Watson girls "got over" (i.e., got through) their schoolwork by doing
a minimum of science and spending most of their time on other things
that interested them more. Like Willis's lads, the Watson group "resisted" the efforts of the school to enlist their investment in IGC (an
arena that could be considered "male"). But in the *way* the Watson girls
resisted—by focusing their attention on attractiveness and romance and
not succeeding in school science—they reinscribed the gender hierarchy of male involvement and female disinterest or subordination that
characterizes the dominant discourse about science. Without consciously doing so, the Watson group behaved in a way that reproduced
the dominant representation of science and of being a scientist as "not
for women," and that locates women's interests elsewhere. Thus the
Watson girls and the lads both reinscribed a social hierarchy and its
associated characteristics. In both cases, the youth's actions were aided
by school personnel who did not recognize what was happening, did
not know what else to do, or did not care.

We wondered whether the same would be true for the women in
our other sites. We wanted to know how the women responded to the
dominant identities and discourses made available in these settings. We
wondered what discontents or critiques the women expressed about the
sites; what struggles they faced to define themselves, find a niche for
themselves, or express their views as they participated in the sites; and
what effects these discontents, critiques, and struggles had on the organizations. To pursue these interests, we concentrated on the ways peo-

ple talked about their struggles "to be themselves" and voiced complaints about their circumstances (see also Holland and Eisenhart 1988).

We will show that the women's efforts at change were few. In the engineering site, EDI, the women mostly ignored the gender differences or disadvantages they faced. This is consistent with the discourse of gender neutrality discussed in the previous chapter. In the environmental action group, ELAC, the women who stayed also seemed to learn to ignore gender differences. In ELAC, women's most potent form of resistance was to leave the organization. Only in CC, where the women were slightly older and the pressures to behave in culturally female ways more salient, was the potential in their presence clear. This is a sad commentary, we think, on how desperately young women want to fit in at sites of historically male privilege, how insecure they are about "sticking out as female," and how little they realize the arbitrariness of the things that disadvantage them. On the other hand, we will suggest that dismissing the transformative potential of the women's efforts, however small, is a mistake. If women were not present in these sites at all, their potential would be much diminished, if not nonexistent.

The Engineering Design Internship, EDI: "I Hate for Them to Notice"

As noted in chapters 4 and 7, we were struck by the fact that the women at EDI did not seem to recognize, at least explicitly, that they embraced and took responsibility for the design work considerably more than the men did. As in other situations when gender differences or biases came up in EDI, there was little serious discussion of them. Both women and men brushed aside blatantly sexist comments as idiosyncratic and irrelevant to their educational experiences. When women wanted to do one thing and men another, preferences were not interpreted by the women in gender terms.

One clear exception to this pattern arose, however: discussions of what to wear. In these discussions, women did not ignore the implications of gender difference, as is evident in the following excerpt from Tonso's fieldnotes about EDI:

> As the student teams prepared for their first client meeting (week 2), they were told to wear "professional dress," but the professors' advice referred only to men's dress clothing—slacks, jacket, and tie; further advice was given about keeping one's jacket on if the client kept his on. However, this directive was entirely too vague for the

women students, and considerable team time was spent negotiating the women's professional dress for all occasions and the men's professional dress for "working" site visits. When one of the male students suggested that they "look nice, but not a suit and tie," one of the female students added "or a jacket and skirt."

Although the professors implied that all client meetings and site visits required the same professional dress, the students decided to modify their attire to fit different situations. For all indoor presentations and on-site tours (requiring only walking through town and talking to their client or to business owners), the students decided to wear their "best" clothing. For the men, this would mean a suit, tie, and dress shoes and, for the women, either a skirt and jacket or dress, nylons, and low-to-medium heels. However, for on-site "work trips," especially the building-by-building survey, the students decided on more casual clothing, even jeans and T-shirts, for everyone. (fieldnotes, January 20, 1993)

But this was not the end of the discussion; the dress-code extended beyond the simple "what to wear" issues. During the team's discussions about the attire for their first field visit, Franci wanted the team to leave for the town at 10:15, instead of immediately after her 9:00–9:50 class. Leaving later would allow Franci to go to class and then return to her dormitory and change into a dress, instead of wearing a dress to class. She remarked that "everybody hassles you" when you wear a dress to class. She was adamant about this, saying, "I hate for them to notice that I am wearing a dress." Doug disagreed with her. He thought that "it's not a big deal. Everybody knows you're in [this class] or have an interview." But the group was persuaded that Franci's needs were important, and they adjusted their travel plans to accommodate her (narrative adapted from Tonso 1993, 56–57).

With respect to clothing, the women and men actively negotiated what constituted professional dress within the group and eventually modified the professors' standards to meet different situations. Women like Franci recognized the need for modifications and argued for them within the group. Although her modifications may seem modest, arguing for them was brave in a context where "sticking out" as a woman goes against strong institutional norms. Certainly Franci's purpose in requesting these modifications was to "fit in" in the larger contexts of school and professional work, but to accomplish her goal, she had to stick out as a woman in the immediate context of her team and stick to her position in the face of Doug's attempt to dismiss it. Franci's effort is a small—but, to her, very important—challenge to norms that disadvantaged women in EDI.

Trying to Be Safe in the Environmental Action Group, ELAC

On the canvass and away from the glare of the organization's directors, some women in ELAC did find small ways to address their concerns about safety. One field manager tried to make certain that female crew members always had a male counterpart nearby. Another assigned women to canvass near the crew car or picked them up first at the end of the evening. However, as in EDI, these modifications were small, usually worked out only in individual cases when a woman complained, and never grew into changes that affected the organization in any systematic or institutionalized way. Women's most effective means of handling their concerns about safety was to leave ELAC. Perhaps because the job was often perceived as temporary, paid poorly, and because the organization was so categorically dismissive of anyone who felt unsafe, women who recognized the threats found it relatively easy to leave.

Kleinman's study of the alternative health clinic, Renewal, also included very few examples of women who criticized the organization and then stayed in it. Like ELAC, Renewal paid its employees very little (sometimes nothing at all for weeks) and dismissed criticism of gender inequalities, and women who recognized these problems and failed when they tried to improve their circumstances simply quit. In these circumstances, women exercise personal power by dropping out or getting out of difficult or abusive situations. Their decisions are no doubt good ones for them, but they do not (or have not so far) affected the organizations in which these women hoped to work, learn, and succeed.

Struggles in the Conservation Corporation, CC

Despite this discouraging picture, we did find two examples of more profound organizational change brought about, we believe, by the presence of women. Both occurred at CC.

Marty's Struggle to Work and Be a Mother at CC

Much of the story of Marty's struggle to work and be a mother at CC was told in chapter 7. We already know that if Marty acts on her desire to be a mother, she will risk her prestige and status within the organization. As a new scientist at CC, she was trying hard to demonstrate her commitment through long hours of extra work and much travel around the state. If she decided to take considerable leave, she could not simultaneously uphold CC's norm of hard work. Further, in expecting CC to support her needs as a mother, Marty would violate the gender-neutral norm that everyone at CC be treated the same. Unless the norms of hard work and the discourse of gender neutrality could be suspended somehow, resentment toward Marty and her privileges could ensue and threaten her hard-earned status in the organization.

Realizing this, Marty did not surrender either her family plans or her career plans. Her situation is similar to one described by Engeström (1993) in his study of medical doctors and their patients. Engeström's analysis focuses on doctor-patient interactions and the contradictions or discoordinations that emerge when the problem presented by a patient does not match the conventional tools for diagnosis at a doctor's disposal. These contradictions or discoordinations are seen as the driving force behind disturbances, innovations, and change in a system. A patient who presents a "problem," that is, names a problem that does not match the doctor's definitions or categories, introduces a (small) force for change in the medical system. When patients continue to do this even when doctors try to overrule them, their actions may eventually result in a creative contribution to (a change in) the system—for example, by forcing doctors into a new way of thinking about a disease or treatment. In Engeström's example, the patient's stated problem—nausea that the patient felt could be caused by lingering effects of neck surgery—is reinterpreted by the doctor as "heartburn." When the patient disagrees by referring to his surgery, the doctor must suggest something else. To the extent that the patient persists in his interpretation, the doctor is forced to offer new and different solutions to the problem.

In a similar way, the protest songs of the Nepali women described by Holland and Skinner (1995) are disturbances with creative possibilities. In their account, women's songs, produced for the annual Tij festival, tended to be structured and presented in familiar ways, yet they sometimes contained novel elements, arising from the individual songwriter's creative use of existing cultural forms, her unique personal experience, or changing sociohistorical conditions. When the village women performed their songs publicly, they added some new and radical elements to the prevailing personal and collective ways of thinking and acting in the world.

By telling her story of wanting a family and a job, Marty was creating such a "disturbance." When Marty told this part of her story, she was creating an opening for change in CC, as Ann had apparently done before her. Other women soon followed their lead. Before the end of Eisenhart's study, three (of six) female scientists at CC had become pregnant and were planning to continue working full-time after their babies were born.

Because the story of how Ann had a baby and managed to continue to work was widely told at CC, Ann had become a kind of cultural icon for younger women in the organization (see Eisenhart 1995a for more details). Her story emboldened them to pursue a course (motherhood *and* a career) that the organization did not (formally) encourage or enable. And although Ann's story was not a happy one for her, and did not itself require the organization to change to meet the needs of mothers, the fact that it inspired more women in the organization to consider motherhood created more pressure on the organization to deal somehow with this woman-centered issue.

It is interesting to compare Ann's position as a cultural icon to the position of Russian women who were activists in the Russian populist movement of the 1870s and 1880s, as reported in a recent historical analysis (Engel 1993). Despite the differences among the many women who were involved in this movement (Engel estimates about six hundred), they were widely portrayed as women who gave up family, personal life, and relationships with men in order to fight for the populist cause. The image of the woman completely devoted to a cause—based on the example of the populist activists—later became an icon manipulated by the Soviet regime to symbolize the kind of people desired in the Soviet state. Of course, this later use of the women populists as cultural icons did not occur by their own choice and captured only some of their characteristics and commitments. Nevertheless, through this imagery these women had a profound effect on the thinking and behavior of women who lived after them. The effect has persisted into the present. Contemporary Russian women are strongly resentful toward these cultural figures, who are now associated with the Soviets and represent a renunciation of distinctly female characteristics and commitments.

Similarly, Ann's own report of her experiences differed from the storied version. Nevertheless, the public version of Ann's story has been added to the culture of CC, and it seems to enable younger women to envision an alternate future within the organization. Thus we can view Marty's and Ann's stories as having small but potentially important effects on the cultural system in which they work. Regardless of their "accuracy," their stories seemed to inspire and motivate women who followed them in CC to take actions that put pressure on the organization to change. It is not unreasonable to expect that the experiences of three new mothers in a small organization will change the conversation in and about CC in ways that help at least some people to be both scientists and mothers.

Another important struggle occurred at CC during Eisenhart's time there. This one did not focus on women's issues, but women played an important part in a struggle that developed over the national organization's decision to adopt a new, more "scientific" procedure for establishing the relative importance of sites that were candidates for CC's protection.

A Representational Struggle in CC

About halfway through Eisenhart's eighteen-month study of CC, the organization held a series of meetings to introduce the staff to a new procedure for calculating the relative priority of conservation sites. The new site-ranking procedure (SRP) was developed by CC's national office to enable state offices to make more systematic and "scientific" decisions about selecting and prioritizing sites. Staff members were eager to learn how their current high-priority sites (identified less systematically) would score in the new SRP. Although no one at CC had used the new SRP, the staff expected it to be a better means of selecting sites than their old procedures. Thus they expected that the SRP would play a major role in constructing the organization's annual work agenda (by determining which sites CC would work to protect in a given year), and strengthen its public discourse about environmental protection (by supporting CC's claim that its work was "science-driven"). This is not exactly what happened.

The Site-Ranking Procedure in CC

The SRP is a formal system, developed and mandated (after a phase-in period) by experts at CC's national headquarters. The SRP generates scores computed from four variables: the "biodiversity" of the site, the threats to preserving it, the requirements of managing it, and the urgency of the need for action. Biodiversity scores (B-scores) are rated on a scale of 1–5 according to the number and quality of species (known at CC as "elements") that are rare globally or in the state. B1, the highest biodiversity score, is defined as "the only known occurrence of any element, the best or excellent occurrence of a G1 (globally most rare) element, or a concentration of . . . occurrences of G1 or G2 elements." Protection threats, management requirements, and urgency are also rated on a scale of 1–5, with 1 being the highest protection threat, management need, or urgency. Once the ratings for a site have been determined, composite site scores are calculated, compared, and rank-ordered. Sites with the highest rank-order are supposed to become CC's highest priorities for conservation during the following year. Component ratings are reviewed and updated once each year.

The SRP is a science-oriented, technically precise, but nonetheless socially produced, means of defining and structuring physical spaces and so-called natural phenomena (Helford 1994). It mathematizes and universalizes space and nature in ways similar to the representations in other privileged discourses (e.g., see Nespor's 1994 discussion of the privileged discourse of physics, and our discussion in chapter 3 of the discourse of genetics). Like other high-status representations, the SRP can name and bound targets of action for the organization, guide its public relations appeals, and provide a yardstick for accountability that transcends local CC offices and their contingencies. The SRP is therefore in a class of powerful representations that are likely to be viewed favorably by people at CC's national headquarters.

The following excerpt from Eisenhart's fieldnotes of October 5, 1993, reveals what happened when the first results of using the SRP to evaluate familiar sites were introduced to CC's staff.

> Today was long-awaited. Today we would finally hear the results of the first use of SRP on the natural history data that CC scientists had been collecting for nearly twenty years. Voices and faces were excited and animated as about fifteen of us filed into the room. Tom, hired a year and a half ago to implement SRP, begins the meeting.

> Tom: After a year and a half, we finally have [SRP]. I think we're a year late, but now we finally have it. [Claps and whistles from the group.]

> Tom laughs, then goes on to explain that the purpose of today's meeting (and those to follow) is to review the [biodiversity] rank-orders and their component scores "to make sure that we have the best and most important things covered in our conservation sites."

[Changes would come from CC scientists' current knowledge about rarity and quality of species and habitats—knowledge that might not yet be in the database that generated the rank-order based on B-scores.]

Bill immediately asks for a definition of what Tom is calling a "conservation site."

Tom: Yes; let me give you some simple definitions. There are "survey sites"—the name given in the field by the person doing the survey work; "conservation sites"—places we've identified as having conservation significance and which may stand alone with a single element occurrence or have several elements. . . . This [the definition of sites] is your "ecosystem tool." . . .

[One thing you should be aware of is] we're finding that we've been overranking many elements—they are not as rare as we thought they were. We're finding them in Utah, Montana, and other places. This will mean lowering the B-ranking on some sites. . . .

[Our work here] is intended to drive next year's, and the next decade's, priorities for [CC] conservation. It's intended to allow us to protect things before they are lost.

Our plan today is to go through each site and have everyone tell whatever they know about protecting it. [This means adding up-to-date information about P (protection), M (management) and U (urgency) to the database.] OK, number one, Anderson Canyon. [Sites are discussed in alphabetical, not rank, order.]

Ed: Wow, this looks like a great one to protect. Let's do it. [A few laughs; Anderson is the target of CC's current capital campaign—a one-time campaign to raise money to purchase and protect a high-priority site, and thus it is already being protected. Tom goes right on, barely acknowledging Ed's joke.]

Tom: Now the rating on this [Anderson] will go down some because the piñon forests are more widespread than we originally thought. Forest rating will go down to a G2.

Ed: Let's not do it until the capital campaign is over! [A few snickers]

Tom: It's still gonna be a good place to save. What about threats, Ann?

Ann: Subdivisions; it's happening right now.

Bill: As we speak, this very day.

Tom: [to Ann] P1? [Ann nods.] Bill, what about management?

Bill: [seems uncertain how to answer] Not a big threat; people are a threat, because we're going to open it to the public.

Tom: I'd say M2 from what I'm hearing. . . . [Observer note: What was he hearing? Bill didn't actually say anything about management needs.]

Ed: Here's a question for us. We could spend all of our efforts rounding out this preserve. But there's lots of [threatening] activity in the area. One of our questions is, Should we pursue trying to do more there or cut our losses, or what? [Tom doesn't pursue Ed's question. He moves quickly onto the second site. Ed says nothing.]

Tom: Arlington Forge. Does anybody know anything about this site?

Ann: [starts talking but seems confused, is flipping through later pages of sites] I think this is our second choice after Mt. James, but I can't find Mt. James in here. Where is it? It's a better site. Isn't it a B1 site? I thought it was a B1 site. . . . It [Mt. James] is the one we really want.

Tom: [tries to get her back to Arlington Forge] It [Mt. James] may just not be in there.

Bill: I think Arlington Forge is a B2 site.

Ann: We haven't done the rich survey work, and it doesn't have the [same] diversity of plants as Mt. James. Where is that? [Observer note: She still seems very agitated about not finding Mt. James.]

Tom: Ok, let's go on. Canyon Gulch.

Jane: I'll be going up near there next week for . . . I'll take a look at it.

Tom: Is there any urgency?

Jane: We don't know until we look at it. I'll call you.

Tom: We'll call it a P4 because we don't know.

Ed: Shouldn't we have an "unknown" category, because P4 indicates low threat when in fact we don't know?

Tom: Because it's a B1, we need to take a look, but our urgency isn't high.

Ed: But we really don't know [whether it's high or not].

Tom: P4 should be read as "no known threat." [Ed seems frustrated with this, but doesn't say anything more.]

Ann: We're thinking of lumping a number of these small sites together into a macro-site. [to Tom] Isn't that what we decided to do with this one? [No clear response] All the rare plants are in a ten-mile area along the top of the cliffs, right? [Jane nods yes.]

Tom: [concludes and moves on] It looks like we need clarification of what's there. Dry Creek. [No one says anything at first. Then Tom mentions evidence of heavy grazing and suggests that they may want to recommend grazing restrictions. He looks to Jane.]

Jane: Well . . . [hesitantly] the cows aren't really the problem [for the rare plants in question there]. It's rabbits. If you could put a few coyotes in there, they would take care of the problem. [Observer note: She said this as if there was no chance of introducing coyotes.]

Tom: [revises] OK, we need to add that grazing does not seem to have a negative impact. [Observer note: Did he add anything about the rabbits? No indication that he did. Later found out that he did not.]

The "Politics of Representation"

This struggle over the SRP can be understood as a case of a general phenomenon in which scientific, technical, "rational" discourse (here, the SRP) communicates with such power that it prevails over other forms of discourse. The special-education placement meetings described by Bud Mehan and his colleagues (Mehan, Hertweck, and Meihls 1986; Mehan 1993) provide an example of one such contest in the "politics of representation," that is, "a competition over the correct, appropriate, or preferred way of representing objects, events, or people" (Mehan 1993, 241). Mehan writes,

> Proponents of various positions in conflicts waged in and through discourse attempt to capture or dominate modes of representation. They do so in a variety of ways, including inviting or persuading others to join their side, or silencing opponents by attacking their positions. If successful, a hierarchy is formed in which one mode of representing the world . . . gains primacy over others, transforming modes of representation from an array on a horizontal plane to a ranking on a vertical plane. (Mehan 1993, 241)

In the interactional sequences of the special-education placement meetings studied by Mehan and his colleagues, the highly technical language used by the school psychologist to describe a child's behavior and needs prevailed over the personal and social language used by parents and teachers to describe the child. Consequently, the child came to be labeled, known, and treated in school in terms of the psychologist's representational scheme. Put awkwardly but tellingly, the school "learned" the child and he "learned" the school in the formal, impersonal, noncontingent, and virtually uncontestable discursive terms of the clinical psychologist. Put more formally, the psychologist's technical mode of representing the child (in terms of diagnostic and standardized test results) achieved a privileged status in the interactions at the meeting when people trying to challenge it were ignored or silenced and when interruptions or requests for clarifications were sustained for other modes of discourse (e.g., bringing in personal, social, or chronological features of a child's behavior) but not for the technical mode (see especially Mehan 1993, 257–58).

In Mehan's case, technical language carries its own special potential for confirming privilege. To define a child in highly technical terminology and theoretical assertions is to make his or her characteristics absolute, scientific, and uncontestable:

> There is a certain mystique in the use of technical vocabulary, as evidenced by the high status that the specialized language of doctors, lawyers, and scientists is given in our society. . . . The use of technical language indicates a superior status and a special knowledge based on long training and specialized qualifications. . . . When technical language is used, . . . the grounds for negotiating meaning [can be] removed from [consideration]. . . . [Many] hearers do not have the expertise to question, or even to interrupt the speaker. To request a clarification . . . is to challenge the authority of a . . . certified expert. (Mehan 1993, 259)

Nespor makes a similar argument about how representations that eliminate contingencies produce power:

> [E]very [contingency] makes a statement more mutable, less mobile, less easily combined with other statements. When [contingencies] are excluded, as in [physics] textbooks [or the laws of physics], a statement takes on the character of a context-independent universal that can be moved across space and time. It is rendered "devoid of any trace of ownership, construction, time, and place. . . . It is, as we say, a fact" (Latour 1987, 23).
>
> By making statements stable and movable in this fashion, it is possible to use them to facilitate communications across distances and tie together networks of practice spread out in space and time. At the same time, the denser and more tightly organized such networks, the more easily they can create and maintain facts. (Nespor 1994, 55)

Mehan suggests that such statements are becoming ever more firmly established as the privileged discourse of modern society and a tool of education:

> More and more often in our increasingly technological society, when a voice speaking in formalized, rationalistic, and mathematical terms confronts a voice grounded in personal, commonsense, or localized particulars, the technical prevails over the vernacular [i.e., language or assertions that are contingent, situational, context-bound]. . . .

When categorizing a student, these educators [in the special-education placement meetings he studied] reproduced the status relations among the different discourses that exist in society. A universalizing language that is given higher status in the meeting and whose variables are read into the child, thereby decontextualizing the child, is the same language we see gaining power and authority in recent times. Thus the concrete face-to-face encounters that generate an instance of a category are constitutive moments and reproduce the relations among categories that we see gaining ascendancy historically. (Mehan 1993, 264)

In the contest at CC, a "technically rational" representation of conservation space—reflected in the SRP—lost ground to a more personal, contingent, and contested representation. This alternate representation seemed to develop (1) in reaction against the SRP's results once the procedure was applied to the sites under previous consideration by CC, and (2) out of CC's local perspective on "what's worth doing." The meeting and its aftermath seemed to supply a "moment . . . of reinterpretation and reformulation" (Moore 1994, 156) regarding the means for prioritizing CC's conservation work. The emergent means (or emergent representation) was modest and not well organized (codified), but it was a potentially consequential challenge to the national-level bureaucracy, including its scientists, that had developed and supported the SRP. It also began to organize a new way of thinking about "doing conservation work" within CC.

Interactional Processes at CC

Interactional processes similar to those described by Mehan were at work at CC. When the first SRP results were presented, interruptions or requests for clarification of the SRP-based decisions were barely tolerated and quickly passed over. Jokes about the results of the SRP were ignored by the leader (Tom), as were questions about other sites or topics that the CC's staffers wanted to discuss. Factors that did not fit the SRP's classification scheme (e.g., rabbits) were disregarded. As the meeting progressed, the challenges diminished; the challengers had been silenced.

But although the SRP prevailed in the meeting, it did not prevail in the long run. The audience at CC (like the teacher and parent in Mehan's example) did not like what they heard. What was available to them technically was not adequate to the work they saw before them, to what they believed CC should do. In CC, some participants, notably women, fought back (unlike the teacher and parent in Mehan's example).

Beyond the Immediate Scene

Resistance by the staff at CC became clearer after the meeting to introduce the SRP. What follows is from an interview with Eileen, in which she talked about a threatened wetlands, which we call Lakes. The interview took place on October 14, 1993, nine days after the SRP meeting. Eisenhart had missed the discussion of Lakes at the SRP meeting, so she asked Eileen to tell her about it. Eileen said

> At that meeting you were at . . . [we started] revisiting the water, when I thought we had already decided. I thought we were saying we might not do the project. I just got frustrated. I thought we were overscrutinizing the water problem, because everyone we talked to said, "Yes, there's some risk [protection threat], but you should do it [protect it] anyway." There are risks and threats to every project, and we need to weigh them and then make a decision. Old site designs would have a section, Risks, and would say one thing: "grazing." They all said that! The SRP still thinks like that.
>
> But now [within CC] we're focused more on ecological processes, so there are [we see] many more threats to elements and ecosystems than when thought of in terms of finding a species, fencing the area, and leaving it alone. In the past, we wouldn't have looked so broadly, or with as much sophistication. . . .
>
> Lakes is consistent with the [broad] orientation [but it received a low rank by the SRP because of the uncertainty of threats, management needs, and urgency associated with the uncertain science and practical projections regarding the water]. Its boundaries are big; water processes [referring to large-scale processes occurring over and beneath large tracts of land] are a key issue but should not be allowed to outweigh everything else . . . especially with the uncertainty. . . .

ME: Were any sites similar to Lakes highly ranked by SRP?

Eileen: You know, I came away from the SRP meeting kind of disappointed. All the B1 sites are single-species, on federal lands, and fairly small acreage. That's not what we do anymore.
Most of our high-priority sites are B3, because plant communities rather than species are our focus. Anderson was our only B1 site, and it will probably be downgraded. You only need one G1 or S1 species to make it a B1 site.

ME: Is the SRP methodology out of synch with what CC's doing now?

Eileen: I'm not sure about that yet; it's kind of what I've been thinking. You know, Ann [was] a big proponent of SRP [before she
saw its results for CC] and has been really upset that we didn't
have SRP before now. She's thrilled to have it, and so am I,
because CC should be driven by a scientific methodology, so
we can justify what we're doing on a site if someone asks us,
"Why are you there?"

Ann has been really concerned about [the question], Are we
working on the things we should be? We thought that we
were, and so did she, because she's a good scientist, but despite that, she wanted the SRP to confirm and justify that.

Now she's wondering why it's so off [i.e., why SRP's priority sites and CC's don't match up]. SRP has been species-
specific, and they're just getting it going, and they haven't
gotten to any community-level stuff. . . . I understand that the
science is changing, that the boundaries are changing, but we
need a framework in which to work. . . . But I don't think we
have it yet.

The upshot of Eileen's and Ann's concerns, and Ed's continuing objections, was that all of the female scientists at CC came to oppose adoption of the SRP as the basis for making decisions about priorities. Although Ed's objections to the SRP were clearly important, no other
men voiced strong support for his position. Thus we believe that the
strong objections of so many women were critical to blocking the SRP.

In raising their concerns after the meeting, the women echoed appeals made at the meeting to think about the sites differently. These
appeals included concerns about how much time CC and landowners
already had invested in conserving a site; whether large-scale ecological
processes (rather than simply the condition of a rare element) had been
taken into account; whether the attitudes of surrounding landowners
were conducive to CC's ownership; and whether factors not covered
by the SRP could be added in. In effect, and unlike what happened in
Mehan's special-education placement meetings, these appeals added
back some contingencies that the SRP was designed to eliminate. Some
of these considerations had long been part of the way scientists at CC
thought about their work. They were part of a discourse reflecting the
local (CC) cultural orientation toward conservation science, and they
were used successfully to block adoption of the SRP.

CC's scientists were not satisfied with the prospect of simply returning to their old procedures, however. Some of the considerations
raised during and after the SRP meeting were new to the organization;

they were made by appeal to landscape ecology—a newer form of conservation science than the one used to develop the SRP and a discourse that had previously received little "air time" within the organization. But despite the availability of means to challenge the SRP, CC was left without a procedure to replace it.

Ann later organized and led a conference designed to pursue the local CC's concerns about the SRP. She brought together experts from across the country for a three-day workshop. She and others thought of this conference as a place to begin talking about an alternative to the SRP. The conference was considered a "success," although it did not produce consensus about what should be done.

If we accept the arguments of people like Mehan and Nespor (discussed above), the local CC took a significant risk in adding contingencies that disrupted the use of the SRP. Knowing what to do, what to argue for, and how to make a decision became difficult. Adding contingencies that interfered with the SRP delayed the local CC's decision making and thus its work; made public presentations about CC's work more difficult (less sure); and made instructing newcomers in the CC's procedures more difficult. These are nontrivial problems for an organization that has a heavy and urgent workload, survives by public appeal based heavily on a stated commitment to science-driven conservation, and expects newcomers to take on responsibilities very quickly (see Eisenhart 1995a for more discussion of this last point). For CC to add contingencies—based on local, situational concerns—to a procedure like the SRP is to begin the construction of an alternative to the technical-rational power represented by the SRP; it is an example of a collective move to produce a reformulation that would alter the practice and culture of this group.

Power in CC

This attempt to construct an alternative to the SRP was impressive. Ed and the women in CC who undertook it were trying to find a way of doing systematic science while keeping science firmly situated in local contingencies. Like Marty's desire to be both a scientist and a mother, the attempt to alter the SRP was a progressive impulse toward institutional change, and the potential of both would probably have been lacking if a significant number of women had not been present in CC.

The responses of women and Ed to the SRP constituted an attempt to reconstruct the technical-rational discourse by which the organization made its most important decisions. Their effort involved more than tinkering at the margins of organizational activities; it went to the heart of them. Constructing an alternative to the technical-rational discourse so influential in contemporary society is no small project; it goes right to the foundation of that dominant discourse. What Ed and the women in the CC were working on was a radical reconstruction of the decision rules by which a national organization determines how to conserve scarce environmental resources in the public interest now and for years to come.

Not surprisingly, the story of the SRP in CC has an ironic twist. The nature of CC's changes to the SRP would seem to make the organization more vulnerable than it would be if it had adopted the SRP. Although Eisenhart's study did not continue long after the events surrounding the SRP's adoption, she did hear women and men express concern about how much more difficult it would be to explain CC's protection agenda to its advisory board, the national office, and local supporters without the SRP. These staff members, including those who opposed the SRP, were worried that various groups, knowing that the SRP was now available, might lose confidence in CC and withhold their much-needed support. Some potential repercussions included the possibility of diminished funding from the national office for failure to comply with the SRP; the problems associated with a slowdown in site approvals and site acquisitions (many of which must be approved by the national CC), which are a major factor in CC's yearly performance reviews and salary increases; and the difficulties of providing clear justifications to affected residents or the public for decisions about site protection. Without the SRP or some similar alternative, CC's appeals to the public did not have the strong, unequivocal "science" backing that they would have with the SRP. For a nonprofit dependent in part on approval from its national headquarters and with an envied public reputation for doing "serious science," these were serious risks.

Thus the progressive potential in the effort to block the SRP seemed to jeopardize the existing status of an organization in which science and women were especially well regarded. As women and some men mounted challenges to the institution, the prestige associated with old practices, specifically those of an organization that prides itself on being science-driven, was in danger of being eroded. As a force for local change, then, the women's actions both pushed the organization toward an alternative, more locally responsive way of doing science and simultaneously disrupted the relations that gave CC its organizational power and enabled its (previous) accomplishments.

Recall, however, that such disruptions are the fundamental in social transformation. If we do not accept the risk to established power relations of changes such as those that Ed and the women at CC supported in response to the SRP (or regarding motherhood), then we cannot be serious about social and cultural change. If all that women in science, engineering, or other traditionally male-dominated professions accomplish (or are allowed to accomplish) is to do more of what men have historically done, they will have gained little.

Discussion

In this chapter we have presented examples of what may at first seem to be two different phenomena. On the one hand, we have illustrated the limited power of young, college-age women in the engineering design internship (EDI) and the environmental action group (ELAC) to alter the circumstances of their lives in these groups. On the other hand, we have focused on the progressive potential that arose from struggles among slightly older women in CC to create a workplace that was more responsive both to their needs or desires as women and to the local conditions of their scientific practice. But both kinds of responses arise in contexts in which the normative principle expressed in a discourse of gender neutrality was strong. The issue for women in both sets of examples is creating a way to be and to act in a place defined as gender-neutral in which gendered differences nonetheless exist. The main response of the younger women in EDI and ELAC was to ignore or downplay features of situations in which they "stuck out" as women. Thus even simple matters such as what to wear were made complicated and risky for them. Matters that were more threatening to women yet almost as easily fixed, such as women's safety concerns, were rarely broached, because their effect on institutional practice made them more visible as "women's special issues." For the older women in CC, who felt pressures from outside the organization (e.g., to be mothers; to be more responsive to local concerns) that they could not ignore, the struggle was to find ways to act on their desires without appearing to ask for special treatment as women and without risking too much of their own prestige or that of the organization. The space in which these women might safely maneuver—without risk to body or prestige—was small indeed.

Yet some of the women took the risks and managed to introduce changes that altered the status quo. This was clearest in the case of the women at CC. Unlike Willis (1977), who found that cultural responses to dominant structures produced ironic reinventions of the status quo, we found women who managed to act in ways that foreshadow progressive changes, at least for themselves, at the site of local activity. Although these changes are small-scale, they challenge powerful forces and are brought about by people who have not historically mounted such challenges. For these reasons, they contain the potential for wider effects, and they may anticipate what women are likely to look for, ask for, and act upon in the future. We need to pay attention to these emergent cultural forms and social practices. Judith Butler, in the quotation that opens this chapter, rightly sees that women's actions are tightly constrained by the "tool lying there"; nevertheless, women's presence and perspective can open up new ways of thinking and acting in institutional contexts, as Tong suggests in the passage that opens chapter 7.

Chapter Nine

Situated Science, the Presence of Women, and the Practices of Work and School

We began this book wondering whether places where women are relatively well represented in science-related activities are actually better places for women than the places of elite science. Our answer is both yes and no. We answer yes because women in lower-status places or niches seem to be more centrally involved in science-related activities, more motivated to learn about science, more satisfied with their work, and more likely to be rewarded in equal proportion to men than has been reported for elite sites. In comparison, entire books—for example, Gornick's *Women in Science* ([1983] 1990) and McGrayne's *Nobel Prize Women of Science* (1993), as well as Rossiter's two volumes of *Women Scientists in America* (1982; 1995)—have chronicled the sorry state of affairs for women in elite science. Studies of conventional school science have found many women disinterested or discouraged. Prior to our engineering study, we found not one documented case of female student engineers or practicing engineers having positive experiences working on teams with men—the most frequently recommended "reform" in engineering education. Although our findings about scientific literacy in the environmental action group are only tentative, we know of no study in which the scientific literacy of girls or young women approached the figures we found there. In the conservation corporation, women's representation in the organization's high-status positions and their central involvement in CC's science-related activities provide a clear contrast to accounts of women's marginal position in elite science (e.g., Traweek 1988). Our lower-status sites are better than elite sites in the ways they attract women to science, engage them in its practice, motivate them, and reward their success.

On the other hand, we answer no because prototypical, white, male-oriented expectations pervaded the lower-status workplaces, and—as in high-status places—these expectations adversely affected women more than men. Furthermore, lower-status places are more financially precarious, more politically tenuous, and more public than elite sites, thereby offering participants less economic security, fewer stable networks, less political clout, and less personal security than elite sites. In these ways, lower-status sites are not better places for women.

We also began this book wondering what accounts for women's concentration in lower-status sites of science and engineering. Others have suggested that the pattern of women's underrepresentation in elite science and engineering is a function of innate proclivities, lack of ability, socialization pressures, poor preparation, overt discrimination, or the accumulation of subordinating interactional routines. In one way or another, singly or in combination, these factors are thought to discourage women from science and engineering. In chapter 2 we argued that the longitudinal and cross-disciplinary patterns in the underrepresentation of women who do pursue some form of science or engineering required a different explanation. We suggested we might find such an explanation in ideas about the reproduction of subordinate status through situated learning, cultural productions, and networks of power.

The Reproduction of Scientific Power through Activity

Applying these ideas in the sites of our study allows us to clarify some aspects of women's participation in science and engineering. First, we found little evidence that the women we studied were uninterested in science, incapable of understanding its subject matter, unwilling to work hard, or discouraged about competing with men in the workplace. Instead, we found women who demonstrated considerable interest, proclivity, and success when science was organized and defined in ways that encouraged participation in immediate, socially relevant and politically contingent activities and networks. Put another way, the women we studied were interested and successful in places where curricular or occupational activities and the meanings of the term *science* that they inspired encouraged broader and more flexible commitments of time, space, and professional identity than the "greedy" activities and meanings of elite science. In sites of elite science, regardless of content, achieving high status requires more of one's time, tighter constraints on appropriate workplaces, and narrower identities and networks of power than in lower-status sites. We suspect that many young women (and many men) find the greedy demands of elite science simply too costly.

For many, this realization probably comes in high school or college, where many young people in the United States first actually confront the power asymmetry of science. They confront it in the form of greedy versus more flexible courses, degree programs, and occupational choices. When this occurs, the differing social and cultural realities of women's and men's lives are likely to send them in different directions, and women move toward more flexible situations than men. We think this is spurred, at least in part, by women's confrontation with the culture of romance.

If, as Holland and Eisenhart suggested (1990), women's prestige and status in high school and college depend primarily on their romantic relationships (whereas men's do not), then young women are less likely than men to be attracted to coursework and degree programs that severely limit time and space for social activities. In demanding situations, women would seem to have two unappealing choices. On the one hand, they can give increasing time, space, and energy to adopting the identities required by high-status science and eschew involvement in the culture of romance that conveys status and prestige on young adult women. On the other, they can try to find small ways to make room for their activities "as women" and risk the lowering of prestige that accompanies such activities. Neither seems an attractive choice for most women.

More flexible situations, like those in the alternative sites we studied, make high demands, too, but not such extraordinary ones and not in ways so likely to disadvantage young women affected by the culture of romance. Degree programs, such as environmental biology (see chapter 2) or science education (Nespor 1994), and occupational positions, such as in the conservation corporation or the technical-expert niche of EDI-engineering, offer participants time, space, and important identities that are more accommodating of social needs and interests than those of elite science or engineering. The alternative sites we studied also rewarded and advanced women in roughly equal proportion to men, an outcome which is not characteristic of elite sites. From women's standpoint, then, lower-status sites of science and engineering appear to be less voracious in their professional demands, less socially costly, and more rewarding than elite sites.

For these reasons, we think that women's current underrepresentation in elite science and engineering can be understood primarily in terms of the limited extent to which young women are willing to accept the narrow, greedy demands of high-status science and engineering when alternative sites, both in school and outside of it, offer more flexible and rewarding professional conditions. But this is not the end of the story. Women pay a special price for rejecting elite science. Our alternative sites of science and engineering *are* lower-status, sometimes unsafe, and financially precarious; they also hide prototypically male characteristics of work behind a discourse of gender neutrality that disadvantages women. Most of the women we studied did not realize that the alternative sites, which offered them some relief from the greediness of elite science and engineering, contained their own limitations. Yet these limitations are subordinating: they ensure that participation in alternative sites leads to subordinate status in science, and they do so in a way that is more consequential for women than men. How does this happen, and why don't women realize it?

So far, we have seen that when women and men refuse (consciously or not) to accommodate the greedy demands of high-status science and engineering, they are rejecting activities in which people's time, space, and identities are monopolized in pursuit of a dispassionate, acontextual, and rational form of science. When women and men participate in our alternative sites of science and engineering, they come to use time and space and to develop their professional identities in more immediately relevant and rewarding ways that rely in part on the science of elite sites. Why do alternatives that entail more immediate and local uses of science, and more equal participation of women and men, also entail subordination?

We can suggest that the characteristics of our alternative sites, *in relation to those of elite science*, make them unwitting contributors to asymmetrical power relations in science. The alternative sites rely on and promote elite science yet do not affect its course. They offer work environments that respond in some ways to the impersonal, inflexible extremes of elite science but are too precarious to challenge them effectively. They engage and reward women in ways elite science does not, but they also hide from view characteristics of the workplace that disadvantage women more than men.

The kind of power formed among participants in elite science is not inherently or necessarily greater than that formed among those in alternative science (consider, for example, the kind of power formed in the conservation corporation), but elite science is *made* more powerful when people, institutions, or corporations privilege abstract, invariant theories over immediate, local needs, and when they offer generous financial and political support to the people and organizations that produce invariant theories and not to those who concern themselves with local, public issues. The generous financial support that elite science receives also stabilizes its networks of participants (by supporting well-funded graduate careers and lucrative permanent jobs, for example) and institutionalizes their power in ways that more precariously financed organizations are unable to support.

Women's increasing participation in activities constrained by these limitations is the other factor that contributes to their underrepresentation in elite science. The more time women spend in lower-status sites, the less likely they are to be able or motivated to move to elite sites.

One reason for this is that participants in our sites got better at different things over time. In each site, they learned different meanings of the terms *science* and *scientist*, and they developed networks and power relations of distinct kinds. The meanings, identities, and social relations they developed were not those of elite science. Although participants in our lower-status sites relied in part on the products of elite science, the skills, orientations, and commitments they developed were not easily transferable to elite science.

Second, in important ways, the organization and priorities of lower-status sites opposed those of elite science. In these sites, science or engineering tends to be applied rather than experimental; contingent and relevant rather than abstract or invariant; and pursued in the messiness of public activity rather than in the more private and controlled spaces of classrooms or laboratories. These "oppositions" are likely to be more comfortable and interesting to women than to men because they are congruent with societal expectations about women, traditional socialization pressures on women, and the cultural demands of women's lives. As participants got better at lower-status priorities, however, they simultaneously got better at and learned to prize their distance from the priorities of elite science.

Third, some of the women in our lower-status sites claimed they were "better places for women" than elite sites. The success and rewards that they achieved in lower-status sites confirmed their claim and were further incentives to stay put. The discourse of gender neutrality in our lower-status sites contributed to women's belief that they were being treated well there.

The Cultural Production of Gender Neutrality

We cannot underestimate the contribution of the discourse of gender neutrality to women's positioning inside science. Among the women we studied, talking and acting *as if* the activities and rewards of their sites were gender-neutral—as if women and men were treated the same—was pervasive. In some limited ways, this discourse reflected a material reality. Women in our three alternative sites performed at least as well as men in their work and were officially rewarded similarly. These organizations and the women in them were justifiably proud and boastful of this accomplishment, especially given the poor track records of other, notably the elite, sites of scientific practice. In other ways, however, the discourse of gender neutrality hid obstacles that affected women more than men. In adopting the discourse of gender neutrality, women did not see how culturally male features of their own workplace jeopardized their continued success and disempowered them as women. Thus they were unprepared for the negative consequences of enacting culturally female characteristics in the context of work. In this contradictory way, the discourse of gender neutrality both supported and undermined women's success in these workplaces.

We have referred to women's engagement in this contradictory context as a "politics of prestige and safety." It is a politics from which women cannot extricate themselves. To act like a woman, or to ask for special treatment as a woman, threatens prestige and status in the local organization. On the other hand, failure to call attention to one's womanhood compromises physical safety and subordinates women's needs and interests to those of the prototypic workplace, which is, as we have indicated earlier, permeated by patriarchy.

As the women in our sites take up this discourse and engage this politics, they are training themselves into—learning—a way of celebrating alternative sites as "better for women," and simultaneously making women's issues and concerns either unappealing, irrelevant, or to put it another way, marginalized. This is what makes resistance or change on behalf of women or women's interests so difficult in these sites. Traces of patriarchy are instantiated in the gender-neutral discourse of work that the women produced, the practices they engaged in, the risks and challenges they faced, and the activist forms in which they thought about trying to influence their workplaces and beyond. In taking up the "tools" the women had available for interpreting their work, charting the course of their identities, and taking actions to effect change and improvement, they learned to accept features of work, prestige, and political action that privilege prototypically male needs, interests, and concerns and, simultaneously continue to marginalize those of women.

In a broader sense, the women's investment in their own success and in the promise of gender neutrality masked some greater dangers of these sites. By constructing these alternative sites as "better places for women" than the sites of elite science, women created a cultural form that could compensate for the lower pay, limited job security, and increased physical dangers of these workplaces. In fact, women would be paid much better, have considerably more job security and flexibility, and regularly engage in work activities that were safer (where colleagues are relatively few, stable, and familiar) if they worked in a university, an industry, or the laboratory sites of elite science or engineering. Women's construction of alternative workplaces as "better," "good," or "fair" places for women—thanks to the contrast with elite sites *and* the rhetoric of gender neutrality—diverts attention from their economic vulnerability and their social and political subordination, as well as from the prototypically male features of the workplaces in which women "do well."

By accepting and enacting the subordinating relationships of non-elite science and the discourse of gender neutrality, the women we studied were inadvertently shaping their work lives in accord with the established furrows of institutional power and patriarchy. Subordinated science and a subordinated role for women were being constructed as these women learned to participate in and to accept lower-status science and the discourse of gender neutrality. In this way, limited institutional power comes to be aligned with women's presence and impotence in the everyday practices of science and work.

The social, political, and cultural arrangements that organize the arena of science-related practice in these ways have been inherited from a particular history. Greater access and interest by women seem to have altered the historical trajectory very little. Women may join, but to do so, they must, for the most part, fit into arrangements that support the continuing dominance of elite science, narrow professional identities, and prototypic white men.

Learning Outside and Inside of School

In *Situated Learning*, Lave and Wenger (1991) argue that authentic learning occurs through sustained, legitimate engagement in the activities of a community of practice. In their examples, authentic learning occurs in contexts such as apprenticeships or on-the-job training, in which newcomers can actually participate over time in the real work of practitioners and truly are preparing themselves for a future identity in that activity. In conventional schools, in contrast, newcomers learn about, but rarely get to practice, real work; for this reason, conventional schools are, in Lave and Wenger's view, not very good places for authentic learning. Their perspective converges with that of other contemporary educational reformers who have argued that schooling could be dramatically improved if its activities were made more "authentic," that is, more like what practitioners really do. This model of school reform has inspired many new programs, including many devoted to improving science education by modeling it after the practice of "real scientists," such as the innovative genetics course (IGC) described in chapter 3.

Our research suggests that it will be insufficient merely to replace conventional school science with approximations of the authentic practice of elite practitioners. Under this conception of reform, "learning" continues to be measured by how well students improve their ability to reproduce the existing power relations in society. This kind of learning enshrines the status quo, with negative consequences for the involvement of historically excluded groups.

Our research, by contrast, suggests that more important educational reforms would loosen the demands of elite science, give more financial and political support to socially and politically relevant science practices, find ways to celebrate those who devote time and energy to applied science, and expose how institutions and discourses can both enable and constrain progressive impulses. None of these insights is likely to be advanced either by the practices of conventional school science or by replacing the latter with activities that better model elite science practice.

The kind of critical learning we advocate requires entirely different kinds of educational activities, in which more expansive meanings of *science* and *scientist* are encouraged. For example, we see no reason why science curricula, degree programs, or occupations must necessarily be as demanding as those of elite science are. We also do not think it justifiable to provide generous support only to tight educational and occupational arrangements that are easier for white men than anyone else to enter and succeed in. Nor is it right to disdain and diminish the activities of alternative sites of science and engineering, which are attempting, against great odds, to make scientific information relevant to immediate, local, public concerns, and which do a good job of equalizing rewards and status for women and men. The models of environmental biology (chapter 2) and the conservation corporation (chapter 6) suggest that requirements can be more flexible, more socially relevant, and more gender-fair without losing scientific credibility as defined by elite scientists. Proficiency in flexible, socially relevant, and gender-fair forms of science must be regarded as a measure of success in school and work that is equal in worth to the mastery of traditional academic science. Similarly, we must support educational activities that build on the science-related interests that girls and young women already have; these activities must be considered as important and valuable as the traditional activities that interest men. Finally, we need educational activities that promote critical inspection and assessment of prevailing discourses such as those of gender neutrality and technical rationality. New kinds of educational activities that right these imbalances must be planned in order to re-envision and reconstruct scientific power.

Where Do We Go from Here?

If our society wants to expand the possibilities in the connections between science, status, and power in contemporary society, then we must encourage and actively support varied, expansive, and new uses of science by diverse people who are trying to make sense of their lives and their futures. Unlike so many young people today, the women in our alternate sites found legitimate public spaces in which to articulate and act on at least some of their critiques of the establishment. Although constrained by existing power relations, most of the women nonetheless appropriated some aspects of science and developed them in social and political contexts with public and personal relevance.

A few of the women we studied—notably in the engineering design internship, EDI, and the conservation corporation, CC—also acted in ways that reveal the possibilities of expanded participation. These women were plowing up some traditional furrows. Their efforts may not be institutionalized, as the attempts to alter the talk about clothing in EDI or the procedures for assuring safety in ELAC were not. Such efforts may not result in outcomes that are easily noticed or quickly realized. Yet the women's efforts are impressive for what they reveal about the potential in women's presence and for how centrally they can challenge the status quo.

This potential is especially evident at CC, where the responses of women (primarily) to the site-ranking procedure (SRP) constituted an attempt to reconstruct the discourse by which the organization made its most important decisions. Cast in terms of technical-rational discourse, as in the special-education placement decisions studied by Mehan (1993), the original SRP was intended to define and direct one of CC's central activities—the way decisions are made about conservation sites. The women in CC were trying to accomplish a reconstruction of the decision rules by which a nationally prominent organization determines how to conserve scarce environmental resources in the public interest now and for years into the future. That their efforts could be curtailed and derailed is obvious; that they are ambitious, potentially far-reaching, locally sensitive, and progressive should be obvious, too.

The women's efforts led us to ask and then try to answer some old questions in some new ways: How might we better organize and support activities that allow young people to engage in credible learning of science and engineering, in conjunction with real-world contingencies? How might science and engineering activities be designed so that people who are (and want to be) women, political activists, and good citizens are encouraged and enabled to learn these disciplines? How can science and engineering work be constituted so that the needs and concerns of diverse people can be expressed, addressed, or allowed to flourish? How can scientific or engineering knowledge be put to use in ways that accrue status and prestige because they are worthwhile, rather than merely because they are the historical province of one elite group? And, finally, What role do the schools have in preparing young people for such (new) forms of science or engineering practice and work? In what follows, we briefly sketch out some of our answers, especially with regard to the role of schools.

Because our lower-status sites are good places for women in the ways they are—because they enable women's participation in science-related activities, reward women in equal proportion to men, and model ways of "doing science" that are important for ordinary citizens in a democratic society—they should be used as sources of information about how to improve science learning and outcomes for women and others. Yet no one would suggest that school science be made to resemble exactly the science in ELAC, the environmental action group, or even the conservation corporation. Nor would we suggest replacing "men's science" with "women's science." What our sites and our evidence about "women's science" offer are strong contrasts to elite, male-oriented science—contrasts that reveal clues to what elite science does and does not do and thus to what a more inclusive and critical science education might be.

Schools should be places that afford students a time and place in which they can learn more robust and complex understandings of science than are available in ELAC or even CC. Schools also should be places where students can learn the content and processes of the sciences, *and* learn to appreciate and use science's strengths and limitations in debates about important social issues. As Lauren Resnick writes, "Building such civic consciousness, by long apprenticeship in the special kind of community that only school has both the distance and the engagement to create, may be the most important challenge facing educational research and reform today" (1987, 19).

Schools are not currently meeting this challenge very well, as Miller's results from simple tests of scientific literacy (1991; see chapter 5) make clear. Our results suggest some ways that schools in general and science educators in particular ought to rethink their practice.

Gender-Fair Science

Schools must, first and foremost, accept the obligation to produce equal outcomes in science. Science and engineering educators should regard as failures all curricula from which boys and girls, women and men emerge with markedly different patterns of success. In our view, this means reforming science curricula in ways that improve the success rate of girls relative to that of boys. This means funding and celebrating the kinds of science-related activities that girls are already interested in and that do not require them to choose between commitment to success in science and involvement in other activities that are important to them. It means finding, creating, and supporting contexts of instruction that will lead girls to extend their command of science beyond the superficial. It also means contributing to consciousness-raising among girls about the effects on them of cultural forms such as the culture of romance (Holland and Eisenhart 1990) or the discourse of gender neutrality.

One place to start is with girls' and women's interests, questions, and criteria for credibility, rather than with what established scientists think women's interests, questions, and criteria should be. Although some proponents of reform in science education (e.g., Aldridge 1992) insist that political and social relevance is too messy to use in science instruction, the women we followed seemed to be more successful at using and learning science in the context of socially relevant activities—with all their inevitably blurred distinctions—than are girls and women in most school science.[1] Thus it seems reasonable to propose that some science-education reforms focus on ways of giving girls and young women the time, spaces, tools, and support to develop sophisticated understandings of the topics that interest them in the contexts that intrigue them. Such attempts at science education reform could benefit from the active collaboration of social science researchers who can assess young women's interests, questions, and criteria of credibility.

Educators must also be alert to the possibility that the apparent lack of interest or ability in science on the part of girls or women is produced more consistently by unappealing school science than by the effects of socialized abilities or overt gender discrimination. When the women we studied were engaged in purposeful activities that demanded scientific or engineering knowledge as part of a desired identity, *and* that did not require them to make drastic, immediate changes in their social lives, they were motivated to learn, and they did as well or better than their male counterparts. Although many of the women we followed had been discouraged from pursuing school science for numerous reasons, they were neither completely disinterested in nor discouraged about the *value* of scientific knowledge. Although some of the women we studied had experienced gender discrimination, their pursuit of scientific knowledge was not necessarily inhibited once they were engaged in activities they found meaningful. Once outside the confines of conventional school science and engaged in more meaningful activities, women seemed to lack neither an interest in science nor the ability to learn it.

Educators must also look closely and separately at men's and women's experiences in schools. The ways that some activities and identities motivate women to learn science or engineering may not apply to men. The engineering internship activities of EDI gave women a rare chance to develop proficiencies in areas they enjoyed. Conversely, the men in EDI saw no need for the course or did not feel that it particularly benefited them. In the genetics class, previously unsuccessful boys found the curriculum challenging, fun, and rewarding; previously unsuccessful girls did not. Educators need to know whether or not the activities they use benefit girls and women in science.

We must also realize that participation by a large number of women is important but not sufficient to assure that women's issues are made visible and dealt with institutionally. In the environmental action group, for example, there were plenty of women and a female director, yet the safety issue could not be dealt with, and could barely even be discussed. In the engineering internship, the genetics classroom, and the conservation corporation, issues that concerned women only were little discussed, even among the women. Educators must find ways to bring these issues to light and help girls and women handle them.

Socially and Publicly Meaningful Science

Schools must give serious attention to the kinds of identities that are implied by school activities. Our cases (and those of other researchers working in the tradition of activity and practice theory) suggest that people change, grow, and learn in the image of identities represented as important in an activity (Chaiklin and Lave 1993; Lave 1988b; Scribner 1984; and Wertsch 1991). If the activities of school science represent identities that are interesting, believable, and possible for students to achieve (given existing demands and expectations), then there is greater likelihood that students will participate in science activities and pursue scientist identities.

In all four of our sites, knowledge of science (or engineering) enhanced one's identity within the group. The person who could use science persuasively and effectively in public forums was given high status by co-workers or peers. Newcomers, regardless of background or job assignment, were encouraged to learn how to use some science in order to raise their own status in the organization. In this sense, high-status identities, including some scientific expertise, guided or "led" the behaviors and aspirations of old-timers and newcomers.

This finding is especially striking when we consider that schools, parents, and school reformers rarely pay much attention to the identities that are represented in activities. Only on rare occasions are students, especially girls and young women, held publicly accountable for scientific knowledge. Rarely are they asked to use science outside the classroom. Rarely are they asked to investigate community problems in which science plays a part. Students are seldom engaged in activities where high status is conferred on persons with scientific knowledge. Instead, most schools (with the support of parents, legislators, and the public) emphasize the procedures students should use to meet school standards, mostly on their own, and regardless of whether anyone else finds the tasks meaningful, credible, or valuable. Our results suggest that schools should spend more time considering how to develop activities in which scientific knowledge is made important to the organizations and communities in which students regularly do or could participate outside of school. This might happen by involving students in projects that connect school science with concerns shared by members of the local community and by making students responsible to community groups for their in-school work.

Schools should also make a variety of science activities and scientist identities important in school science. Why are school science activities so often patterned on dispassionate research inquiry? Why is the model of practicing scientist embodied by school activities so often that of a laboratory scientist (e.g., as in the innovative genetics class we studied)? As Jane Roland Martin ([1982] 1994b) tells us, curriculum is socially constructed; thus it does not have to be the way it is or always has been. Yet we continue to privilege dispassionate, distanced, basic, conventional school science even when we know it is useful to only a few and discourages many, especially women and minorities.

Of course, some activities and even curricula in schools are organized around socially relevant science—some of them very similar to the activities of EDI, ELAC and CC. Yet these activities are almost always marginalized. They are often designed for, or come to be used for, students who are not supposed to be "up" to conventional science; they become "field trips"—excursions away from the "real" activities of science; they are perceived as deviations from the kind of school program that assures high test scores, acceptance at the best colleges, and job opportunities in the future.

Our case studies underscore that the laboratory (research) scientist is only one kind of person who uses or needs scientific knowledge. Laboratory scientists use scientific knowledge in one way—to further basic knowledge, and they may do so with little attention to social, political, or ethical implications. Most ordinary citizens face the issues of how to obtain accurate scientific information, how to make informed decisions about socially and politically relevant issues, and how to engage in debate about social and political matters in constructive and responsible ways. Given the need for scientifically informed citizens and the enthusiasm for learning more science that we found among women in our sites, it seems incumbent on educators and others to find ways of making similar activities and identities more central to school science.

We consider such changes essential. The following example illustrates how this approach could help more students come to see science as a meaningful social activity.[2]

Foundations of Science (FOS) is an alternative science program being developed by four teachers at a midwestern public high school (Huebel-Drake et al. 1995). Working closely with researchers from the University of Michigan and modeling their initial project on the Global Rivers Environmental Network (GREEN) publication, *Field Manual for Water Quality Monitoring* (Mitchell and Stapp 1994; Susskind and Finkel 1995), these teachers have created an integrated context in which students work with community members to investigate and take action on a local environmental issue: the quality of the water in a small stream. As a part of this program, students and their teachers have "adopted" a local stream, where they spend most of a semester collecting and analyzing the macroinvertebrates that inhabit the creek, describing and evaluating the habitats that exist within the creek, and measuring and analyzing the quality of the creek's water. Students write and revise a series of reports on their findings, and they present their analyses to members of the local environmental agency that monitors other parts of the same watershed. In addition, students' presentations are videotaped and aired on a local cable television station.

Students in FOS are continually made aware, by their teachers and through the involvement and interest in their work by members of their community, of the relevance of their work to themselves and to others in the community. Students know that no one else is monitoring the creek they are studying and that their analyses will be used by local officials. Through their work in this activity, students appear to develop a sense of themselves (an identity) as concerned citizens who can use scientific information to understand local environmental issues. As the following story indicates, students' involvement as concerned, participating citizens extends beyond the school year and school assignments, and encourages them to develop considerable scientific knowledge.

Toward the end of the 1994–95 school year, the local public transportation authority contacted the FOS teachers with a plea: A pond located on their property was in poor health, stagnant, and smelly; was there anything that the FOS students could do to help? The agency had hired an environmental consulting firm to conduct a series of tests, but wanted a second opinion. The teachers issued a request for interested students, and a group of eight high school students and two teachers visited the pond. In the words of the students, "We went out to the pond . . . [and] performed the same tests as [the consulting firm], plus a few extras. We read [the consulting firm's report] and made a few of our own observations." In addition, the students designed a survey to discover how employees of the agency wanted to use the site, developed a restoration plan based on the response that "people wanted a more natural look to the area . . . [and thought] it should be clean enough to have picnic tables," and offered to continue working at the site. The transit authority accepted the students' offer to help, and over the summer, student volunteers began their restoration project.

The students' restoration plan included three suggestions to improve the pond water's quality. These suggestions included (1) monthly testing of pond water during the summer when algal growth was at its maximum; (2) reducing the use of fertilizers on the lawn surrounding the pond; and (3) introducing biological controls that would make use of the excess nutrients that promoted algal growth. Their suggestions were based on a series of tests conducted and interpreted by the students: chemical tests to determine dissolved oxygen, fecal coliform, pH, biological oxygen demand, total phosphate, and nitrates; and physical tests to determine turbidity and total solids.

In order to interpret the results of these tests and develop the restoration plan, students had to be familiar with a variety of scientific concepts, including the connections among oxygen concentration, photosynthesis, and plant growth; sources of fecal coliform and pathogenic organisms; the link between oxygen concentration and algal and bacterial growth; the meaning of the pH scale; and the sources and effects of nitrates and phosphates in freshwater systems.

Of the eight students who volunteered to participate in the project, five were girls. All four principal authors of the restoration plan were girls. Finkel's observations of two of the girls suggested that prior to their participation in FOS (and even at several points during the academic year), these girls were not interested in science. In interviews conducted the previous September, Angela (a pseudonym), one principal author of the restoration plan, indicated her distaste for science, commenting that science in school and science teachers were "boring" and that science had no impact on her outside of school. In early February, Angela continued to indicate her aversion to science, responding to positive feedback in class with "Yeah, but I still hate science." Not until an interview conducted in May did Angela express a positive attitude toward science, describing the use of a computer program (designed to help students model the creek ecosystem they studied) as "interesting" and something that "she understood . . . a lot better." Shortly after this interview, Angela volunteered to work on the transit authority project.

When one of the researchers met Angela during the summer, her excitement over the work on this project was clear. The following is from the fieldnotes recording the meeting:

> [Angela] . . . told me she was expecting a phone call from [one of her teachers] . . . about the [transit authority project]. She was very excited about the report she helped write (asked me if I'd read it yet) and was also anxious to get the phone call about their next task. She was very excited about going back to do some follow-up water testing.

Angela's excitement and enthusiasm for this project was a remarkable change from her earlier pronouncements that she did not like science and found it irrelevant to her life outside of school.

Although FOS is only one program, we think that its activities connect students to the community, to other people, and to science in ways that are distinctly different from those of conventional school science. FOS requires students to situate their tasks in a local community context, establish relationships and identities with experts and community members beyond the school, and develop ways of talking and writing that are useful and persuasive in a real-world setting. In this motivating context, the students also cultivate understandings of scientific concepts and ideas that are both locally useful and technically sophisticated. In addition, girls seem to find this activity especially motivating.

Beyond providing opportunities for students to engage in this sort of authentic scientific inquiry and investigation, schools should take responsibility for practicing and modeling serious and conscientious uses of scientific knowledge in a social or political context. Although the out-of-school sites we studied motivated science learning, the extent of the science available to be learned there was sometimes less than desirable. Information about the scope and depth of scientific knowledge, its complexities, and its limitations was not always available. The environmental action group (ELAC) in particular provided few opportunities for discussion and debate of scientific issues. Although participants were primed to learn science, the only resources they had available were meager, superficial, and in some cases misleading. In contrast, in IGC (the conventional school site) and in EDI (the internship guided by professors and experienced practitioners), more sophisticated knowledge was available and was practiced. If schools can find ways to prime their students by conducting meaningful science in authentic settings, and then *provide opportunities to learn more* about science and to thoughtfully discuss and debate scientific issues, they would seem to be even better places than our study sites to present and practice science or engineering. The FOS program described above is one example of a school program that both primes students to learn and gives them access to activities and identities that encourage them to extend their knowledge of science.

Exposing Cultural Forms

Cultural forms like the culture of romance and the discourse of gender neutrality must be exposed and challenged in schools and elsewhere. Cultural obstacles to women's participation and advancement in science and engineering exist even when women can do well. One of these obstacles is the culture of romance (Holland and Eisenhart 1990), which focuses young women's attention and energies on making themselves attractive to men, and can therefore make it hard for them to give serious attention to school work. Curricula with greedy demands, such as those in physics, genetics, and engineering, only exacerbate the tension for young women. Such curricula are virtually impossible for women to pursue, if they also want to participate in social and romantic activities that give them status and prestige among their friends and family members. But it will not be enough to ask for looser curricula; women must find better ways to balance the competing demands of their lives. The culture of romance monopolizes young women's time and energies in negative ways, too, as it requires young women to subordinate their own interests, careers, and futures to those of male romantic partners. Educators and parents must help young women to understand how cultural forms like the culture of romance affect their decisions and actions. Without some critical discussion with adults about both the enabling and disabling features of cultural forms, young women will be left on their own to handle very pervasive cultural forces.

Another cultural obstacle to women's success is the discourse of gender neutrality. As discussed above, gender neutrality is double-edged for women. On the one hand, women may have been attracted to the sites we studied because the sites were viewed as gender-neutral. On the other hand, an expressed commitment to gender neutrality by women, men, or the organization itself could hide the fact that workplace norms privilege prototypically male behavior. Whether they recognize it explicitly or not, women are more vulnerable to assumptions of gender neutrality than are men. For example, defining gender differences as irrelevant creates the danger that no one will inquire how women are faring compared to men, no one will ask what women are particularly enthused or frustrated about, and no one will notice what women fear.

Gender neutrality can disadvantage men and families, too. If one's availability to work long hours and travel frequently without the distractions of child care, parent care, cooking, or housekeeping is taken for granted, have conditions improved overall for women, men, or families? Even though women may be far more numerous in professional occupations than they were in the past, is it acceptable for them (or men) to have to suppress traditional "female" interests or concerns in order to be successful at work? In short, when school, citizenship, and employee identities are cast in gender-neutral terms, these identities may constitute institutional justification for ignoring culturally female issues to the detriment of all.

This situation presents a paradox for policy makers. Is it good or bad, fortunate or unfortunate, for organizations to approach gender issues in this way? On the one hand, we can view moves toward gender neutrality positively, as attempts to create professional environments in which gender does not matter. On the other hand, we can view gender neutrality negatively, as a tactic that permits institutions to ignore the hard issues concerning existing male privilege and female needs in the workplace. Many women and men seem to embrace both positions uneasily—they want to believe that gender should not and does not matter in the workplace, yet they also seem to harbor an uneasy feeling that special circumstances cannot and should not be ignored. The same issues exist in schools: Should education aim to be gender-neutral or gender-sensitive? Should gender differences be handled as an individual "problem" or as a group "need?" These questions deserve considerably more attention than they have thus far received from educational policy makers.

At the very least, however, educators and parents have an obligation to expose cultural forms such as the culture of romance and the discourse of gender neutrality. Students, both women and men, need to know how cultural forms both enable and constrain individual decisions and actions. Surely one way democracy proceeds and grows is by giving voice to and permitting debate of the issues that frustrate and bedevil individuals and groups. Here again, the active collaboration of social scientists, humanists, and science educators could be especially helpful in schools.

Schools, Science, and Power

In conclusion, schools must find ways to develop and encourage uses of science and the scientist identities that contribute to a substantive democracy and broad participation in it. This is a daunting charge, but the women whose experiences we have followed in this book suggest some important directions in which to proceed. As Iris Marion Young observed,

> Groups with different circumstances or forms of life should be able to participate together in public institutions without shedding their distinct identities or suffering disadvantage because of them. The goal is not to give special compensation to the deviant until they achieve normality, but rather to denormalize the way institutions formulate their rules by revealing the plural circumstances and needs that exist, or ought to exist, within them. (1990, 134)

The women we studied make clear that we can envision science and the meaning of being a scientist in ways that contribute to, rather than work against, democratic participation. Although the forms of science in which many of these women were engaged are lower-status and precarious, they also foster uses of science, the expression of local concerns, and the development of networks of power that are more consistent with broad participation in a substantive democracy than those of elite science. Concerned citizens, both inside and outside of school, must do more than they are doing now to support—both politically and financially—the kinds of organizations, school-reform efforts, and networks of power in which many of the women we studied are participating.

In this book we have tried to make sense of how and why women participate in and learn from the margins of science. Although we found that this is where women usually participate, we also found that what they do, learn, and accomplish there is an impressive alternative to the hegemony of the hard sciences. At the same time, however, their efforts are compromised by structural features that limit their power, threaten their prestige, and jeopardize their safety. Our results suggest that this is not the time to say that the women's movement is no longer needed, to cut off affirmative action opportunities for women, to turn away from special science opportunities that focus on girls' interests, or most important, to ignore the power of encouraging women's critical consciousness regarding the circumstances of their lives. Girls and women need to be able to take stock of their experiences, opportunities, and discourses; they must be able to scrutinize them for what is valuable and necessary and what is not; they must have meaningful access to the powerful tools and networks of our society; and they must have a language for articulating what will not work for them and why. These are necessary tools for moving girls' and women's "learning from the margins" to a more central place in our collective conversation and consciousness.

Notes

Introduction

1. Although many scholars argue that standardized, multiple-choice or short-answer tests, such as Miller's survey of scientific literacy, are not strong measures of sophisticated knowledge, few would deny that findings of such low levels of scientific literacy on a test as basic as Miller's are striking and alarming.

2. More recent scores, reported in 1997 from the Third International Mathematics and Science Study (TIMSS), place U.S. students (fourth and eighth graders) near the top in international comparisons. Yet concerns remain due to the much lower twelfth grade rankings (for current information, see the TIMSS website: www.ed.gov/NCES/timss).

3. Practice theories are a group of theoretical orientations developed by anthropologists, sociologists, and cultural psychologists who have joined the ideas of Russian psychologist Lev Vygotsky with American social and cultural theories to develop a sociocultural theory of knowing and learning (see, for example, Cole 1990; Lave 1988a, 1988b; Lave and Wenger 1991; Mehan, Hertweck, and Meihls 1986; Nespor 1994; Wertsch 1991; and the articles in Chaiklin and Lave 1993; D'Andrade and Strauss 1992; and Forman, Minick, and Stone 1993). Our earlier discussion of situated learning is one form of practice theory. A key proposition of all practice theories is that social context anticipates the objects, products, or endpoints of knowing and becoming; and "[s]ocial practice (not internalization) is the most important vehicle for transmitting the experience the world has to offer" (Lave 1988b, 14; see also Lave 1993, and Nespor 1994). We discuss these issues in more detail in chapter 2.

4. By *discourse*, we mean an accepted way of talking *and* acting about a given topic that is characteristic of a group and mediates (i.e., both enables and constrains) the group's understanding of the topic and actions regarding it.

5. The system that defines prototypically white male (or female) behavior is a cultural-historical phenomenon, that is, a matter of collective, durable action and interpretation—not biologically fixed. Biological males may exhibit culturally female behaviors, and biological females may exhibit culturally

male behaviors. In the United States, however, our cultural-historical legacy has marked organizations and institutions with gender, class, and race—as in the examples given above—in ways we often take for granted as "just the way things are" but which, in practice, make it easiest for people who can and do exhibit certain behaviors to do well, learn, and gain power in a particular organization or institution (see also Littleton 1987). In the cases we describe in this book, people who demonstrated prototypically white male work behaviors were the ones who tended to be differentially rewarded and to gain prestige and status at work.

Chapter One

1. We should also note that women in science or engineering are predominantly white. The numbers of nonwhite women in science and engineering are very small, although in comparison to their percentage in the population, their representation is not as dispiriting as for white women. In 1991, minority women, approximately 8 percent of the population as a whole, earned about 5 percent of all bachelor's degrees in the physical sciences and about 7 percent of all bachelor's degrees in the biological sciences (NSF 1994, 231–34). Numbers at the doctoral level are far lower, with black, non-Hispanic women (5 percent of the population) earning just 1.1 percent of all science and engineering doctorates in 1992, and American Indian/Alaskan Native women (0.5 percent of the population) earning 0.2 percent of those degrees (NSF 1994, 345–46). These figures suggest why, when we did find women working in science or engineering, most of them were white.

2. Some readers will no doubt think that the inequities facing women in the science and engineering workforce have more to do with discrimination against women or with women's decisions about family matters than with education. We take up these issues in chapter 2. Here we focus on the current, large-scale, national effort to improve women's opportunities through education.

3. Scott Marion contributed to this review of educational reforms. A longer critique of the reforms can be found in Eisenhart, Finkel, and Marion (1996).

Chapter Two

1. Karen Tonso assisted with this review of the history and popular explanations of women's participation in science.

2. Portions of this section originally appeared in Eisenhart (1996); they are reproduced here by permission.

3. Portions of this section originally appeared in Eisenhart (1995b); they are reproduced here by permission.

Introduction to Part Two

1. It is important to note that the figure on girls' participation in IGC is for an advanced science *elective* at the high school level. While 40 percent

would be a low proportion for girls' overall participation in high school science courses, overall figures include many courses that are required for graduation. When considering only advanced or elective courses, as IGC is, 40 percent is quite high (NSF 1996).

2. Of employed environmental scientists with master's or doctoral degrees, only 14 percent are women; of employed life scientists with master's or doctorates, 33 percent are women (NSF 1996, appendix table 5–1, 223). Thus, 46 percent is high for female (environmental) biologists in comparison to national figures. And although we do not have figures on women's participation in nonprofit organizations, the fact that 50 percent of employees were women in a science-oriented nonprofit organization is at least surprising in light of women's supposed disinclination to learn about or to be interested in science.

Chapter Three

1. See, for example, Computer as Learning Partner (C.L.P.) and Knowledge Integration Environment (KIE), two projects developed under the supervision of Marcia Linn at the University of California at Berkeley; Learning Through Collaborative Visualization (CoVis), developed by Roy Pea and colleagues at Northwestern University; Computer Supported Intentional Learning Environment (CSILE), developed by Marlene Scardamalia and Carl Bereiter at OISE/Toronto; Communities of Learners (COL), developed by Ann Brown and her colleagues at UC-Berkeley; and Project-Based Science (PBS), developed by Joe Krajcik and colleagues at the University of Michigan and by researchers at the Technological Education Research Consortium (TERC) in Boston, MA.

2. Lave and Wenger (1991) suggest that there are always "vast differences between the ways high school [science] students participate in and give meaning to their activity and the way professional [scientists] do" (99). No doubt many would agree with them. While the IGC course was explicitly modeled on the idea that science is a process of discovery, three characteristics limited the ways in which the practices modeled for students were like those of professional scientists. First, time constraints, including a class period less than fifty minutes long and a course that met only for nine weeks, meant that, unlike practicing scientists, students had both a limited daily period in which to think about and work on science and a limited number of days to struggle with a given problem. This set of constraints also affected the design of the course, which assumed more or less predetermined limits on the length of time students could spend on a particular problem.

Second, students in this class used the computer simulation instead of live organisms as a means of generating data. Thus instead of dealing with the vagaries of living organisms (including the problems of organisms that do not reproduce as expected, the observational difficulties inherent in studying tiny and often similar-looking organisms, and the length of time required to collect adequate data for model building), students were presented with a computer-generated representation of an organism. Although the organism modeled by the computer is very much like the fruit flies studied by geneticists, the computer-generated organisms were represented by male and female symbols, and the variations and inherited traits were represented only in textual form. This meant that although students could use the computer simulation to produce tens of crosses in as many minutes, thus producing considerable data for model building, the variations and traits that they were comparing across generations were not connected to any "real" picture of an organism. Thus, unlike geneticists, who work with real organisms and who must name and describe traits that they see, students in this class worked with computer-generated organisms described with abstractions, and they had to take at face value the notion that the words attached to traits and variations did indeed describe something worth describing and modeling.

Third, students had a different relationship with their teacher than scientists have with a supervisor or research director. They worked on predetermined problems in a sequence set by their teacher. While this may be somewhat like what happens in a research setting (in which a research director assigns particular tasks to particular scientists), unlike scientists, students were aware, despite claims that a "right" answer was not what she wanted, that their teacher knew an answer, and that she would, eventually, be responsible for assigning them a grade. As the teacher's expectations for students in this class were considerably different from the expectations of other teachers in other science classes, these students spent considerable time and effort attempting to determine what the teacher wanted them to do so that they could earn a good grade.

While it is important to understand these differences and to acknowledge their existence, the science practiced by students in this classroom was still like that practiced by professional scientists in several important ways. Science in both the laboratory and in this classroom requires participants to identify problems and develop solutions to those problems based upon their perceptions of what is important within a given context, using the specific tools available to them. Science in both the laboratory and in this classroom is an open-ended activity; it is up to scientists and students to decide when and if a problem has been adequately solved. These features of the practice modeled in this classroom were clearly different from those of traditional science classes, where both the problems and their answers are determined by the teacher or the book, and questions about the adequacy and importance of solutions (or problems, for that matter) are rarely discussed. In other words, despite some significant differences between the practice of science by professional scientists and that of students in this classroom, in many ways the practice of science in this classroom was more like that of professional scientists than like that practiced in most high school science classes.

3. More heterogeneous groupings of students (in which not all the students in a group were previously successful or unsuccessful) might have affected outcomes; however, because students were allowed to self-select their

groups and because we do not have data on group composition in previous classes, we cannot determine whether the type of grouping was associated with success in IGC over time.

Chapter Four

1. Pseudonyms are used throughout.

2. While women's overall success in EDI is impressive, women's experiences in other areas of the college's curriculum were not so successful, particularly when only one woman was involved in a team activity (e.g., Robin on Team B). See Tonso 1996 for a discussion of these situations.

3. This vignette is a composite of fieldnotes taken during classes from January 11 through January 27, 1993.

Chapter Five

1. Our data about ELAC (and the conservation corporation; see chapter 6) differ in an important way from the data collected about IGC and EDI. Because Behm pursued her work with ELAC just as any beginning canvasser would—becoming a trainee and then participating as a member of the canvass and in after-canvass social activities, she was not able to assume the role of detached observer that allowed Finkel (IGC) and Tonso (EDI) to record detailed notes about groups, group processes, and informal conversations as they occurred. Her data consist primarily of fieldnotes, written from memory after each day's work, about her experiences at ELAC and semistructured interviews with other staff there. For these reasons, the data presented in this chapter are more descriptive and personal than in the two previous chapters.

2. Most so-called tests of "scientific literacy," like Miller's, measure general knowledge of science using true-false, multiple-choice, and open-ended items. Although a standardized measure such as Miller's has limitations, its use both with the ELAC sample (by Behm) and with larger and more varied populations (see Miller 1991) gave us a practical means of comparing the ELAC participants to other groups.

Chapter Six

1. Like Behm's study of the environmental action group, ELAC, Eisenhart's study of CC was conducted primarily through her role as an active participant in the organization. The data reported in this chapter are taken from her fieldnotes of her own experiences (written from memory after each day spent working at the organization), supplemented by semistructured interviews with employees of CC and by documents for and about the organization.

2. Eisenhart originally formulated this scheme as a means of comparing the uses of science in the communities of practice that Behm, Lawrence, and she were studying and after reading about communities of practice (e.g., Lave and Wenger 1991), work-group cognition (e.g., Levine and Moreland 1991; Scribner 1984), and science as culture (e.g., Ross 1991). Many previous studies of knowledge or learning in workplaces (and schools) have focused on single

activities—and on the tasks and skills that comprise them—without as careful attention to the larger forms in which these activities are embedded.

3. This vignette was developed from Eisenhart's fieldnotes from a day-long observation on March 6, 1993.

Chapter Seven

1. Portions of this section were adapted from Tonso 1996.

2. The data in this section come from Behm 1994.

3. Because Behm was not initially aware of the safety issue, she did not probe participants about it. Thus any expressions of safety-related concerns to Behm were unsolicited, suggesting that the number of women who had them could have been greater than half.

4. The crew car is driven by the field manager, who makes the street assignments for a canvassing team. After each canvasser has been dropped off at a "turf," the field manager parks the car near his or her own turf. Thus, the car might be located several miles from most of the canvassers.

5. The vignette was adapted from Behm 1994, 141–42.

6. Most of the material in this section and the next ("Marty's Experiences") was previously published in Eisenhart 1995c, and is reproduced here by permission. The narrator in this account is Eisenhart.

7. Ann knew better than Marty what the law required and how CC responded to needs like Marty's. Unfortunately, Ann never discussed these issues with Marty (and neither did anyone else). When questioned about this by Eisenhart, Ann explained that she did not want to disappoint Marty and that she had been too busy with her own struggles to find time to talk.

8. Since the time of Eisenhart's study, the Family Medical Leave Act has been passed by the U.S. Congress. It offers greater protections for both mothers and fathers.

Chapter Nine

1. We are not the only ones to object to the idea that narrow definitions of *science* and *being a scientist* are required for successful science instruction. Others, notably those associated with the Science/Technology/Society [STS] approach (e.g., DeBoer 1991; Gallagher 1971), have argued for years that students should learn science by becoming "familiar with the social interactions of science as well as the structured disciplines themselves" (DeBoer 1991, 178). Although STS was prevalent in the literature about science education in the 1980s and still has its proponents, the approach has been overwhelmed by standards-based approaches to science education reform in the 1990s (see also Eisenhart, Finkel, and Marion 1996).

2. The discussion of this example originally appeared in Eisenhart, Finkel, and Marion (1996). It appears here in slightly modified form.

References

Aisenberg, N., and Harrington, M. 1988. *Women of academe: Outsiders in the sacred grove.* Amherst, MA: University of Massachusetts Press.

Aldridge, B. 1992. Project on scope, sequence, and coordination: A new synthesis for improving science education. *Journal of Science Education* 1 (1): 13–21.

American Association for the Advancement of Science. 1989. *Science for all Americans: A Project 2061 report on literacy goals in science, mathematics, and technology.* Washington, DC: American Association for the Advancement of Science.

———. 1993. *Benchmarks for scientific literacy.* New York: Oxford University Press.

American Association of University Women. 1992. *How schools shortchange girls: A study of major findings on girls and education.* Washington, DC: Author.

Anyon, J. 1981. Social class and school knowledge. *Curriculum Inquiry* 11 (1): 3–41.

Apple, M., and Weis, L., eds. 1983. *Ideology and practice in schooling.* Philadelphia, PA: Temple University Press.

Astin, A. 1985. *Achieving educational excellence: A critical assessment of priorities in higher education.* San Francisco: Jossey-Bass.

Astin, A., and Astin, H. 1993. *Undergraduate science education: The impact of different college environments on the educational pipeline in the sciences.* Los Angeles, CA: Higher Education Research Institute, UCLA.

Atkinson, P., and Delamont, S. 1990. Professions and powerlessness: Female marginality in the learned occupations. *Sociological Review* 38 (1–2): 90–110.

Baker, D., and Leary, R. 1995. Letting girls speak out about science. *Journal of Research in Science Teaching* 32 (1): 3–27.

Behm, L. 1994. A study of informal science education in a PIRG Group. Unpublished Ph.D. Dissertation, University of Colorado, Boulder.

Belenky, M.; Clinchy, B.; Goldberger, N.; and Tarule, J. 1986. *Women's ways of knowing: The development of self, voice, and mind.* New York: Basic Books.

Bourdieu, P. 1977. *Outline of a theory of practice.* Trans. Richard Nice. Cambridge: Cambridge University Press.

———. 1988. *Homo academicus.* Stanford, CA: Stanford University Press.

Bowles, S., and Gintis, H. 1976. *Schooling in capitalist America.* New York: Basic Books.

Burkam, D.; Lee, V.; and Smerdon, B. 1997. Gender and science learning early in high school: Subject matter and laboratory experiences. *American Educational Research Journal* 34 (2): 297–331.

Butler, J. 1990. *Gender trouble: Feminism and the subversion of identity.* New York: Routledge.

Chaiklin, S., and Lave, J., eds. 1993. *Understanding practice: Perspectives on activity and context.* New York: Cambridge University Press.

Chodorow, N. 1978. *Reproduction of mothering: Psychoanalysis and the sociology of gender.* Berkeley, CA: University of California Press.

Cole, M. 1990. Cultural psychology: A once and future discipline. In T. J. Berman, ed., *Cross-cultural perspectives. Nebraska symposium on motivation, 1989.* Vol. 37, pp. 279-335. Lincoln, NE: University of Nebraska Press.

College Entrance Examination Board. 1992. *College handbook, 1993.* New York: College Board Publications.

Connell, R. 1987. *Gender and power: Society, the person, and sexual politics.* Stanford, CA: Stanford University Press.

———. 1993. Disruptions: Improper masculinities and schooling. In L. Weis and M. Fine, eds., *Beyond silenced voices: Class, race, and gender in United States schools,* pp. 191–208. Albany: State University of New York Press.

Connell, R.; Ashendon, D.; Kessler, S.; and Dowsett, G. 1982. *Making the difference: Schools, families, and social division.* St. Leonards, Australia: Allen and Unwin.

Culotta, E. 1993. Curriculum reform: Project 2061 offers a benchmark. *Science* 262: 498–99.

D'Andrade, R. G., and Strauss, C., eds. 1992. *Human motives and cultural models.* Cambridge: Cambridge University Press.

DeBoer, G. 1991. *A history of ideas in science education.* New York: Teachers College Press.

Dinnerstein, M. 1992. *Women between two worlds: Midlife reflections on work and family.* Philadelphia, PA: Temple University Press.

Downey, G.; Hegg, S.; and Lucena, J. 1993, November. Weeded out: Critical reflection in engineering education. Paper presented at the American Anthropological Association, Washington, DC.

Eccles, J. 1987. Gender roles and women's achievement-related decisions. *Psychology of Women Quarterly* 11: 135–72.

Eccles, J., and Jacobs, J. 1986. Social forces that shape math participation. *Signs: Journal of Women in Culture and Society* 11: 367–80.

Eckert, P. 1989. *Jocks and burnouts: Social categories and identity in the high school.* New York: Teachers College Press.

———. 1993, November. Status and subordination. Paper presented at the Annual Meeting of the American Anthropological Association.

Eder, D., and Parker, S. 1987. The cultural production and reproduction of gender: The effect of extracurricular activities on peer-group culture. *Sociology of Education* 60 (3): 200–213.

Educational Testing Service. 1988. *Science learning matters: The science report card interpretive overview.* Princeton, NJ: Educational Testing Service.

Eisenhart, M. 1993, April. Science, gender, and the business of conservation. Paper presented at the Annual Meeting of the American Educational Research Association, Atlanta, GA.

———. 1995a. The fax, the jazz player, and the self-story teller: How do people organize culture? *Anthropology and Education Quarterly* 26 (1): 3–26.

———. 1995b. Learning as movement in networks of knowledge and power. *Educational Researcher* 24 (7): 35–36.

———. 1995c. Women scientists and the norm of gender neutrality at work. *Journal of Women and Minorities in Science and Engineering* 1 (3): 193–207.

———. 1996. The production of biologists at school and work: Making scientists, conservationists, or flowery bone-heads? In B. Levinson, D. Foley, and D. Holland, eds., *The cultural production of the educated person: Critical ethnographies of schooling and local practice,* pp. 169–85. Albany, NY: SUNY Press.

Eisenhart, M.; Finkel, E.; and Marion, S. 1996. Creating the conditions for scientific literacy: A reexamination. *American Educational Research Journal* 33 (2): 261–95.

Eisenhart, M., and Holland, D. 1983. Learning gender from peers: The role of peer groups in the cultural transmission of gender. *Human Organization* 42 (4): 321–32.

———. 1992. Gender constructs and career commitment: The influence of peer culture on women in college. In T. Whitehead and B. Reid, eds., *Gender constructs and social issues,* pp. 142–80. Urbana, IL: University of Illinois Press.

Eisenhart, M., and Lawrence, N. 1994. Anita Hill, Clarence Thomas, and the culture of romance. In A. Kibbey, K. Short, and A. Farmanfarmaian, eds., *Sexual artifice: Persons, images, politics,* pp. 94–121. New York: New York University Press.

Engel, B. 1993. Sister of their sisters? Russian women, the revolutionary legacy, and the denial of personal life. First Annual Elizabeth Gee Outstanding Scholarship Award Recipient Presentation, University of Colorado, Boulder, CO.

Engeström, Y. 1993. Developmental studies of work as a testbench of activity theory: The case of primary care medical practice. In S. Chaiklin and J. Lave, eds., *Understanding practice: Perspectives on activity and context,* pp. 64–103. New York: Cambridge University Press.

Evetts, J. 1996. *Gender and career in science and engineering.* London: Taylor and Francis.

Finkel, E. 1993. The construction of science in a high school genetics class.

Unpublished Ph.D. dissertation, University of Wisconsin–Madison. *Dissertation Abstracts International*, 54/08, p. 2970.

Foley, D. 1990. *Learning capitalist culture: Deep in the heart of Tejas.* Philadelphia: University of Pennsylvania Press.

Forman, E.; Minick, N.; and Stone, C. A., eds. 1993. *Contexts for learning: Sociocultural dynamics in children's development.* New York: Oxford University Press.

Friedman, M. 1991. Feminism and modern friendship: Dislocating the community. In J. Arthur and W. Shaw, eds. *Justice and economic distribution*, pp. 304–19. Englewood Cliffs, NJ: Prentice Hall.

Gallagher, J. 1971. A broader base for science teaching. *Science Education* 55: 329–38.

Gaskell, J. 1985. Course enrollment in the high school: The perspective of working-class females. *Sociology of Education* 58: 48–59.

Gilligan, C. 1982. *In a different voice: Psychological theory and women's development.* Cambridge, MA: Harvard University Press.

Goffredson, L. 1981. Circumscription and compromise: A developmental theory of occupational aspirations. *Journal of Counseling Psychology* 28: 545–79.

Gornick, V. [1983] 1990. *Women in science: Portraits from a world in transition.* New York: Simon and Schuster.

Greider, M. 1992. *Who will tell the people? The betrayal of American democracy.* New York: Simon and Schuster.

Green, K. 1989a. A profile of undergraduates in the sciences. *The American Scientist* 78: 475–80.

———. 1989b. Keynote address: A profile of undergraduates in the sciences. In *An exploration of the nature and quality of undergraduate education in science, mathematics and engineering*, National Advisory Group, Sigma Xi, the Scientific Research Society. Racine, WI: Report of the Wingspread Conference.

Haber-Schaim, U.; Abegg, G.; Dodge, J.; and Walter, J. 1982. *Introductory physical science.* 4th ed. Englewood Cliffs, NJ: Prentice Hall.

Hall, R., and Sandler, B. 1982. *The classroom climate: A chilly one for women?* Washington, DC: Association of American Colleges, Project on the Status and Education of Women.

Hafner, R. 1991. High school student's model-revising problem solving in genetics. Unpublished Ph.D. dissertation, University of Wisconsin–Madison.

Harding, S. 1991. *Whose science? Whose knowledge? Thinking from women's lives.* Ithaca, NY: Cornell University Press.

Haraway, D. 1989. *Primate visions: Gender, race, and nature in the world of modern science.* New York: Routledge.

Helford, R. 1994, August. Rediscovering the presettlement landscape: Making the oak savannah "real." Paper presented at the American Sociological Association, Los Angeles, CA.

Hochschild, A. 1983. *The managed heart.* Berkeley, CA: University of California Press.

Holland, D., and Eisenhart, M. 1988. Moments of discontent: University women and the gender status quo. *Anthropology and Education Quarterly* 19 (2): 115–38.

———. 1990. *Educated in romance: Women, achievement, and college culture.* Chicago: University of Chicago Press.

Holland, D., and Lave, J. Forthcoming. *History in person: Enduring struggles and identities in practice.* Santa Fe, NM: School of American Research Press.

Holland, D., and Skinner, D. 1995. Contested ritual, contested femininities: (Re)forming self and society in a Nepali women's festival. *American Ethnologist* 22 (2): 279–305.

Holland, J. 1985. *Making vocational choices: A theory of vocational personalities and work environments.* Englewood Cliffs, NJ: Prentice Hall.

Howe, K. 1993. Equality of educational opportunity and the criterion of equal educational worth. *Studies in Philosophy and Education* 11: 329–37.

Huebel-Drake, M.; Finkel, E.; Stern, E.; and Mouradian, M. 1995. Planning a course for success. *The Science Teacher* 62 (7): 18–21.

Hutchins, E. 1993. Learning to navigate. In S. Chaiklin and J. Lave, eds., *Understanding practice: Perspectives on activity and practice*, pp. 35–63. New York: Cambridge University Press.

Jacobs, J. 1995. Gender and academic specialties: Trends among recipients of college degrees in the 1980s. *Sociology of Education* 68: 81–98.

Johnson, S., and Stewart, J. 1990. Using philosophy of science in curriculum development: An example from high school genetics. *International Journal of Science Education* 12: 297–307.

Jones, L.; Mullis, I.; Raizen, S.; Weiss, I.; and Weston, E., eds. 1992. *The 1990 science report card.* Washington, DC: Educational Testing Service.

Jungck, J., and Calley, J. 1993. Genetics Construction Kit. In J. R. Jungck, P. Soderberg, J. Calley, N. Peterson, and J. Stewart, eds., The BioQUEST [software] library. College Park, MD: University of Maryland Press.

Kanter, R. 1977. *Men and women of the corporation.* New York: Basic Books.

Keller, E. 1982. Feminism and science. *Signs: Journal of Women in Culture and Society* 7 (3): 589–602.

———. 1985. *Reflections on gender and science.* New Haven, CT: Yale University Press.

Kleinman, S. 1996. *Opposing ambitions: Gender and identity in an alternative organization.* Chicago: University of Chicago Press.

Kymlicka, W. 1990. *Contemporary political philosophy: An introduction.* New York: Oxford University Press.

Latour, B. 1987. *Science in action.* Cambridge: Harvard University Press.

Lave, J. 1988a. *Cognition in practice: Mind, mathematics, and culture in everyday life.* Cambridge: Cambridge University Press.

———. 1988b. The culture of acquisition and the practice of learning. Report No. 88-007, May, 1988. Palo Alto, CA: Institute for Research on Learning.

————. 1990. Views of the classroom: Implications for math and science learning research. In M. Gardner, J. Greeno, A. Reif, A. Schoenfeld, A. DiSessa, and E. Stage, eds., *Toward a scientific practice of science education,* pp. 203–17. Hillsdale, NJ: Erlbaum Associates.

————. 1993. The practice of learning. In S. Chaiklin and J. Lave, eds., *Understanding practice: Perspectives on activity and practice,* pp. 3–34. New York: Cambridge University Press.

Lave, J., and Wenger, E. 1991. *Situated learning: Legitimate peripheral participation.* Cambridge: Cambridge University Press.

Lawrence, N. 1993, April. The language of science and the meaning of abortion. Paper presented at the Annual Meeting of the American Educational Research Association, Atlanta, GA.

————. 1994. The choice of language and the language of choice: Public/private discourse about abortion and education in the early 1980s. Unpublished Ph.D. dissertation, University of Colorado, Boulder.

LeCompte, M. 1980. The civilizing of children: How young children learn to become students. *The Journal of Thought* 15 (3): 105–27.

Levine, J., and Moreland, R. 1991. Culture and socialization in work groups. In L. Resnick, J. Levine, and S. Teasley, eds., *Perspectives on socially shared cognition,* pp. 257–79. Washington, DC: American Psychological Association.

Levinson, B.; Foley, D.; and Holland, D., eds. 1996. *The cultural production of the educated person: Critical ethnographies of schooling and local practice.* Albany, NY: SUNY Press.

Levinson, B., and Holland, D. 1996. The cultural production of the educated person: An introduction. In B. Levinson, D. Foley, and D. Holland, eds., *The cultural production of the educated person: Critical ethnographies of schooling and local practice,* pp. 1–54. Albany, NY: SUNY Press.

Littleton, C. 1987. Reconstructing social equality. *California Law Review* 25: 1279–1337.

Maccoby, E., and Jacklin, C. 1974. *The psychology of sex differences.* Vols. 1 and 2. Stanford, CA: Stanford University Press.

Marcus, G., and Fischer, M. 1986. *Anthropology as cultural critique: An experimental movement in the social sciences.* Chicago: University of Chicago Press.

Martin, J. 1989. What should science education do about the gender bias in science? In D. Herget, ed., *The history and philosophy of science in science teaching,* pp. 242–55. Tallahassee, FL: Florida State University.

————. [1981] 1994a. Sophie and Emile: A case study of sex bias in the history of educational thought. In J. R. Martin, *Changing the educational landscape: Philosophy, women, and curriculum,* pp. 53–69. New York: Routledge.

————. [1982] 1994b. Two dogmas of curriculum. In J. R. Martin, *Changing the educational landscape: Philosophy, women, and curriculum,* pp. 187–99. New York: Routledge.

Mason, C., and Kahle, J. 1989. Student attitudes toward science and science-related careers: A program designed to promote a gender-free environment. *Journal of Research in Science Teaching* 29: 167–77.

Mason, J. 1991. The invisible obstacle race. *Nature* 353 (19): 205–6.

McDermott, R. 1993. The acquisition of a child by a learning disability. In S. Chaiklin and J. Lave, eds., *Understanding practice: Perspectives on activity and practice*, pp. 269–305. New York: Cambridge University Press.

McGrayne, S. 1993. *Nobel Prize women in science: Their lives and momentous discoveries.* New York: Birch Lane Press.

McIlwee, J., and Robinson, J. 1992. *Women in engineering: Gender, power, and workplace culture.* Albany, NY: SUNY Press.

McNeil, L. 1986. *Contradictions of control.* New York: Routledge.

McRobbie, A. 1978. Jackie: An ideology of adolescent femininity. Occasional Paper No. 53, Women's Series. Birmingham, England: Centre for Contemporary Cultural Studies.

Mehan, H. 1993. Beneath the skin and between the ears: A case study in the politics of representation. In S. Chaiklin and J. Lave, eds., *Understanding practice: Perspectives on activity and practice*, pp. 241–68. New York: Cambridge University Press.

Mehan, H.; Hertweck, A.; and Meihls, J. 1986. *Handicapping the handicapped: Decision making in students' educational careers.* Stanford, CA: Stanford University Press.

Miller, J. 1991. The public understanding of science and technology in the United States, 1990. Report to the National Science Foundation. DeKalb, IL: Public Opinion Laboratory, Northern Illinois University.

Mitchell, M., and Stapp, W. 1994. *Field manual for water quality monitoring: An environmental education program for schools.* Dexter, MI: Thomson-Shore.

Moore, H. 1994. *A passion for difference: Essays in anthropology and gender.* Bloomington: Indiana University Press.

Morine, D. 1990. *Good dirt: Confessions of a conservationist.* Chester, CN: Globe Pequot Press.

National Research Council. 1994, November. *National science education standards: Draft.* Washington, DC: National Academy Press.

———. 1996. *National science education standards.* Washington, DC: National Academy Press.

National Science Board. 1993. *Science and engineering indicators, 1993.* Washington, DC: U.S. Government Printing Office (NSB 93-1).

National Science Foundation. 1994. *Women, minorities, and persons with disabilities in science and engineering, 1994.* Arlington, VA: National Science Foundation (NSF 94-333).

———. 1996. *Women, minorities, and persons with disabilities in science and engineering, 1995.* Arlington, VA: National Science Foundation (NSF 96-311).

National Science Teachers Association. 1992. *Scope, sequence, and coordination of secondary school science.* Vol. 1. Washington, DC: Author.

———. 1995. *Scope, sequence, and coordination of secondary school science.* Vol. 3. Arlington, VA: Author.

Nelkin, K. 1987. *Selling science: How the press covers science and technology*. New York: W. H. Freeman.

Nespor, J. 1990. Curriculum and conversions of capital in the acquisition of disciplinary knowledge. *Journal of Curriculum Studies* 22 (3): 217–32.

———. 1994. *Knowledge in motion: Space, time, and curriculum in undergraduate physics and management*. London: Falmer Press.

Noddings, N. 1990. Feminist critiques in the professions. *Review of Research in Education* 16: 393–424.

Oakes, J. 1988. Tracking in mathematics and science education: A structural contribution to unequal schooling. In L. Weis, ed., *Class, race, and gender in American education* pp. 106-125. Albany, NY: SUNY Press.

———. 1990. Opportunities, achievement, and choice: Women and minority students in science and mathematics. *Review of Research in Education* 16: 153–223.

Ortner, S. 1984. Theory in anthropology since the sixties. *Comparative Studies in Society and History* 26: 126–66.

O'Sullivan, C., Reese, C., and Mazzeo, J. 1997. *NAEP 1996 science report card for the nation and states*. Washington, DC: National Center for Education Statistics.

Peterson, N., and Jungck, J. 1988. Problem-posing, problem-solving, and persuasion in biology education. *Academic Computing* (March/April): 14–17, 48–50.

Pierce, J. 1995. *Gender trials: Emotional lives in contemporary law firms*. Berkeley, CA: University of California Press.

Phillips, P. 1990. *The scientific lady: A social history of women's scientific interests, 1520–1918*. London: Weidenfeld and Nicolson.

Resnick, L. 1987. Learning in school and out. *Educational Researcher* 16 (9): 13–20.

Rhode, D. 1997. *Speaking of sex: The denial of gender inequality*. Cambridge, MA: Harvard University Press.

Ross, A. 1991. *Strange weather: Culture, science, and technology in the age of limits*. London: Verso.

Rossiter, M. 1982. *Women scientists in America: Struggles and strategies to 1940*. Baltimore, MD: Johns Hopkins University Press.

———. 1995. *Women scientists in America: Before affirmative action, 1940–1972*. Baltimore, MD: Johns Hopkins University Press.

Rutherford, J., and Ahlgren, A. 1990. *Science for all Americans*. New York: Oxford University Press.

Sadker, M., and Sadker, D. 1994. *Failing at fairness: How America's schools cheat girls*. New York: Scribner.

Scardamalia, M.; Bereiter, C.; Brett, C.; Burtis, P.; Calhoun, C.; and Smith, N. 1992. Educational applications of a networked communal database. *Interactive Learning Environments* 2 (1): 45–71.

Scribner, S. 1984. Studying working intelligence. In B. Rogoff and J. Lave, eds., *Everyday cognition: Its development in social contexts*, pp. 9–40. Cambridge, MA: Harvard University Press.

Seager, J. 1993. *Earth follies: Coming to feminist terms with the global environmental crises.* New York: Routledge.

Seymour, E., and Hewitt, N. 1997. *Talking about leaving: Why undergraduates leave the sciences.* Boulder, CO: Westview Press.

Sieber, R. 1979. Classmates as workmates: Informal peer activity in the elementary school. *Anthropology and Education Quarterly* 10: 207–35.

Smith, E., and Tang, J. 1994. Trends in science and engineering doctorate production, 1975–1990. In W. Pearson Jr. and A. Fechter, eds., *Who will do science? Educating the next generation*, pp. 96–124. Baltimore, MD: Johns Hopkins University Press.

Stromquist, N. 1993. Sex-equity legislation in education: The state as promoter of women's rights. *Review of Educational Research* 63 (4): 379–408.

Susskind, Y., and Finkel, E. 1995, April. Socially responsible science. Paper presented at the American Educational Research Association, San Francisco, CA.

Tittle, C., and Weinberg, S. 1984. Job choice: A review of the literature and a model of major influences. Paper presented at the American Educational Research Association, New Orleans, LA.

Tobias, S. 1990. *They're not dumb, they're different: Stalking the second tier.* Tucson, AZ: Research Corporation.

Tong, R. 1989. *Feminist thought: A comprehensive introduction.* Boulder, CO: Westview Press.

Tonso, K. 1993. Becoming engineers while working collaboratively: Knowledge and gender in a nontraditional engineering course. Paper prepared for the Final Report to the Spencer Foundation entitled The Construction of Scientific Knowledge Outside School.

———. 1996. The impact of cultural norms on women. *Journal of Engineering Education* 85 (3): 217–25.

———. 1997. Constructing engineers through practice: Gendered features of learning and identity development. Unpublished Ph.D. dissertation, University of Colorado, Boulder.

Traweek, S. 1988. *Beamtimes and lifetimes: The world of high energy physics.* Cambridge, MA: Harvard University Press.

Tsing, A. 1993. *In the realm of the diamond queen: Marginality in an out-of-the-way place.* Princeton, NJ: Princeton University Press.

Valli, L. 1986. *Becoming clerical workers.* Boston: Routledge and Kegan Paul.

Vandervoot, F. 1985. Women's roles in professional scientific organizations: Participation and recognition. In J. Kahle, ed., *Women in science: A report from the field*, pp. 124–47. Philadelphia, PA: Falmer Press.

Vetter, B. 1992. What's holding up the glass ceiling? Barriers to women in the science and engineering workplace. Occasional Paper 92-3, Commission on Professionals in Science and Technology.

Weis, L. 1990. *Working class without work: High school students in a de-industrializing economy.* New York: Routledge.

Wertsch, J. 1991. *Voices of the mind: A sociocultural approach to mediated action.* Cambridge, MA: Harvard University Press.

Wexler, P. 1992. *Becoming somebody: Toward a social psychology of school.* London: Falmer Press.

Willis, P. 1977. *Learning to labor: How working-class kids get working-class jobs.* New York: Columbia University Press.

———. 1981. Cultural production is different from cultural reproduction is different from social reproduction is different from reproduction. *Interchange* 2 (2/3): 48–67.

Yates, J., and Finkel, E. 1996, March. Girls and computing: Gendered experiences in a nontraditional science classroom. Paper presented at the National Association for Research in Science Teaching, St. Louis, MO.

Yoder, J. D. 1991. Rethinking tokenism: Looking beyond numbers. *Gender and Society* 5 (2): 178–92.

Young, I. M. 1990. *Throwing like a girl and other essays in feminist philosophy and social theory.* Bloomington, IN: Indiana University Press.

Zuckerman, H. 1977. *Scientific elite: Nobel laureates in the United States.* New York: Free Press.

———. 1991. The careers of men and women scientists: A review of current research. In H. Zuckerman, J. Cole, and J. Bruer, eds., *The outer circle: Women in the science community,* pp. 28–56. New Haven, CT: Yale University Press.

Index

Abegg, G., 123
academic knowledge, xi–xii
activity theory, and reproduction of scientific power, 229–33. *See also* practice theory
Ahlgren, A., 3, 4, 23–24, 25, 123
Aisenberg, N., 39
Aldridge, B., 23, 170, 238
American Association for the Advancement of Science (AAAS), 23, 46
American Association of University Women (AAUW), 80
Anyon, J., 39
Apple, M., 43
Ashendon, D., 40
Astin, A., 5, 37
Astin, H., 5
Atkinson, P., 8
authentic learning, 56–57, 234–35; and apprenticeships, 56, 235; and social relevance, 236, 240–45; in schools, 235–36; sites of, 235. *See also* situated learning theory

Baker, D., 4
Behm, L., xv, 138, 141, 254n.2 (chap. 7), 254n.5
Belenky, M., 37
Bourdieu, P., 8, 28, 29, 43, 54
Bowles, S., 39
Burkam, D., 79
Butler, J., 207

Calley, J., 62
Chaiklin, S., 240, 249n.3
Chodorow, N., 37
Clinchy, B., 37
Cole, M., 249n.3
College Entrance Examination Board (CEEB), 91
Connell, R., 40, 43, 55
Conservation Corporation (CC) (case study): compared to other case studies, 167–68; constituencies, 156–58; data collection, 146, 253n.1 (chap. 6); definition of "scientist" in, 148–50, 159–66; description, 10, 57–58, 145–46, 147–48; gender neutrality, 12, 192, 197–203, 204–5, 213; as a "good" place for women, 192–95, 197, 199–203, 204, learning trajectories, 161–66; meaning of "good" work, 195–96; norm of "hard" work, 196–97, 213; power, connections to, 166–68, 224–26; prestige, 201, 202; prototypical white male behavior, 192, 195, 203; resistance, 210, 222–24, 226; role of women in organizational change, 212–15, 224–25; science in practice, 148–50; Site Ranking Procedure (SRP), 215–16, 237; status, 201, 202; values, 150–51; women at, 58, 146, 164, 193–95, 198–99; women's and